BLIND JUSTICE

PETER FLANNERY

Peter Flannery studied drama at Manchester University before joining Contact Theatre there and writing his first play for them, *Heartbreak Hotel* (1975). There followed *Last Resort* (Sidewalk Theatre Company, 1976; Royal Exchange, Manchester, 1978), *The Boy's Own Story* (Rat Theatre Company, 1978), *Savage Amusement* and *Awful Knawful*, a play for children co-written with Mick Ford (both staged at the RSC Warehouse in 1978). From 1979–80 he was Writer in Residence at the Royal Shakespeare Company in London, for whom he wrote *Our Friends in the North* 1982), which won the John Whiting Award that year. *Blind Justice*, his first venture in television, shown on BBC-TV in 1988, won both the Royal Television Society Award and the Samuel Beckett Award. His play, *Singer*, opened at the RSC Swan Theatre, Stratford-upon-Avon in 1989 and transferred to the Barbican, London, in 1990. He is currently adapting *Our Friends in the North* as an eleven-part television series and working with Mick Ford on a film about Romania, both for BBC-TV.

also by Peter Flannery

Our Friends in the North
Savage Amusement
Singer

For children
The Adventures of Awful Knawful (co-written with Mick Ford)

PETER FLANNERY
BLIND JUSTICE

FIVE SCREENPLAYS

Series created by

HELENA KENNEDY with PETER FLANNERY

NICK HERN BOOKS

A division of Walker Books Limited

A Nick Hern Book

Blind Justice, screenplays from the BBC Television series created by Helena Kennedy with Peter Flannery, first published in 1990 as an original paperback by Nick Hern Books, a division of Walker Books Limited, 87 Vauxhall Walk, London SE11 5HJ.

British Library Cataloguing in Publication Data
Flannery, Peter
  Blind justice.
  I. Title
  822.914

ISBN 1 85459 063 4

Introduction

The creation of *Radical Chambers* (as *Blind Justice* was initially
known) grew out of long animated evenings of discussion about
life at the Bar. Most people start conversations with criminal
barristers by asking how they square it with themselves acting for
people they know to be guilty. My answer to that question
changed with the company and the years. It was partly true that
I cultivated gullibility, but the real truth was that I had problems
with the whole idea of guilt. Was it enough to apply the narrow
tests of a criminal justice system which often ignored the reality
of people's lives beyond the door of the courtroom? Who are the
truly guilty?

I have always bitterly resented representations of the legal
profession which confirm the old myths and stereotypes: Charles
Laughton figures who spoke with marbles in their mouths and
had clients who fainted away in the witness box. The old forms
are changing and being challenged in a way which never seemed
to appear on the screen. There are lawyers who see themselves
as more than hired guns, who do wonder at the role they play in
the larger scheme of things. The legal fiction that justice is blind
and all who come before her get impartial consideration is fatally
flawed, and the best way of showing that has always been in the
stories that emanate from the courts.

As lawyers in practice we are all constrained from going into
print on our own cases, since we are bound by professional
ethics about divulging our clients' dark secrets, but drama
provides a vehicle for exploring some of the myths about the law
without breaking any of those rules. I drafted the outline of a
television drama series explaining its purpose and intentions. I
included in it a cast of characters and a number of story lines. I
was rather keen that my main protagonist should be a woman
because that was what I particularly knew about but also because
there are particular ambiguities about a woman working in a
male institution which remain unexplored. They relate to
feelings of discomfort about women functioning like men and of
glee when they fail to function like men. I was also keen that the
series showed the contradictions of being a 'radical lawyer'. Every
lawyer worth his or her salt wants to win and enjoys the roar of
the crowd, which fits uneasily with the heroic pose.

But most of all I wanted people to share my anger. I wanted the audience to feel in their bones that this was the truth, that here was the law in action and it was not good enough. That message had to be tough and unconditional; Michael Wearing, a producer at the BBC, promised me it would be.

Michael had been sent the 'treatment' – as such things are called – and had championed its development. I indicated from early on that I wanted to collaborate with a writer as I could not take time out of practice. However I wanted to work very closely with everyone involved because the project was too close to my heart to be cast to the creative winds without some kind of control. Michael Wearing works miracles in his ability to bring together people who make the right kind of creative energy together. I immediately liked Peter Flannery and after just a few meetings knew he understood how I imagined the series and why it was so important to me. We come from very similar backgrounds and made each other laugh – always a good sign. In the weeks, months, nay years, that followed we talked long and hard about every aspect of legal practice, the stories, the intrigues, the politics, the relationships. We thrashed out storylines, tested how they held up forensically, corrected the legal language and argued over the nuances. Michael Wearing was midwife to all this, playing Devil's advocate, prodding us towards larger themes. We decided at an early stage that we had to create a contrast between how the Bar traditionally functions and how alternative ways of working exist in some chambers: a device had to be found to keep that contrast alive. This was done by having our female lawyer, Katherine, start off firmly ensconced in a very conservative set of chambers from which she moves on. It was also agreed that several cases should be happening at the same time so as to give a hint at the kind of turnover and caseload existing at any one time.

Peter spent some time in different sets of chambers and in the courts. He has a great gift for dialogue and hears the rhythms in language. Very quickly he was able to recreate the class conflicts of the courtroom in the most wonderful exchanges. After bursts of time we spent together he would go off on his own and emerge some time later with a script which would startle me with its power. He could harness together all the ideas we had discussed – great and small – and add his own genius for playwriting. Occasionally I had to anchor his flights with the dull reality of legal possibility and assure him that the lawyer would be struck off if she took a particular course. We would go back to the drawing board and search for a way out of the ethical mess.

I had felt a desperate need to distance myself from the main character, anticipating that comparisons would be made. I wanted her personal life to be as unlike mine as possible whilst raising some of the problems that are always present when people do a job they love almost too much. The price of that is high and we wanted that cost to be included. Our only ripples of combat arose over Katherine's private life.

My major preoccupation in the law is with the cases which are the harder to win because of the additional problem of unspoken prejudice that is bubbling away just below the surface. You get this in Irish cases and cases involving black defendants, in rape cases and sexual abuse cases. There is a hidden agenda which has to be challenged if there is to be a fair trial. But sometimes passions are running too high, and you are struggling with a monster that is too powerful for any barrister to subdue. We have seen that happen in some Irish trials, and I wanted the series to confront the strange way that the burden of proof, which is supposed to remain firmly with the Crown, shifts when the subject matter is highly sensitive. It falls to the defence to do that which is always denied: prove the innocence of those standing trial. From the outset we knew that tackling anything Irish was likely to summon up the furies, but an Irish case had to be at the core of the series.

The scripts were stronger and stronger as we became more sure of our relationship and respective roles. Going back to the original treatment, it is interesting how the themes and ideas are all just as they were in the final product. Yet it was only as we worked that it developed its superstructure which was a reflective consideration both of Britain in the eighties and of the erosion of liberty. Almost by stealth it became a piece about the state of the nation, but then the law does hold up a mirror to society if you look at it clearly enough.

What came as a revelation was the way the protagonists we'd invented began to take on their own momentum and dictate their own behaviour. Katherine and Frank and Bingham all became very coherent characters, whose lives became closely interconnected with ours. We would sometimes wrestle and argue over what they would feel and do, and their independence was finally asserted when the directors and actors became involved. I now find it impossible to think of Katherine Hughes as in any way anything to do with me, and I had to have it pointed out to me recently that Peter was playing a writer's joke by inverting my initials to create hers.

The fruition of the project was all that I could have wished. The more I hear of producers the more I realise how privileged

we were to have Michael Wearing pilot the series. He really is in
a special league as of course were the actors and directors.
Everyone rejoiced in Peter Flannery's fine scripts and remarked
on a quality which is rarely present in television drama. For me
the collaboration was enormously successful and left no
unrequited feelings, only respect and a lasting gratitude that
Peter took on the job.

Helena Kennedy
June 1990

At the end of the final episode of *Blind Justice*, Katherine
Hughes, exhausted by the fight against the state and in
temporary despair, turns to camera and says, 'In this country
we've forgotten the meaning of liberty and that's why we don't
care about justice'. The lines were meant to startle the audience
dramatically and to worry it politically.

The 1980s was not a decade we will come to associate either
with justice in our courts or with outspokenness in television
drama. Both the Temple and the ranks of television producers
are too full of timeservers and apparatchiks for those things to
have flourished in the land. That *Blind Justice* was outspoken in
its attack on injustice is the achievement of its producer, Michael
Wearing, and of its instigator, the barrister Helena Kennedy. A
measure of this achievement – and also a measure of how deeply
resented have been this government's attacks on dissenting voices
– is the large number of people who have said to me since
transmission: 'I was half way through watching *Blind Justice* and I
suddenly thought, "I can't be seeing this. *You* are not allowed to
say things like this on TV these days, and *I* am not allowed to
hear it".' Such comments are also a measure of the erosion of
audience expectations in the field of television drama.

So rather than describe here how *Blind Justice* got made, I'd
like to outline one or two reasons why it nearly didn't get made;
or, if you like, why things like *Blind Justice* get made so rarely.
Let me point out here that in television *most* projects fall by the
wayside. Maybe four out of every five that are actively
considered fail to make it into production. Such had been my
own experience of television before I undertook to write *Blind
Justice*. I had written a six-part serial about corruption in British
public life, and a single film screenplay about the Falklands war.
Neither had been produced. The serial – representing two years
work on my part – had been swept off the desk when one BBC-

1 Controller was suddenly replaced by another. No explanation was ever offered me for Michael Grade's decision. I suspect it was simply the sweep of a new broom. The Falklands screenplay was rejected by the producer who had commissioned it because he simply didn't like it and found it to be, amongst other things, 'un-British'. He later went on to produce *Tumbledown*, which was a telling indictment of war in general but not, as I remember, an attempt – as my play was – to question and ridicule the origins and political conduct of a particular war. Was there not room for both? Or were we really living through times when two television plays about such a momentous event was one too many? Well, as far as some commentators were concerned even one was one too many.

The fact is that both of my pieces of work happened to be in the wrong place at the wrong time and fell victims to individual taste. There is no conspiracy as such against serious work, but there is a built-in and ever more arduous obstacle course in the way of anything ambitious or contentious. Ambitious usually means expensive and that sends the producer scuttling to find co-production finance. This in turn means that the project will fare better if it is attractive to investors from abroad. There was no co-production money available for *Blind Justice* or for *Boys From The Blackstuff*, but they got made. Other things did not. There *was* money available for *Edge Of Darkness*, and it didn't suffer thereby. Other things have. The fact is that one of the first questions any TV drama producer now asks about a project is, 'Will it attract co-production?'. I would like to ask, 'Isn't there something glaringly wrong when a nation of fifty-odd million people apparently cannot afford to make television drama to please itself without having to find out whether the folks in Kalamazoo or Perth will chip in?'.

In turn, contentious usually means political; and this sends the television producer scuttling in a rather different direction – not for foreign finance but for legal clearance. Of these two pernicious influences on the future of television drama, it is this latter – the growing influence of lawyers – which poses the more serious threat. Part Three of *Blind Justice* was read by such a vast number of people – because it dealt with the thorny problem of whether or not members of the IRA could expect a fair trial in a British court – that at one stage its transmission seemed almost superfluous. In the end it was indeed transmitted, minus the lines which questioned the reliability of the convictions of the Guildford Four, the Maguire family, and the Birmingham Six. A clear case of fair comment in my opinion, but according to the lawyers a clear case of defamation of police officers. One doesn't of course expect lawyers to be blessed with 20/20 foresight – leave that to writers – but a bit of common sense and a little boldness might not have gone amiss.

And what price boldness three years on? My serial about corruption, having crawled back onto the desk from whence it was so abruptly swept in 1984, is once again in difficulties. Its entire basis – fictional characters engaging the gears of recent historical events in the police force, Parliament, and local government – is thought to be *automatically* defamatory. The lawyers are clear and getting clearer: drama equals fiction, full stop. If allowed to gather influence at their present rate, they may eventually force into existence a new breed of drama never foreseen by Aristotle: a drama from which all reference to public life has been eradicated; a drama in which no character exists who could possibly be confused with anybody now alive on the planet with a profile higher than that of the average public librarian. What should we call this new species of entirely private drama in which nothing happens which might remind anybody of anything that really *has* happened except those things that have happened to everybody? There's no need, of course, to invent a name. The species is already here and has been for years. It's called *Neighbours* or *Coronation Street* or, just as often, *Play For Today*, God help us. I'm not against it. I just don't want to watch it, let alone have to write it. A colleague has recently taken a potentially contentious idea to the BBC. He's been asked to talk to the lawyers *before* he starts writing!

Why the jeremiad? *Blind Justice* got produced, without having to compromise itself for co-production money and without having to take too much notice in the end of lawyers. It got transmitted, in a prime evening slot. We all won prizes. The BBC might repeat it, though it's rather expensive. They might even be interested in a second series, if I could find the time to do it. And perhaps I should make time. *Blind Justice* was exhilarating to write. Its stories gripped millions of people and its unabashed voice of dissent gave cheer to many many people whose own voices had become tired or hoarse in the late 1980s. Scores of people who worked on it found *Blind Justice* worthy of their complete professional commitment, and I find very often that they are still, like me, inordinately proud of their connection with it.

Michael Wearing once called me a brontosaurus. This was less a comment on my shape and eating habits than on my clear position among that small band of writers which still wants to write about the big picture. He fears, I suppose, that I'm facing extinction in a changing climate. But I'm very young as brontosauri go, and anyway I favour the evolutionary theory that says the dinosaurs grew wings and survived as birds. Television drama has big, big problems, and there is reason enough to fear the future. But compared to the complete asylum of the film world or a commercial theatre dominated by musicals and trivia, it remains a major arena for the serious dramatist. There are many more things about which to raise one's voice; many more thrilling stories to be attempted; many more battles to be fought for the right of access to the airwaves and to defend the liberty to remain an intelligent, disagreeable and incongruous misfit. Like a brontosaurus in a tree.

Peter Flannery
June 1990

Blind Justice was first shown in five parts on BBC Television in September 1988. Full cast lists are given at the beginning of each episode. The Production Team for the series was:

Producer	Michael Wearing
Director	Rob Walker (1,2,3)
	Michael Whyte (4,5)
Production Assistant	Maggie Stevens (1,2,3)
	Barbara Gibson (4,5)
Production Manager	David Mason (1,2,3)
	Michael Darbon (4,5)
	Tony Redston (4,5)
Associate Producer	Peter Norris
Script Editor	John Chapman
Location Manager	Betsan Morris-Evans (1,2,3)
	Simon Cellan Jones (4,5)
A.F.M.	Julie Edwards (1,2,3)
	Sarah Lee (4,5)
	Mark Scantlebury
Cameraman	Alec Curtis (1,2,3)
	Ian Punter (4,5)
Sound Recordist	Dick Manton (1,2,3)
	Barry Tharby (4,5)
Designer	John Hurst (1,2,3)
	Roger Cann (4,5)
Costume Designer	Brian Willis
Make-up Designer	Linda McInnes (1,2,3)
	Di Roberts (4,5)
Film Editor	Ardan Fisher (1,2,3)
	Jim Latham (4,5)
Dubbing Mixer	Rob James
Music composed by	Colin Towns

EPISODE ONE

Crime and Punishment

Cast

KATHERINE HUGHES	Jane Lapotaire
FRANK CARTWRIGHT	Jack Shepherd
MR JUSTICE LANGTRY	Charles Gray
DET SGT McCABE	Peter Postlethwaite
CORA DAVIS	Anna Manahan
JAMES BINGHAM	Julian Wadham
LORRAINE	Caroline Hutchison
HUGH	Eamonn Walker
COMMANDER STANTON	John Ringham
HOLLAND	Barrie Houghton
ALTON PHILLIPS	Clarke Peters
DAVID FRANKLAND	Donald Churchill
HENRY	Vas Blackwood
PROSECUTING COUNSEL	Ian Lowe
DEFENDING COUNSEL	Michelle Copsey
PAM HOLLIS	Shirley Stelfox
LEONI MASON	Tilly Vosburgh
MIRANDA FRANKLAND	Diana Katis
ARNOLD FLOWERS	Roger Booth
TOM	Sam Cox
EDWARD	Duncan Bell
ALAN ACKROYD	Toby Salaman
PATRICIA SWALES	Janet Palmer
ITALIAN	Vincenzo Nicoli
ROBERT	David John Pope
COLIN CAMPBELL-JOHNSON	Robin Hooper
DET CON SISSONS	Roger McKern
CUSTOMS OFFICER	David Rose
COURIER	Clare Hudson
SERGEANT	Martin Oldfield

MAGISTRATE   Brian Vaughan
COURT CLERK   Joan Campion
MRS McCABE   Janet Amsden
USHER   Margaret Stallard
MOTORWAY POLICEMAN   Christopher Gray
ANGELA   Maria Warner
MIRIAM   Mia Soteriou
DILIP   Aftab Sachak

1. Exterior. Street outside Inner London Crown Court. Day.

KATHERINE HUGHES *and* ALTON PHILLIPS *are walking towards the court building.*

KATHERINE. Sometimes I feel I'm inside a machine. The day before yesterday I defended a man called Clayton. This bloke had taken a bottle, broken it, and twisted it into another guy's face, nearly killing him. I'd defended this bloke once before. He's actually a sweetie.
They go into the court building.

2. Interior. Crown Court corridors. Day.

KATHERINE *and* ALTON *walk towards the* BARRISTERS' *Robing Room.*

KATHERINE. Till he drinks. Then he's a psychopath. The evidence against him was overwhelming. I had no chance.
A BARRISTER *passes by.*
BARRISTER. Good afternoon.
KATHERINE. Oh, hi. He'd insulted the victim till the guy couldn't stand it anymore. The guy lurches across the table at my client and Clayton bottles him.
The courts are in full swing. They are walking past a throng of POLICEMEN, SOLICITORS, BARRISTERS, WITNESSES, BAILED DEFENDANTS, FRIENDS *and* RELATIVES. *They occasionally nod at a familiar face.*
His defence was 'self-defence'. When the surgeon gave evidence a woman juror had to be given attention.
KATHERINE *and* ALTON *go upstairs towards the Robing Room. She speaks discreetly.*
KATHERINE. Have you ever come across a ridiculous little piss artist called Rhodes?
ALTON *shakes his head.*
He's an assistant Recorder. He sits in little places when everybody else is too busy. He's never going to be made into a proper judge but that hasn't dawned on him yet, so he's still worried about what they think of him in the Lord Chancellor's office. He's a total incompetent. It would be nice to believe that's why he's been passed over, but total legal incompetence has never been a bar to Judicial office before, so . . . Won't be a minute, Alton.
She goes into the Robing Room.

3. Interior. Crown Court building. Day.

KATHERINE *comes out of Robing Room in her gear.*

ALTON. Patricia's arrived.

KATHERINE. OK.

They walk quickly downstairs and down more stairs to the cells below the courts.

KATHERINE. So anyway, this bloke Rhodes does his summing up for the jury – in which he's practically ordering them to lock my client up and throw away the key – and he gets so carried away he forgets to sum up self-defence. I don't know whether he was pissed or what, but . . . So I'm on my feet before he can get the jury out. I says 'Excuse me, your Honour, aren't you forgetting your duty to sum up self-defence for members of the jury?' He goes beetroot. He starts blustering. 'Oh well', he says, 'they've already heard all that from you, Miss Hughes, it's very fresh in their minds'.

ALTON *is laughing.*

I says 'Pardon me, your Honour, it's hardly fresh in their minds when they've since had to sit through a very lengthy prosecution speech. In fact' – get this bit, Alton – 'in fact, they've had to sit through two prosecution speeches if we count yours as well!' He was apoplectic. But what can he do? He knows he's screwed it up and I'm going to be into the Court of Appeal like a rat up a drainpipe if he won't do it. So he rattles off self-defence and out goes the jury for the four and a half seconds they need to consider the case.

They have reached the cell area.

4. Interior. Crown Court building. Cells. Day.

ALTON *and* KATHERINE *find* PATRICIA SWALES *in a cell. She is pregnant, young and very worried.*

PATRICIA. Hello Alton.

ALTON. Hello, Patricia. This is Katherine Hughes.

KATHERINE. Hello Patricia. Have you had some breakfast?

PATRICIA. Yeh, they gave me some in Holloway. I couldn't eat much, you know.

ALTON. We're going in first, so not a lot of hanging about. Don't worry. Just keep cool. You won't have to say anything. Katherine will do all the talking.

KATHERINE. That's what I'm paid for, Patricia. I'm going to make you sound like a cross between Joan of Arc and Little Orphan Annie, so don't blush and give the game away.

She's smiling.

PATRICIA *eases a bit. She smiles and nods.*

KATHERINE. OK? See you in a minute?

ALTON. OK, love.

PATRICIA. Yeh.

ALTON *and* KATHERINE *go out of cells and upstairs towards the courts.*

5. Interior. Courtroom. Day.

KATHERINE *and* ALTON *take their seats. The court is getting ready for the judge's appearance through the following:*

KATHERINE. So the jury comes back. Guilty with knobs on. Clayton knows he'll have to cancel the milk for seven years or so. He's got five previous for assault and this is it this time: the big league for nutters, and he's quite looking forward to it. Rhodes gave him two and a half so I wouldn't appeal it. Clayton'll be out in twelve months and he'll undoubtedly kill somebody very soon after that. He blew me a kiss as they took him down. The victim wept with frustration. If you can imagine tears dripping down a face that looks like three different heads sewn together.

MR JUSTICE LANGTRY *enters with two* MAGISTRATES.

USHER. Court rise.

LANGTRY *sits.* MAGISTRATES *sit on either side of him. He ignores them throughout.*

Oh ye, oh ye, oh ye to all manner of persons who have anything to do at the Crown Court at Inner London Sessions house draw near and give your attendance. God save the Queen.

They sit.

ALTON. Do you know him?

KATHERINE *shakes her head. She's scribbling her name on a piece of paper, passing it to the* CLERK, *who passes it to* LANGTRY.

CLERK. Patricia Swales.

PATRICIA *is brought up from the cells. She immediately looks for* ALTON *and* KATHERINE. *They smile at her. She is put into the dock.*

Your Honour, the defendant Patricia Swales was found guilty at Clerkenwell Magistrates on four counts of shoplifting.

LANGTRY. Mr Bartholomew.

PROSECUTING COUNSEL *stands.*

6. Interior. Cells below courts. Day.

A jail delivery from Brixton. A dozen DEFENDANTS *arriving.* HENRY GRIFFITHS *is taken into a cell.*

7. Interior. Courtroom. Day.

LANGTRY. Does she understand that she's been sent here to be sentenced because the Magistrates in the Lower Court felt they had insufficient means with which to deal with her?
KATHERINE stands.

KATHERINE Your Honour. I represent Patricia Swales in this matter. She does understand that.
He nods and settles down to hear a good speech, a pleasant smile playing about his lips.
Your Honour, you'll have before you three documents which no doubt you have read.
LANGTRY *is non-committal about this.*
One is a psychiatric report, one a social services report and the other is from her Probation Officer.
LANGTRY *nods. He has them before him.*
There was no dispute about the facts of this case: my client admitted the offences. The reason Clerkenwell Magistrates saw fit to commit her to this court for sentencing is no doubt because of my client's rather distressing record of petty theft. I say 'distressing', your Honour, because it distresses Patricia as much as anybody. Patricia is seventeen years old. She comes from a broken home in which her father was an alcoholic and her mother suffered severe bouts of depression. She's been in care since she was eleven. Her problems with the police date almost exactly from that time. She was twice fostered unsuccessfully.
LANGTRY *is yawning deeply.*
And it's the fact that she stole property from both sets of foster parents which I think gives you a very big clue as to what exactly is the problem here. Your Honour, if you care to look at the psychiatric report, you will see that it talks in its concluding paragraph about a common enough syndrome in which a child who feels rejected and insecure will often indulge in petty crime and indeed in other forms of antisocial behaviour –
LANGTRY *isn't interested in the report. He is polishing his spectacles methodically.*
– as a way of saying to its parents. 'WOULD YOU MIND TAKING A BIT OF NOTICE OF ME?'
At last LANGTRY looks at her. He smiles.
Typical adolescent behaviour in fact. But with Patricia, stealing became a problem and led her into repeated trouble with the authorities. The crucial thing about Patricia – and all of the reports refer to this, your Honour –

To her astonishment he's talking to the CLERK. *He hears that she has stopped. He looks up.*

LANGTRY. Well do carry on, Miss . . . (*He looks at paper.*) . . . Hughes.

KATHERINE (*trying not to explode*). – is that since she was twelve or thirteen she has really not cared about what happened to her. She never felt secure enough in her situation to feel a sense of hope for the future. Your Honour, the reports will also tell you what you may not have noticed; Patricia is now five months pregnant. This could have been a devastating new problem.

LANGTRY *peers at* PATRICIA, *who is seated.*

KATHERINE. In fact it's had quite the opposite effect. For the first time in years, this young girl *wants* her life. She wants her future. She wants the baby. And that, Your Honour, is why everybody who's been trying to help Patricia for the last six years would say to you now: we know that Patricia has been living dangerously: we know that her behaviour has been inviting a court somewhere sooner or later to pass on her a custodial sentence; but if ever a young girl deserved and needed at this point in her life to be given another chance, then it's Patricia today. Thank you, your Honour, that's all, but may I remind you about the three reports?
She sits.

LANGTRY. Have you finished?

KATHERINE *nods politely. He smiles. He turns his gaze on* PATRICIA. Stand up.

She stands up.

Patricia Swales, I've listened very carefully to your counsel. I now have to decide what to do with you. What your counsel has said has made my decision much easier for me.

LANGTRY *smiles graciously at* KATHERINE.

KATHERINE *smiles a little bit.* LANGTRY's *not such a bad stick after all.*

LANGTRY. I'm going to give you one last chance. (*Pause.*) I'm sentencing you to youth custody for nine months because that's the only chance someone like you has of ever turning into a decent citizen. Will you take her down, please?

PATRICIA *is led away, bewildered and afraid. Her eyes are glued to* KATHERINE *who can only stare back in horror.*

CLERK. Court will rise.

She looks in disbelief at LANGTRY. *He gives her a little smile that says, 'That surprised you, didn't it, dear?' He leaves the court.*

KATHERINE *is speechless.*

8. Interior. Cells below courts. Day.

KATHERINE *watches as* PATRICIA, *who has gone berserk, is restrained by several* WPO's. *They manage to grip her tightly enough to stop her moving everything but her head. This she uses as a battering ram.* ALTON *is trying to calm her.*

ALTON. Patricia, Patricia, cool it. Come on now. Cool it. We'll appeal it. Come on now.
ARNOLD FLOWERS, a solicitor carrying two bulging briefcases, arrives and notices the commotion. He has to squeeze past KATHERINE *and the crowd round* PATRICIA *as he looks for his client. The area is by now overflowing with remand prisoners. There are some open cubicles housing* PRISONERS *waiting to go before the Bench.*
A wagonload of PRISONERS *has just arrived from Brixton. Meetings with briefs are going on wherever there is a space to sit, stand, or squat. In one of the cubicles, handcuffed to a radiator, is* HENRY GRIFFITHS. FLOWERS *finds him.*

FLOWERS. Hello, Henry.
He looks about, pissed off.
Was there a chair in here?
Somebody is sitting on it outside. He squats and takes papers from his case.

HENRY. Mr Flowers, you got to tell them this time. I can't stand no more of Brixton. It's wrong I'm there, you know?
FLOWERS's *eyes glaze over.*

FLOWERS. Christ knows I know how you're feeling. (*He belches.*) Sorry, pardon. My God, it's a scandal. Do people care?

HENRY. But what I'm saying: I fink I could get bail, you know, if I could just tell them my case, you know, this is what I've been finkin'. I wasn't dealing in it. I mean it was just my own personal stuff –

FLOWERS. When the time is right, your case will be put. Believe me.

HENRY. What about bail?

FLOWERS. I'm going to do my level best, son. Can't say more than that. I better get up there.
He leaves.
HENRY *sits alone and depressed in the cubicle.*

9. Interior. Crown Court Cells. Day.

HENRY *is taken from his cell by two* PRISON OFFICERS *and led up a flight of stairs directly into the dock.*

10. Interior. Courtroom. Day.

HENRY *enters the dock and looks around. He sees* FLOWERS *and his barrister,* GALSWORTHY. FLOWERS *gives a smile.*

CLERK. Are you Henry Earl Griffiths? Sit down please. Your
Honour, the defendant Henry Earl Griffiths was remanded in
custody on April 3rd on a charge of supplying controlled
drugs: namely cannabis. Bail was refused by the Magistrates
Court and the application is now being made before this court.

LANGTRY. Yes.

GALSWORTHY *gets to his feet.*

GALSWORTHY. Your Honour, I appear on behalf of Henry Earl
Griffiths. This is a case in which, in my submission, bail ought
to be granted. Mr Griffiths doesn't hold a passport, he isn't
charged with a grievous offence, the only witnesses are police
officers, so there are no witnesses to be interfered with and
he's not likely to re-offend.

LANGTRY. Is anyone representing the Crown?

A POLICE SERGEANT *stands at the side.*

Are there police objections, Sergeant?

POLICE SERGEANT. Yes, your Honour.

JUDGE LANGTRY. I thought perhaps there might be. Perhaps you
could let me hear them.

11. Exterior. Exit from cells below courts. Day.

HENRY *is loaded back on to the bus for Brixton. He looks back and sees*
FLOWERS *looking on sympathetically from the cell area.*

12. Exterior. Gray's Inn. Day.

Teeming rain. KATHERINE *walks towards her chambers. She's weeping.*
Two male BARRISTERS *scuttle across in opposite directions.*

FIRST BARRISTER. Hello! How'd it go?

SECOND BARRISTER. Twelve years but we're appealing!

KATHERINE *takes refuge in a porch.*

13. Exterior. Porch on Gray's Inn Buildings. Day.

KATHERINE *gathers her wits and finds* FRANK CARTWRIGHT *watching*
her, further back in the porch. Still a bit tearful.

FRANK. Turned out nice again.

KATHERINE. Yeh. I'm having a bad day.

He nods sympathetically.

FRANK. Busy?

KATHERINE. Well you know me, Frank. Anything for a bit of money.

They laugh for two seconds.

KATHERINE. You finally did it. Great.

FRANK. Yeh. I've signed the lease. Fetter Court. Drop in. Right across from the Bailey.

KATHERINE. Your own chambers. It's wonderful.

FRANK. It's a democracy.

KATHERINE. Well it would be.

FRANK. Come and have a look.

She realises he means now.

KATHERINE. Oh, I dunno, I . . .

He really wants it.

KATHERINE. OK.

14. Interior. The big room. Fetter Court. Day.

FRANK *and* KATHERINE *come up a central staircase into what is really no more than a bare space. A loft. They walk around. The rain teems down the windows and occasionally drips on to the floor through the roof.*

FRANK. Good, isn't it?

KATHERINE. Is this a chambers – or are you thinking of racing a few pigeons?

FRANK. No, it'll be great. Course it all depends on who comes in with me.

KATHERINE. Don't be pissed off with me, it's boring.

FRANK. I'm not.

KATHERINE. You are. I've given you my reasons.

FRANK. You haven't actually. All you said – and I admit you were paralytic – but all you actually said was: you didn't want to sit drinking your Maxwell House listening to half a dozen second-rate barristers banging on about Nicaragua.

Silence. She remembers it now. She laughs. He laughs.

KATHERINE. Who's in so far?

FRANK. Well, a lot of first-rate young barristers. The sort of people who get crapped on in straight chambers. Tessa Parks. Alison Rye. David Milner.

KATHERINE. How are you going to pay the rent, Frank, if you're the only one earning any money?

FRANK. No, no: Ken Gordon, Michael Khan . . . James Bingham.

KATHERINE. Oh. The radical toff himself.

FRANK. James is excellent. But what I really need is a

heavyweight woman. Someone with a good practice in heavy crime and political stuff.

KATHERINE. Why not ask Margaret Wharton?

FRANK. Because I want a stayer. A genuine lawyer. Not someone passing through on her way to a safe Labour seat.

KATHERINE. Who's clerking for you? Whoever it is better be good.

FRANK. She is. And – she's on a salary. No ten per cent for the clerk.

KATHERINE. Very egalitarian. But it might've been cheaper to put her on ten per cent.

FRANK. So that's the big attraction of Grimshaw's, is it? The company of other big earners? Or is it that you love the clerking there so much? They carve you up, you know.

KATHERINE. Grimshaw's is no worse than most. I know where I stand there because Grimshaw supports me. Sort of. He believes troublemakers like me should be allowed a corner to live in because he thinks he believes in making room for the dissenting voice, blah, blah.

Footsteps start arriving up the stair-well.

But really because it makes him look good, makes him look broad-minded, you know. So I'm left in peace and I don't have to fake anything or make any deals with people who think they're radicals. People like –

BINGHAM's *head appears coming up the stairs.*

FRANK. James.

BINGHAM. Hi. (*Shaking out his brolly.*) Katherine. Hello.

KATHERINE. Hello, James.

Awkward silence.

Well, look . . . Good luck. Really. Fingers crossed.

KATHERINE *goes.*

BINGHAM. No go?

FRANK. No.

BINGHAM. Pity.

FRANK *studies him. Does he think it's a pity really?*

FRANK. Well. Early days.

15. Interior. Grimshaw's. Day.

KATHERINE *enters the building and goes up flights of stairs. She opens the door to her shared room. She sees people inside. She comes out.*

KATHERINE. Sorry.

She goes into the Clerk's room.

16. Interior. Grimshaw's. Clerks' room. Day.

DOREEN *sits typing.*
It's quite a large room with modern office equipment.
KATHERINE *sits drying her hair on a towel.*
TOM, *the clerk, fifties, comes in and bustles to his desk.*
Behind him comes EDWARD, *nineteen, the junior. Both in pin-stripes.*
They are looking for something and talking.

TOM. I mean I ask you: how can I get the man briefed if he's
  going to lose easy cases like that one? Miss Hughes. How did
  your girl do?

KATHERINE. She got Borstal. Still. Langtry had a chance to act
  out his sadistic fantasies. That's the main thing. That's what
  we're here for.

TOM. Lily up to her tricks again?

  EDWARD *laughs, impressed with* TOM.

KATHERINE. Lily?

TOM. Langtry.

  He makes a limp wrist.

  EDWARD *again appreciates the joke.*

  They're the worst in my view. They're all a bit vicious, aren't
  they?

  EDWARD's *agreeing.*

KATHERINE. You know what Langtry thinks? He thinks he's an
  English eccentric, but he's really just another senile delinquent
  on the bench.

  ALAN *and* DICK, *who share* KATHERINE's *office, enter with three
  other* BARRISTERS *from other chambers.*

ALAN. Sorry, Katherine. Coast's clear.

KATHERINE. You should've seen his face, Edward. The way he
  enjoyed it. That's the business you're coming into.

DICK. Who's this?

EDWARD. Lily Langtry.

DICK. Oh! He's an absolute swine! I defended a bloke in front of
  him once who had that same week buried his daughter. He
  was up in front of Langtry on a pretty pathetic embezzlement
  charge that was going to cost him his job whatever. The bloke
  had elected for trial. Langtry wanted to send him to prison.

  Laughter from the men.

DICK. We had to appeal it.

TOM. The poofs are all the same.

KATHERINE (*quietly*). Oh, for God's sake. Is this for me, Edward?

  She picks up a brief from his desk.

ALAN. He did the same to me once. I finished what I thought
  was rather a good mitigation. He said 'Are you quite finished?'

I said 'Yes, your Honour' – thinking he might be going to congratulate me or something. He said 'I suppose you want me to feel *sorry* for your client? Well I don't!'
Big laughs from the men.

TOM. I hear your thief didn't do terribly well this morning, Mr Ackroyd.

ALAN (*embarrassed*). Ah. Well.
They all rib him. He's squirming as KATHERINE *quietly leaves the room with her new brief.*

17. Interior. Grimshaw's. Katherine's office. Day.

KATHERINE *goes through into her room. She sits at her desk. She picks up a little figure which usually sits on her desk. It's a monkey on a stick, but the monkey has a full-bottomed wig on. She makes him somersault.*

18. Exterior. Heathrow Airport. Day.

An Air India jumbo jet lands.

19. Interior. Heathrow Airport. Day.

HOLLAND *and* O'NEILL, *two* CUSTOMS OFFICERS, *walk slowly past a row of people suspected of having swallowed drugs on smuggling runs. These* PEOPLE *are nearly all black men who've come in on a run from Lagos. They are all handcuffed and sitting on toilet pans.*
Other CUSTOMS OFFICERS *are watching them for signs of bowel movements.*

HOLLAND. Remember: I want you to stay as close to her as possible. We don't know where she might take it. We've got to know exactly who she talks to at any given moment until she disposes of her consignment. OK, let's get cracking. Colin.
An OFFICER *nearby comes quickly.*
HOLLAND *points to a straining Nigerian who appears to be about to drop himself in it.*
COLIN *pulls on surgical gloves.*

20. Interior. Heathrow Passport Control. Day.

Milling crowds plus all their luggage from the Indian arrival. They are all making their way towards the channels. Many of the PASSENGERS *are Asian, including whole families. The usual confusion and anxiety. Tired children are crying.*

A large woman stands serenely. She wears the outfit of a nun. This is
CORA.
Near CORA *is an* INDIAN WOMAN. *She's distracted by the noise and*
bustle and the problem of her trolley of luggage. She's looking after three
CHILDREN, *including a baby in her arms. Another of the* CHILDREN *is*
crying.
CORA *comforts the* CHILD *with a smile and a caress. The* MOTHER *looks*
thankful. CORA *smiles at her.*
Across the other side of the hall, O'NEILL *surveys the milling throng.*

CORA. It won't be long I shouldn't think.

21. Interior. Heathrow. Day.

The concourse, beyond customs desks. FRIENDS *and* RELATIVES *waiting*
for the Indian arrivals to start coming through customs.
HOLLAND *makes his way to a vantage point. He surveys the crowds. He*
moves off and stands beside two more CUSTOMS MEN, *also in plain*
clothes like himself. They talk and look at the people waiting.
The first of the arrivals start coming through customs and are greeted by
relations.

HOLLAND's *two* OFFICERS *take up new positions nearer to the arrival*
point.

22. Interior. Heathrow customs. Day.

The green channels are closed. All bags are being searched and there are
huge queues already building up as CORA *arrives within sight of the*
desks, carrying only a small suitcase and an overstuffed shoulder bag.
She looks on in dismay. There is chaos as the place fills up.
O'NEILL *again watchful.*

23. Interior. Heathrow concourse. Day.

HOLLAND *looks on. His* TWO OFFICERS *position themselves to be near*
CORA *when she comes through.*
We see for the first time among the crowd McCABE *and* SIMPSON.
McCABE *has a discreet look around, looking for customs men.*

24. Interior. Heathrow customs desk. Day.

CORA *puts her case and bag up for inspection.*
OFFICER. Sorry, love.
CORA. That's all right. It isn't locked.
  He opens her luggage and rummages in a cursory way.

OFFICER. Thank you.

CORA. Thank you. God bless you.

25. Interior. Concourse. Day.

CORA *appears with her bags.*

HOLLAND *and his* MEN *move and so do* McCABE *and* SIMPSON.

CORA *makes her way through the groups of arrivals and relatives.*

The CUSTOMS MEN *stay close to* CORA *but they are obviously not intending to arrest her.*

Suddenly McCABE *and* SIMPSON *step in front of* CORA *and produce their warrant cards and an arrest warrant.*

McCABE. Cora Davis?

HOLLAND (*twenty yards away*). What in God's name –?

  CORA *is too stunned to reply.* SIMPSON *already has her suitcase and is taking her shoulder bag too.*

  People look on in amazement, not least the TWO CUSTOMS MEN *who are only six feet away.*

  The TWO CUSTOMS MEN *look to* HOLLAND.

McCABE (*loudly*). We're police officers. We're arresting you. This is the arrest warrant.

  They lead her towards the exit.

CORA. What's this?

McCABE (*softly*). You're nicked, sweetheart.

They escort her away with maximum speed and minimum fuss.

HOLLAND *and his men look on in dismay and anger.*

HOLLAND. Who the hell *are* they?

CORA. I think you're making a mistake, officer. Surely this is a mistake?

26. Exterior. M4 Motorway. Day.

A police car heading from Heathrow towards London. A POLICE DRIVER *in front.*

In the back seat, D.S. McCABE, D.C. SIMPSON, *and* CORA.

D.C. SIMPSON *rummages in the bag and in the suitcase.*

CORA. Why don't you just tell me what you want?

  They ignore her.

  Can't you see this is a mistake? My Mother Superior's going to want a very good explanation for this.

  Her luggage obviously doesn't contain what they seek.

  D.C. SIMPSON *looks to* D.S. McCABE *for instructions.*

  D.S. McCABE *looks at her, hard.*

McCABE. Where is it?

CORA *is apparently baffled.*

CORA. I don't understand. I'm sorry. Could you please tell me what you want from me?

D.S. McCABE *takes a knife from his pocket.*

D.C. SIMPSON *tips the contents of the suitcase on to the floor.*

D.S. McCABE *rips the lining.*

For Heaven's sake!

In the front, the DRIVER *is worried about all this. The search again reveals nothing.* CORA *trembles and closes her eyes.*

It doesn't matter. We don't need suitcases or clothes. All we need is enough to eat and a roof over our heads.

She seems to be praying silently.

D.S. McCABE *tips the contents of the shoulder bag on to his knees.*

D.S. McCABE *picks out a paper bag. He opens it and takes out an unused sanitary towel. He looks at it, at* D.C. SIMPSON, *and at* CORA. *He holds it up and studies it.*

McCABE. If you were a customs man looking for naughty substances, would you search a nun?

SIMPSON. I might.

McCABE. If you were a customs man looking for naughty substances would you search a nun if you thought she might be having her period?

SIMPSON. Oh, leave it out.

D.S. McCABE *looks at her with a raised eyebrow.*

CORA. You can't be serious. I don't think you *are* a policeman.

McCABE. I don't think you're a nun.

CORA. That man in the front, you seem like a decent man. If you have any Christian feelings, stop this car.

McCABE. Keep your eyes on the road, driver.

SIMPSON. Get in the fast lane and put your foot down.

The car speeds up.

CORA *is worried.*

McCABE. Anorak.

We now concentrate on the DRIVER *and his view of the proceedings in his rear view mirror.*

We hear the anorak taken off.

D.C. SIMPSON *checks it quickly.*

Skirt.

CORA. I refuse.

McCABE. You take it off or I'll do it for you.

She starts to remove her skirt.

27. Exterior. M4 Motorway. Day.

A coach heading into London from Heathrow. On board is a party of AMERICAN TOURISTS. *The* COURIER *stands up and switches on the* P.A. *system.*

COURIER. Hi. I'm Sherry. You'll be seeing quite a lot of me in the next six weeks. Welcome to England and thank you for choosing to vacation with Victoria's England Tours. This year is a very special one. It marks the hundred and fiftieth anniversary of the accession of Queen Victoria to the throne. So we'd like to start off your holiday with a champagne toast to that great monarch.
A WAITRESS *starts passing out plastic cups of champagne.*

28. Exterior. In the police car on M4. Day.

CORA. I am not removing my underwear. Have you got no feelings? What sort of men are you?
McCABE. Look, I'll give you three seconds to get those drawers off, starting now. One.
DRIVER (*muttering*). Bloody hell.
McCABE. Two. Three.
A struggle breaks out in the back.
CORA. Get your filthy hands off me!
There is a tremendous ripping noise.
Oh, you rotten bastard!

29. Exterior. In the coach on the M4. Day.

COURIER *and* PASSENGERS *raise their plastic cups.*

ALL. To Queen Victoria!
They drink.
COURIER. And here's to you. Congratulations. You've chosen a great holiday and I can promise you some fascinating sights.
This is appreciated. But one or two people in window seats overlooking the fast lane have already begun to notice something. They point in astonishment at a police car attempting in vain to overtake.
In the back seat, two men appear to be trying to pull the knickers off a nun. Some of the women passengers start to scream.

30. Interior. Police cell. Lewisham Police Station. Day.

DAVID FRANKLAND, *fifties, enters cell.*
He sees CORA.

She's no longer wearing the outfit or the sanguine expression of the nun. She's subdued and tearful, anxious and depressed.

FRANKLAND. Mrs Davis? David Frankland. Mrs Hollis telephoned me. I'm a solicitor.

CORA. Oh, thank God. (*She stands up eagerly.*) Can I go now?

FRANKLAND. Well, it isn't quite so easy as that.
He sits and takes out pad and pen.
She sits reluctantly.

FRANKLAND. It's often remarked how much easier it is to get *in* to custody than to get out.
He smiles.
CORA *doesn't.*
Now I understand that you've been charged already and that you've made a statement.

CORA. Yes.

FRANKLAND. Were you told that you could choose to remain silent?

CORA. Oh yes, they said that.

FRANKLAND. What exactly did you say – can you remember?

CORA. Only that I did it.
FRANKLAND *does his best not to look dismayed.*

FRANKLAND. I see. And why did you say that?

CORA. Well. I did do it. They found the stuff *on* me, you see. So I didn't see any point really in . . .
He nods and scribbles.

CORA (*hopefully*). How long will I be kept in, do you think?

FRANKLAND. Well . . .

CORA. Only Leoni, my daughter, she needs me at home really. She's expecting. Her fourth.

FRANKLAND. Well, overnight at least. You'll be brought before a magistrate tomorrow morning and the question of bail will be decided.

CORA. Will you be there?

FRANKLAND. Oh yes. I'll be taking good care of your interests from now on.

CORA. Oh good. Overnight, that's not too bad. She's a grown woman, for goodness sake, she can manage another night.
FRANKLAND *is worried about her unrealistic view of the future.*

FRANKLAND. Mrs Davis, looking ahead, I wouldn't wish to encourage you to be over-optimistic.

CORA. No, no, I realise that.
FRANKLAND *is a bit happier.*
But at the same time, I mean, I'm an old woman. I'm a

granny. They won't be too hard on a granny, now will they?
(*She smiles.*)

31. Exterior. Holloway Prison. Evening.

Establishing shot of the prison.

32. Interior. Holloway Prison. Evening.

CORA *alone in her cell. Baffled, frightened.*
The narrow strips of her cell windows are pushed open to allow in the evening air. The window gives out on to a deep courtyard.
All around the courtyard are windows. Many have arms sticking out of them. Many of the windows have been kicked out and lie broken in the yard. The WOMEN *are having shouted conversations across distances. Ten different conversations are going on. To* CORA *it sounds like a cacophony until she discerns that one of the voices is addressing her.*

WOMAN'S VOICE. You. The new one. Oy, the new one. What are
  you in for? The new one. What are you in for?
   CORA *is drawn to the window.*
WOMAN'S VOICE. The new one! What are you in for?
CORA. Heroin!

33. Exterior. London Docklands. Evening.

McCABE *sits waiting in his lovely BMW. The place is deserted. Beside him is* PAM HOLLIS.

PAM. What you going to tell them?
   McCABE *doesn't speak.*
   Well you'll have to explain. I mean we can't be left with
   nothing. George. What are you going to –?
McCABE. Will you shut your crack please, Pam? I get enough ear-
   ache from her indoors.
   They sit in silence.
   McCABE *notices a speck of dust on the interior trim. He polishes it off*
   with a wet finger.
   A top of the range Mercedes approaches swiftly and parks close to
   them.
   Out of the passenger seat steps a man who could easily pass for an
   ITALIAN. *He walks over as* McCABE *unrolls his window.*
   The ITALIAN *holds out his hand.* McCABE *thrusts a package into it.*
McCABE. Just one thing. A slight problem.
ITALIAN. Problem?
McCABE. I mean a slight shortfall.

ITALIAN *looks alarmed.*

No, no, no. It's all there. Only mine isn't. You see, we had to –

ITALIAN. What you do with yours is your problem.

He gets back in the Mercedes. It roars away, splashing mud all over the BMW.

McCABE *leaps out and looks at it.*

He gets back in the car. He lets his head fall into his hands. He sits up. He takes a deep breath.

PAM. Well now what, George?

McCABE. Shut up.

He starts the car.

34. Interior. Visiting room. Holloway Prison. Day.

LEONI MASON, *early thirties, four months pregnant, sits glumly waiting. Other visits are taking place in the room.*

An OFFICER *shows in* CORA.

LEONI *puts a cheerful look on her face.*

The PRISON OFFICER *stands with her colleagues.*

CORA *sits opposite* LEONI.

CORA. Well, you took your bloody time.

LEONI. Oh Mum, I couldn't. I'm so upset.

Silence.

CORA *apologetically mouths the words.*

CORA. Have you got any cigarettes?

LEONI. What?

CORA. Have you got any cigarettes?

LEONI (*diving for her cigarettes*). Oh, sorry. I'll leave these for you.

CORA *smokes avidly.*

LEONI *is a bit distressed but keeping on top of it.*

CORA. Baby all right?

LEONI (*feeling it*). Yeh.

CORA. Kids?

LEONI. Yeh. They think you're at Hayling Island.

LEONI *tries to be cheerful for* CORA's *sake.*

Pam drove me over to the Scrubs yesterday. Broke the news to Martin. Course bein' Martin he saw the funny side first.

This makes CORA *burst into sobs.*

CORA. Oh yeh! Funny. I don't think it's funny. He leaves you with debts and I try to do something about it and . . .

This is barely intelligible.

LEONI *cries too.*

LEONI. Don't blame him, Mum. I knew you would.

CORA. I don't know how you could marry a criminal.

This is all done through tears and snot and sobs.

LEONI. He wasn't a criminal when I met him.

CORA. Well he is now, isn't he? He's a thief. He's a swindler. I'm ashamed.

LEONI. Well what's smugglin' heroin then? Bloody Duke of Edinburgh Award Scheme?

WPO is walking towards them.

35. Exterior. Outside Holloway. Day.

LEONI, *sobbing her heart out, is helped into a car by* PAM HOLLIS. *In the back are* LEONI's *three kids. The youngest starts crying.*

PAM. How is she?

LEONI. She wants to know if promises are going to be kept, even though it went wrong.

PAM. Has she said anything to her solicitor?

LEONI. Only that she's guilty.

She breaks down in tears.

All the KIDS *start crying.*

36. Grimshaw's. Katherine's room. Day.

KATHERINE *at her desk.* ALAN ACKROYD *getting his papers together to go to court. He looks like a man about to face the death squad. He's sweating and mentally incoherent.*

ACKROYD. Erm . . . yes . . . and . . .

He's twitching.

She's trying not to add to his misery by noticing it.

KATHERINE. Alan, screw it, it's only another case. Murder's no harder to do.

ACKROYD. Why – do I look nervous?

KATHERINE. It'll only be submissions. You've got good briefs handling the other defendants. Just do what they do.

ACKROYD. I think I can handle it actually. Thanks all the same.

KATHERINE *thinks 'Fuck you then'.*

ACKROYD *goes out.*

She goes into the Clerks' Room to TOM.

KATHERINE. Look, why did you get him briefed in this? He can't do it. He's not a barrister. He can't cope. He makes speeches that make the jury laugh. Just because his grandfather was a barrister and his father was a barrister, why does he have to be a barrister? Why can't he sell soft toys or something?

TOM. Have you finished? Would you like a granny who smuggled half a million quids worth of heroin into Heathrow? Pleading to it. Not a lot for you to do.

KATHERINE. Yes. Anything else for me?
TOM. No.
KATHERINE. Any money?
TOM. No.

37. Interior. Katherine's flat. Morning.

ROBERT *and* KATHERINE *in bed. Radio playing music.*
ROBERT *coming out of a doze.* KATHERINE *is up on one elbow facing away from him. She's chuckling to herself. He starts licking her back. She chuckles. He thinks she's enjoying it. He licks her some more.*

KATHERINE Sixty-year-old woman here charged with bringing in half a kilo of heroin stuffed inside her knickers! Know what she says?
He's biting the back of her neck.
She says she's got lots of Asian shops near her house and she's always wanted to go to India!
She laughs. He's trying to get his tongue in her ear. She reads and sort of gives him a little nuzzle with her back. He thinks he's on to something. She laughs out loud.
KATHERINE. She dressed up as a nun so the Indians wouldn't pester her!
ROBERT *gives up. He gets up and makes some coffee.*
You're for the high-jump, Granny.
She can't help noticing from the angry clatter of dishes and cups and spoons coming from the kitchen that ROBERT *is pissed off.*
He comes in and starts setting the table for breakfast for two.
She puts down the brief.
Robert. Come on. Come and see me a minute.
Rather sulkily he sits on the bed. She kisses him.
Mmm? Come on. Come on.
ROBERT *gets back in bed and they start to get it on.*
The telephone rings.
KATHERINE. No, no, just ignore it.
She and ROBERT *try this for a few seconds.* ROBERT *disengages and picks up the telephone.*
ROBERT. Yeh? Yeh.
He hands her the telephone and starts to get dressed.
KATHERINE. Hello? Who? Oh, right, right. Yeh. I've got it in front of me, actually.
She fishes for the brief she was reading.
FRANKLAND (*on telephone*). I wondered what were your first impressions.
KATHERINE. Well. I think it's as well she's pleading guilty. There

isn't a lot here in terms of a defence.

FRANKLAND (*chuckling*). Nothing whatever, I'm afraid. What we'll be looking for therefore is something elegant in the way of mitigation.

KATHERINE (*chuckling*). Well. I can talk about how she needed the money and all that. Beyond that though . . . Since the LCJ has made it perfectly clear to judges that there is no mitigation full stop in cases of drug smuggling, you know . . . So I'll do my best. But I think she's facing a long stretch.

ROBERT *leaves noisily.* KATHERINE *doesn't notice.*

FRANKLAND. Oh, there's no doubt about that.

KATHERINE. Does she realise that? Have you told her what she's facing?

FRANKLAND. Well . . . I've certainly not hidden the gravity of the thing . . . Perhaps you'd like to meet her?

KATHERINE. Yes, OK. I think I better. Get your clerk to ring my clerk, will you?

FRANKLAND. She's a jolly old dear, I'm sure you'll enjoy her.

KATHERINE. Oh, just one thing: has she given you any clue about who she was running it for?

FRANKLAND. No. I'm afraid she's not interested in talking about that.

She puts down the telephone. She looks around for ROBERT.

38. Interior. Scotland Yard. Office. Day.

The office of COMMANDER STANTON, *head of the Robbery Squad.*
STANTON *looks up from paperwork as* D.S. McCABE *is shown in by*
STANTON'S CLERK. (*Uniformed.*)
D.S. McCABE *sits.* CLERK *leaves.*
STANTON *looks at him for a while.*

STANTON. Well, I don't know what to say. You're an arsehole, that's obvious, but it's not a full explanation of a cock-up of this dimension.

D.S. McCABE *can't think what to say.*

You find out about a major heroin smuggling operation so you just swan out to Heathrow and arrest this old woman. Didn't it occur to you to ask anybody? Didn't it occur to you that other people might've been interested in seeing where she was going?

D.S. McCABE *can't think what to say.*

STANTON. How did you know about her?

McCABE. Information received, sir.

STANTON. Don't give me 'information received, sir!' I want to

know who told you, why, what and when. Where's the
bleeding paperwork? I've got this bugger Holland from
Customs and Excise going apeshit in the DAC's office.
Bananas are being gone on the tenth floor and there's not a
piece of paper in here that tells anybody how you knew. I
want it on my desk by four o'clock today or I'll put you in a
room with the Customs and Excise and you can explain it to
them yourself. Now get out.

39. Interior. Inner London Crown Court. Cells. Day.

ARNOLD FLOWERS *picks his way through the sea of human misery to
find* HENRY GRIFFITHS *once again handcuffed to a radiator in a
cubicle.*

FLOWERS. Hello, Henry. How are things?
  HENRY *is so depressed he can't speak.*
  Ah. Well. Look I better get up there. I'll see you in a bit.
  FLOWERS *goes.*

40. Interior. Inner London Magistrates Court. Day.

Courtroom.
HENRY *is making another remand appearance.*

FLOWERS. There has been a change of circumstances. I
  understand that the police are no longer objecting to bail.
MAGISTRATE. Is that true?
SERGEANT. Your Honour. He has now obtained a fixed address
  and gone to live with his sister, we now accept that bail is
  unlikely to cause us any difficulties. We accept that.
MAGISTRATE. Very well.
  HENRY *is amazed.*

41. Exterior. Outside court building. Day.

HENRY *emerges. It takes him a second or two to believe that he really has
got a temporary reprieve from the nightmare. He's just beginning to cope
with the idea when he sees* D.S. MCCABE *across the road, beckoning him.*

42. Exterior. Travelling in city centre. Day.

In a car in the middle of London. Heavy traffic. D.C. SIMPSON *is
driving* D.S. MCCABE *and* HENRY *in back.*

MCCABE. Well don't say thank you. You can go back any time you like. All I have to do is pick you up for doing your gas meter or whatever and you've broken your bail, haven't you?

HENRY. I ain't got gas, I'm all electric.

D.C. SIMPSON *laughs.*

McCABE. Oh, Henry, you are a pitifully stupid specimen. Let's keep it simple. Did you like it in Brixton?

HENRY. No.

McCABE. No. It's awful, isn't it? Totally out of order up with what the scum have to put. I've written to my MP about it but he doesn't give a toss. Would you like to stay out then?

HENRY. Yes.

McCABE. Yes.

He hands him a statement.

HENRY. What's this?

McCABE. It's a statement you forgot to sign. Don't read it. Just sign it.

HENRY. I don't know a woman called Cora Davis. Oh, no, no.

He tries to give it back.

I ain't signing that.

McCABE. Let's start again, shall we? Did you like it in Brixton?

HENRY *wrestles with himself.*

You won't have to give evidence. She's pleading guilty anyway. It's just a bit of paperwork.

HENRY *signs.*

They stop the car and chuck him out.

43. Interior. Cubicles. Holloway. Day.

KATHERINE *sits waiting to meet* CORA.

With her is an outdoor clerk, MIRANDA FRANKLAND, *twenty, who's doodling on a pad.*

KATHERINE *is sizing her up.*

KATHERINE. What made you join a solicitors, Miranda?

MIRANDA. Oh, no I just help out. It's a bit of pin money for me. Actually I've just started an acting training course.

KATHERINE *tries hard not to dislike her.*

KATHERINE. Oh. I see.

MIRANDA. My Uncle David's a partner, so . . . David Frankland.

KATHERINE. Oh right. So you're not really interested in the law?

MIRANDA. Oh yeh, I mean, yeh.

KATHERINE. But not as a career.

MIRANDA. Erm . . . no. I mean I know there's a lot of money in it and everything. But . . . I dunno . . . it's a bit of a slog if you're a woman, I bet.

KATHERINE. Women can slog.

MIRANDA. Oh yeh, I mean I'm not saying that.

KATHERINE gives this up as a waste of time.

Pause.

One thing always fascinates me. When a barrister gets somebody off, when you know they're guilty . . . I mean . . .?

She looks expectantly at KATHERINE.

KATHERINE. What's the question?

MIRANDA. How do you cope?

KATHERINE. Cope? I don't need to cope. I'm celebrating.

Door at the end of the room opens.

Footsteps.

44. Interior. Cubicle. Day.

CORA *is now sitting with them.*

KATHERINE. Cora. I'm just going to ask you some things and talk a bit about the case. OK? Now, your statements to the police and to Mr Frankland admit that you brought in the heroin. You *knew* you were a courier.

CORA. Yes.

KATHERINE. OK. Take a minute to think about this. Did you know for certain *what* you were carrying?

CORA looks shifty.

CORA. Well . . .

KATHERINE butts in before CORA commits herself.

KATHERINE. I mean: could it be that you might've been told it was . . . jewellery, say?

CORA. Well. (*Obviously lying.*) I thought it might be cannabis.

KATHERINE nods, but isn't encouraging.

But surely cannabis isn't as bad, is it? I mean: surely the judge must take that into account?

KATHERINE. Believe me, Cora, that's a non-starter. You're admitting you brought in a proscribed drug. The fact is it was heroin. You don't score any points in court by saying you thought it was one proscribed drug, not another. But I'll mention it. You never know. OK.

CORA insinuates her cigarettes out of her pocket.

CORA. Alright if I smoke, ladies?

KATHERINE shrugs her assent as she thinks about the next bit.

CORA lights up.

MIRANDA *eyes the cigarette.*

KATHERINE. OK. Now, you were –

MIRANDA. Actually, Cora, could I bum one?

CORA. Course, dear, help yourself!

Which she does, not catching KATHERINE's *steely gaze.*

KATHERINE. You were given this stuff in a hotel in Bombay. Who gave you it?

CORA (*shrugging*). A little Indian bloke.

KATHERINE. He didn't introduce himself. OK. You concealed the stuff in your underwear before boarding a flight back to London.

CORA. Well . . .

KATHERINE. What?

CORA. *He* did it as a matter of fact. They didn't tell me *that*.

KATHERINE. Who?

CORA. Who what? I told you: he never said what his name was.

KATHERINE. No. Who didn't tell you?

But CORA's *not having any of this.*

CORA. Tell me what?

KATHERINE. Who didn't tell you before you went that you'd have to open your legs to a little Indian feller so he could tape the stuff to you?

CORA. Nobody. That's what I'm saying: nobody told me.

KATHERINE *letting it go for now.*

KATHERINE. OK. And you wore this stuff all the way back like that?

But CORA *is now suspicious of* KATHERINE.

CORA. I've been through all this with Mr Frankland.

Pause.

KATHERINE. How many hours? Twelve hours? With all that polythene stuck to you, sitting on a plane? Must've been awful. I can't imagine it.

Pause.

Can you imagine that, Miranda?

MIRANDA. Must've been really uncomfortable.

CORA *warms up to* MIRANDA.

CORA. It was shockin'. When I think back! I dunno . . . the things you do for money, eh?

She laughs and makes an 'Oooh' face.

They laugh with her.

It's not the worst I've done for money – but it was the most uncomfortable!

More laughing.

I can tell you: twelve hours or no twelve hours – I didn't move about much!

More laughing.

MIRANDA (*laughing*). Not surprising with half a kilo of smack inside your undies.

CORA. Half a kilo? Three kilos if you don't mind! Half a kilo. My shape, you wouldn't know half a kilo was there, love!
She laughs.
KATHERINE *is still smiling, but she's checking the papers.*
KATHERINE. Cora, you're in enough trouble with half a kilo. And since we're on the subject: whereabouts exactly *did* you put it?
CORA *is confused.*
Silence.
KATHERINE *re-checks.*
Cora. You are charged with importing a half a kilo of heroin.
CORA (*shaking her head*). Three kilos.
KATHERINE. Let me get this right. How many strips of polythene did the little Indian feller tape inside your drawers?
CORA. Six.
KATHERINE. Did you remove any between Bombay and London?
CORA. No.
KATHERINE. So how many did they find when you were searched?
CORA. What – the first time or the second time?
KATHERINE. Whoa, hold it, I'm lost. Hang on.
She speed-reads to the relevant bit in the papers.
Yeh: according to the police you were searched at Lewisham police station where they found – this is the two women police officers, yeh? – they found one bag of heroin weighing a half a kilo.
CORA. Yes, but, the other two – the men, the ones who arrested me – they'd already found the six bags in the car on the motorway when they ripped my knickers off with all those peope lookin' in on the bus. That's why we had to stop at Marks and Spencer.
KATHERINE *and* MIRANDA *are both dumbfounded and confused.*
KATHERINE. I'm sorry, Cora . . .?
CORA. So they could get me some new ones. The old ones were in shreds. Then we parked near the station and they had some new sticky tape and they put one bag back on me because I had to be searched formally they said. But they couldn't get it all in again they said, but they said that didn't matter though, and I got the new knickers on and in we went. And these two young lady police – they were lovely actually, like nurses – they searched me properly. And there was the stuff. Surprise, surprise.
Pause.
KATHERINE. Were they surprised? The WPCs?
CORA. Very. I was still dressed as a nun, you see.
MIRANDA *bursts out laughing.*

KATHERINE. Miranda. But not the two male detectives? Were
they surprised when they found the stuff on you in the car?

CORA. Oh, no, they were looking for it. Pigs.

Silence.

KATHERINE *thinks. She sighs.*

KATHERINE. Cora, it would be best if I just forget that I heard
any of this. You're charged with a half a kilo. Let's just forget
the rest.

CORA. Well where did it go?

KATHERINE *hesitates.*

KATHERINE. It's not our problem.

CORA. But surely, if we tell the judge –

KATHERINE. I'm not going into that court and saying 'my client
wishes it to be known that she didn't bring in a half a kilo of
heroin, she brought in three kilos.' No way. Forget it. You're
in deep enough trouble. I didn't hear it, OK. Nor did
Miranda. Christ. Now. Where were we?

CORA. What do you mean – deep enough trouble? You're giving
me palpitations here. Mr. Frankland says to me 'there's no
reason for despair'.

KATHERINE *decides to bite the bullet.*

KATHERINE. That's true, but . . . Mr Frankland has maybe not
wanted to upset you too much. You're admitting a very serious
crime and you couldn't've picked a worse time. I promise you
my level best with the mitigation speech. But, Cora, you've got
to realise that we're looking at . . . well five years minimum.

This is a bodyblow to CORA.

45. Interior. Holloway. Day.

KATHERINE *and* MIRANDA *are waiting to be let out.*
Families of prisoners are waiting to be admitted.

KATHERINE. Did I say *five* years? What we need here is a good
account from Cora about Mr Big and threats to her family if
she names names, which I'm sure is the truth of it. Blah, blah.
Mitigation. Tell Uncle David, will you?

MIRANDA. But I mean: surely we should be doing something
about those cops?

KATHERINE. Like what?

MIRANDA. Well they've obviously taken five bags of heroin, God!

KATHERINE. What I don't understand is if the police decided to
help themselves why didn't they take the lot? You know: half a
kilo's worth a lot of money, right?

MIRANDA. But . . .

KATHERINE. What?

MIRANDA. But they took it, didn't they? I mean: God! Can't we do something?

KATHERINE. What do you want me to do about it? Ask them to put it back in Cora's knickers and re-write the charge sheet?

MIRANDA is chastened.

And don't bum cigarettes off an old granny doing time!

PO arrives to pass them out.

One more thing. Write this down. I want you to ask your Uncle David: How come those detectives – who aren't even Drugs Squad – knew about Cora? How did they know? Do they hang around Heathrow Airport all day looking for suspicious old biddies or what? There's nothing about it in the papers, but somebody must've tipped them off. Who?

Out they go.

46. Interior. A West London Law Centre. Day.

A busy scene with people coming and going from offices leading off the reception area. People waiting to be seen, sit on chairs.

ANGELA, a young black, is arguing with somebody on the telephone at the reception desk.

HENRY has come in from the street and now stands wondering what to do. He has a crumpled piece of paper clutched in his hand.

A woman SOLICITOR comes out of an office and puts a large envelope on ANGELA's desk for posting, making sure that ANGELA sees what she's doing. On her way back, she sees HENRY.

WOMAN. You want some help?

HENRY is slow to respond. He looks at her. He looks at the piece of paper in his hand. He gets his thoughts sorted out and opens his mouth. But by now ANGELA has put down the telephone and is ready to deal with him.

ANGELA. OK, Miriam. Can I help you?

MIRIAM goes into her office, watched by HENRY.

Can I help you?

HENRY focuses his attention on her. He looks again at the piece of paper.

HENRY. Alton Phillips.

ANGELA picks up telephone.

ANGELA. Is he expecting you, Mr . . . ?

HENRY. I saw him on the telly.

Down goes the telephone.

ANGELA. OK, well he's very tied up just now. He won't be long. You need legal advice of some kind, yeh?

HENRY *thinks and nods. He's a very troubled man.*

HENRY. I'm on a hell trip.

Suddenly he's almost in tears. He chokes back a big sob. He takes big breaths to steady himself and dabs his eyes on his overcoat sleeve.

ANGELA *thinks he's on something.*

ANGELA. Well, sit down a minute, eh? I'll get you a cup of coffee, in a minute, OK?

He goes and sits down. He stands again immediately and slowly paces the floor, locked in his own thoughts.

ALTON PHILLIPS *bursts from his office and puts a brief on* ANGELA's *desk.*

ANGELA. Gentleman here wants a word, Alton.

ALTON (*friendly, straightforward*). OK. Give me five minutes, right, and I'll be with you. Angie, this must get to Frank Cartwright before he goes to Bristol tonight.

ANGELA. I'll put it in a taxi.

She's already dialling.

ALTON. Four minutes. Would you like a coffee? Angie, get him a coffee, yeh?

He disappears back into his office.

DILIP *comes out of his office, startling* HENRY. DILIP *has a sheaf of papers in his hand concerning a landlord dispute. He makes a wrong assumption about* HENRY.

DILIP. Pilecki?

HENRY *gawps at him.*

DILIP *checks the papers.*

DILIP. Is it 'Pilecki' or . . .

DILIP *searches for the name.*

ANGELA *breaks off her telephone call.*

ANGELA. Hang on a sec, can you? Dilip, Mr Pilecki's a Hungarian. That's right. Fetter Court, near the Old Bailey.

DILIP (*beginning to understand*). You're *not* Mr Pilecki?

ANGELA. Pilecki's *gone*, Dilip. Miriam spoke to him. Hello? Great. Thank you.

Telephone down.

DILIP *goes back into his office.*

HENRY *looking decidedly jumpy.*

ANGELA *gets to her feet.*

Tea or coffee?

HENRY. I'll come back I fink.

HENRY *heads for the street door.*

ANGELA. No, look, he'll be free in a minute.

But HENRY's *gone.*

47. Interior. Law Centre. Day.

ALTON *comes out of his office into reception area. He's expecting to find* HENRY.

ALTON. OK. Sorry.

ANGELA *looks up at him.*

  Where is he?

ANGELA. Gone.

ALTON. Why?

ANGELA. I dunno. I think he was on something. Man, he was weird.

ALTON. What did he want?

ANGELA. He didn't say.

ALTON. Did you ask him?

ANGELA. Not specifically. You said five minutes.

ALTON. What was his name?

  ANGELA *sighs. She forgot to ask.*

ALTON. Well we sorted him out, didn't we?

ANGELA. He said he'd come back.

ALTON (*heading for his office*). Yeh.

48. Exterior. Streets near Law Centre. Evening.

It's getting dark as ALTON *walks away from the Law Centre towards his car. He passes a figure squatting on the pavement. It's* HENRY. ALTON *sits down beside him. It's cold.*

ALTON. You're in big trouble, right? Shall we go back to the centre? Or I'll buy you a beer if you like.

HENRY *still mute.*

  Are you hungry?

  HENRY *thinks and nods.*

49. Interior. A greasy spoon. Night.

HENRY *and* ALTON.

ALTON *just with a coffee.*

HENRY *is finishing off a monsterburger.*

Now he's post-prandial. He leans into ALTON *and checks out for eavesdroppers.*

ALTON *is still not sure if this bloke is all there.*

The PROPRIETOR *is wiping down the tables.*

HENRY. I ain't a choirboy, Alton. I ain't saying that.

  ALTON *accepts this in a man-of-the-world way.*

  Well. Ever come across a cop called George McCabe?

  ALTON *nods, surprised.*

ALTON. Friend of yours, is he?

HENRY. Friend of mine, you must be jokin'. This bloke puts his fags out on your legs.

HENRY's so scared his voice goes loud.

The PROPRIETOR *looks over.*

HENRY *breathes deep to steady himself.*

ALTON. I've come across him once or twice. He's not nice. How do you know him?

HENRY. I know him 'cos he's sittin' on my back, Alton. He's a killagorilla. Even when I fink I've got bail, McCabe's got his fist down my throat.

PROPRIETOR *comes over to clear the table.*

HENRY *holds his peace till he goes away again.*

ALTON. What's he nicked you for?

HENRY. Dealin'. But it ain't what I'm nicked for that's worryin' me. It's this other thing. Cora Davis.

50. Interior. Cubicles. Holloway. Day.

CORA, KATHERINE *and* MIRANDA, *in silence.*

KATHERINE. Are you going to answer?

Silence.

Who were you running it to? Cora?

Silence.

Well maybe the judge will come to his own conclusions about that. He'll maybe think: 'This old bird has got herself a little business'.

CORA *'Ha's' quietly.*

Well it's up to you. It seems all you have to say is that you're guilty. So what? You're guilty. Great. Now tell me something interesting. Give me something to build a case on – or I can't help you.

CORA(*angry*). Well I better have another barrister then.

KATHERINE. Fine. Is that what you want?

CORA. Well you can't defend me you say. Over and over and over.

KATHERINE. OK. You can get your solicitor to ask me to return the brief if you want. You've a perfect right to do that, if that's what you want.

CORA *nods.*

I'll bugger off then, shall I?

CORA. Yes. Do. Bugger your*self* while you're about it. I don't need you. I plead guilty.

KATHERINE. Miranda, stop writing. Have you got any cigarettes?

MIRANDA. Mm.

KATHERINE. Well get them out.

MIRANDA. Oh. Yeh, sorry.

She puts them on the table.

CORA *smokes.*

KATHERINE *smokes.*

CORA. I didn't know you smoked.

KATHERINE. When I want.

CORA. So typical of your generation. What I want when I want. No idea about sacrifice.

KATHERINE. Sacrifice? OK, let's talk about sacrifice. Is Leoni being taken care of?

CORA. I hate people like you.

KATHERINE. Let's leave me out of it. I didn't walk through Customs with heroin up my fanny.

CORA. I know you. I know all you're interested in is winning a case.

KATHERINE. Thank your lucky stars.

CORA. I brought that girl up without a father, so don't take the piss out of me!

KATHERINE. I'm sorry. OK.

She has nothing more to say. She stubs out her cigarette.

CORA. I've never expected anything from life, so whatever happens doesn't matter.

This kind of talk drives KATHERINE *up the pole.*

I got myself into this mess, so I'll have to pay the consequences.

KATHERINE. Bollocks. How much are they giving Leoni?

Silence.

CORA *taken aback.*

CORA *stubs out her cigarette. She has nothing more to say.*

KATHERINE. Is it a lump sum, a weekly allowance or what? I hope it's a lump sum, in advance of the trial, because once you go down, Leoni will never see them again.

Silence.

CORA *is rattled but she says nothing.*

Well I probably won't see you again until we get to court. Is there anything you need?

CORA. No thank you. I have everything I need. We don't need much when it comes down to it.

MIRANDA *is damp-eyed.*

KATHERINE *could strangle.*

51. Interior. Holloway. Day.

MIRANDA *and* KATHERINE *are waiting to be passed out.*
KATHERINE *is angry and agitated.*

KATHERINE. I don't know if Cora's all there or not, but I know
one thing: she's driving *me* round the bend. Does she think she
really is a nun?

MIRANDA. Yeh, but I mean it's all to do with sacrifice. Like she
said.

KATHERINE (*exasperated*). Well if she wants to suffer for her sins,
we've got a criminal justice system that'll happily oblige her.
I've done all I can.

52. Interior. Fetter Court. Day.

Clerks' room.

HUGH *and* LORRAINE *are babysitting* HENRY *while* FRANK *and* ALTON
confer in FRANK'*s office.*
*They have given him a cup of tea and they are getting on with paper
work.*
HENRY *can't sit down. He gets up and wanders about. He's much
more relaxed now.*

HENRY. So like what goes on in here then?

HUGH Well this is the Clerks' room. Really the nerve centre of
the chambers. All the work comes through here. We negotiate
with solicitors and that, don't we, Lorraine?

LORRAINE. Yeh, basically we get work from people like Alton for
people like Frank. And we negotiate their fees and make sure
the right brief arrives in the right place at the right time . . .

HUGH. We do all the hard work basically.

HENRY *hasn't understood a word.*

HENRY. Amazing. So you're sort of . . . like judges and that?

HUGH. No.

LORRAINE. No, not really.

HENRY. Oh right. What are you then?

LORRAINE. Well I'm a barristers' clerk and Hugh is a junior
barristers' clerk.

HENRY (*sympathetic to* HUGH). Oh but still it's great. It's a job,
innit? Do you have to have any bits of paper, Hugh?

LORRAINE *can't stay any longer without laughing so she picks up some
briefs and goes.*

LORRAINE. Back in a minute.

HUGH. Erm . . . no, not really.

HENRY. So I could apply.

HUGH. Yeh.

HENRY. Oh, brilliant. I'll get a form then.
HUGH. Right.
  Pause.
HENRY. Fancy some spliff?
  HUGH *hesitates.*
HUGH. Yeh, all right.

53. Interior. Fetter Court. Day.

FRANK's *room.*
ALTON. They've leaned really hard on this little man, Frank; he's
  done nothing to deserve this. They find him with a few
  grammes of grass, do a bit of agriculture and charge him with
  dealing just to make their figures look good. They refuse him
  bail so whatever happens in his case, he's done a bit of time,
  you know, another nigger off the streets. And he could get
  five in front of the wrong judge. And I mean he's just a nice
  little space cadet. If he wants to spend his Giro to stay spliffed
  out of his head all week why should anybody care? He says
  reality is for people who can't handle drugs.
  FRANK's *got a problem though.*
FRANK. I can do something for him on the drugs thing when the
  time comes. But this other thing . . . Why not ring C4?
ALTON. And say what? 'One of your nice policemen is using the
  bail laws to blackmail my client' – he isn't even my client –
  'into verballing some woman called Cora Davis. Please arrest
  him straightaway.' There must be something better than that.
  Come on, Frank, I know this advice is free, but shit.
FRANK (*after thought*). OK. Maybe we can give the legal process a
  helping hand.

54. Interior. Frank's office. Day.

ALTON, FRANK, HENRY.

ALTON. Henry, this is Frank Cartwright. He's a barrister.
  HENRY (*as if congratulating him*). Oh, fantastic, yeh.
FRANK. Hello, Henry. You've got a bad problem.
HENRY. Oh yeh, it's a bummer. I'm havin' really bad dreams. I'm
  only twenty-two.
  FRANK *nods sympathetically, as if* HENRY *were talking sense.*
ALTON. We've had a talk and Frank wants to help.
HENRY. Fantastic. I fink to myself: I can't lose with *two* good
  people on my side. McCabe better watch out, eh? Wait till I
  tell my mother, eh?
ALTON. Well hang on. There's the slight problem that you

already have a solicitor.

HENRY's *face darkens.*

FRANK. What we're worried about is you leaving Flowers to go to Alton, McCabe finding out about that – and we have to presume that he *would*, I think – and coming down on you again. I mean the last thing we want is your bail to be rescinded.

HENRY. Yeh. Yeh. But I mean: I can't go back to Flowers now, can I?

He's starting to panic.

I mean: I need help, you know.

ALTON. Calm down, Henry. That's a boy.

He calms down.

FRANK. What you *can* do quite legitimately when the time comes is tell Flowers to brief me and I will accept if I possibly can.

HENRY *doesn't like the sound of this word 'possibly'.*

I mean: I will.

ALTON. If Flowers says 'Why Frank Cartwright?' Just say 'Why not, I had a friend who had him and he got him off'. OK? OK?

HENRY. When would I get Frank then?

FRANK. When they set a rough date for the trial, then we all jiggle with dates, and . . . Not that long I wouldn't think.

HENRY. See, Frank, I'm not a dealer –

FRANK *is unhappy about this.*

ALTON. Frank's not allowed to talk to you about the actual case yet.

HENRY. Why?

ALTON. It's just the rules. All that will happen later.

HENRY. Sorry, Frank.

FRANK. No, no. Let's try in the meantime and do something about this false statement. I know a man called Holland who works in Customs and Excise. Give me a day or two to get alongside him, OK? Let me see if he knows anything about Cora Davis and George McCabe.

55. Exterior. Holloway Prison. Day.

D.S. McCABE *and* PAM HOLLIS *arrive in the BMW.*
They sit.

PAM. What am I supposed to say to her?

McCABE. She was your bright idea. Tell her the baby'll end up in a Bolognaise sauce if she opens her trap.

PAM. Oh that'll really settle her nerves, won't it?

D.S. McCABE *rests his head on the steering wheel and thinks. He straightens up.*

McCABE. She's got to see sense. Tell her twenty-five grand is out of the question now. See if she'll take ten.

PAM. Where you going to get ten grand?

McCABE. I dunno.

She gets out. He notices sweat marks on the leather trim on the steering wheel from his forehead. He wipes it.

56. Interior. Holloway cubicles. Day.

CORA *is brought in.* PAM *waiting. They sit.* CORA *looks awful.*

PAM. Oh my God, Cora.

CORA. This place is a madhouse. A girl killed herself day before yesterday. Hung herself. I can't stand it. I just keep thinkin' about the money. Are they sorting it out?

PAM. Yeh. Oh yeh. Only there's a little bit of a problem. You see they say you didn't make the delivery so you shouldn't get the full whack.

CORA (*steely*). Those kids need that money. Without that money all they've got in the world is Leoni and a father who's a halfwit doing seven years in Wormwood Scrubs.

PAM. But, Cora. If you take me down with you it won't make any difference to what you get from the judge.

CORA. That's not what my barrister thinks, I can promise you that.

PAM. But naming me would be pointless. It wouldn't hurt them.

CORA. No but it might make you try a bit harder, love. And I want some on account. Leoni needs money *now*.

57. Exterior. Holloway Prison. Day.

HOLLIS *gets back in the car.*

HOLLIS. I got her down to twenty.

D.S. McCABE *is aghast.*

McCABE. Oh well done.

HOLLIS. You could get fifteen for the car.

McCABE *nods.*

58. Interior. Hospital maternity ward. Morning.

There are dads and grannies. etc. visiting various new mums.
KATHERINE *finds a* NURSE. *The* NURSE *points to* LEONI.

LEONI *is lying on her side, gazing happily at her baby in the cot beside the bed.*

KATHERINE *stands at the foot of the bed, holding the flowers, looking at how happy* LEONI *is.*

KATHERINE. Leoni?

LEONI *looks at her.*

Katherine Hughes.

LEONI *sits up and smiles.*

LEONI. Oh yeh, hello. Nice of you to come.

KATHERINE. She's lovely. Hello, little Cora.

LEONI (*smiling*). You got any?

KATHERINE. I hope you like roses.

LEONI. Oh lovely. Thanks. Really sweet of you. Mum says you've been ever so good to her.

KATHERINE (*guilty, touched*). Did she say that?

LEONI. She says you really care.

KATHERINE *doesn't reply.*

Will it be long for her now?

KATHERINE. No. No, it won't be long now. I'll get a vase or something, shall I?

She goes to the end of the ward to get a vase.

PAM HOLLIS *arrives in the ward and goes to* LEONI's *side.*

She pecks her on the forehead.

PAM. Hello. How's that little chicken? Oh, look at her! Leoni, I've just spoken to sister and she says if you have a good night's sleep tonight she'll let you come home to my place tomorrow, OK?

LEONI *is not totally in favour.*

LEONI. I don't want to. I want to go home.

PAM (*firm*). Now, Leoni. Don't complicate things now. You know the arrangement. After the trial you can do what you like. And you'll be able to afford to. That's settled then.

KATHERINE *arrives back for the end of this.*

LEONI. Pam, this is Katherine Hughes. Katherine, Pam Hollis.

The names mean nothing to them.

Katherine's Mum's barrister.

PAM (*trying to look mildly interested*). Oh. Nice.

KATHERINE. No, not really. I don't like it when the wrong people go to prison.

She goes to BABY CORA *and looks at her.*

She's lovely.

LEONI. Did you say you had one?

KATHERINE (*answering as a lawyer*). No.

59. Interior. Katherine's flat. Night.

KATHERINE *is alone, drinking. She's a bit pissed and a lot depressed.*
The door opens.
ROBERT *comes in. He doesn't speak. She doesn't speak.*
He sizes up the situation. He takes off his coat. Quietly, he removes the
wine bottle.

KATHERINE. Don't do that, please.
He puts it back in front of her. He gets himself a sandwich.
Listen. I'm sorry. I'm more than sorry. You deserve better
than this.
He's going to respond. She stops him. He listens.
I don't know if you can imagine, if I have any right to ask you
to imagine, but . . . day after day, week after week, year after
year: the same desperate people being sent down for the same
desperate reasons. The same stories. The same fit-ups.
Punishment, punishment, punishment. Slap them down. Bang
them up. Forget about them. Pass some more laws if these
ones won't do. Catch more people in the net. Fill up the
prisons till the roof blows off. And I'm in this; I do this for a
living. I help process them through the machine. I look at
these faces staring out at us from the docks and the jury boxes
and galleries, looking at us as if we're talking Latin. Which we
are half the time. While their lives get chopped into pieces.
And do you know the question I always think they'll ask but
never do? 'How fucking dare you do this?' But do you know
what they *do* ask? 'Why the fancy dress?' And I say 'Oh it's
part of the history of the Bar' blah, but the real reason for the
fancy dress is so that you can stop feeling like a real person
because if you had to be yourself you'd die.
ROBERT. How much have you had to drink?
She doesn't reply.
He relents. He gives her a hug. It starts to get serious. He checks her
out.
How much *have* you had to drink?
KATHERINE. Just enough.
They are about to get it on.
The doorbell goes.
Oh that'll be Frank.
ROBERT *can't believe it.*
KATHERINE. No, it's nothing, just somebody he wants me to
meet.
ROBERT. Well sod that and sod you, I'm going out.
KATHERINE. No, please, please. It's a quickie.

She kisses him.
The door bell goes again.

60. Interior. Katherine's flat. Night.

KATHERINE *is sitting close to* ROBERT, *stroking his neck as she listens to* FRANK.

HOLLAND *sits sizing up the flat.*

FRANK. I'm briefed for a guy called Henry Griffiths. He had a little bit of dope planted on him by George McCabe.

KATHERINE. I know him.

FRANK. I know you do. Is Cora Davis pleading to the heroin charge?

KATHERINE. Pleading? She's going beyond guilty. A totally new concept in self-flagellation. How do you know about Cora?

FRANK. McCabe made my client sign a statement saying he tipped off McCabe about your client.

KATHERINE. Why?

FRANK. He needed a reason for arresting her.

KATHERINE. You know he helped himself to most of the stuff? He must be worth five million quid.

FRANK. We think maybe he was running her.

KATHERINE. No. I can tell you that's not on. I mean I've talked to her about the way he took the stuff off her in the car. I mean you couldn't invent that.

HOLLAND. Has she told you who was running her?

KATHERINE. No. Nor will she now. The case is warned. It'll be over for her in a week or two. Apart from five years inside.

HOLLAND *and* FRANK *are disappointed.*

ROBERT *is bored with all this and fed up with having the back of his neck scraped.*

He shuffles away from her.

KATHERINE. Why don't you make some coffee, Robert?

ROBERT *goes into the kitchen.*

FRANK. You're still convinced it's McCabe?

HOLLAND. He's got all the credentials. He's been crooked for years. He's got woman trouble, he's got money trouble, he's got all sorts of trouble. He's in hock to everybody. Trying to live like a stockbroker on policeman's pay.

ROBERT. I'll see you later.

KATHERINE. OK, love.

ROBERT *goes.*

What's his woman trouble?

HOLLAND. He left his wife, he went back, he got chucked out, he

went back, he left again; he lives half the time with her
indoors and half the time with a piece on the side with a little
sweet shop in Acton. This has been going on for years. She
also operates as his gofer into prisons to do deals for him with
people on remand: 'You plead to this and George'll see his
way to dropping that'. Pamela Hollis her name is.

KATHERINE. Say that again.

HOLLAND. Pamela Hollis.

KATHERINE. Oh this is brilliant.

61. Interior. Clerks' Room. Grimshaw's. Day.

DOREEN, TOM, EDWARD *all working. Other barristers in and out. It's
first thing in the morning.*
KATHERINE *comes in like a whirlwind from outside.* KATHERINE *picks
up a telephone and dials.*

KATHERINE. Edward, could you get hold of David Frankland –
tell him I'm going to do the business of Cora's knickers after
all, can he ring me, he'll know what I mean. (*To telephone,
ringing:*) Come on.

TOM. Oh my goodness they'll be selling tickets for this one.

KATHERINE (*to* TOM). Is Cora Davis listed?
He ignores her.
EDWARD *is already ringing* FRANKLAND.

EDWARD. Yes. Next Tuesday. Langtry it is.

KATHERINE. Oh, give me a break. Can you remember who's
prosecuting? I've got to have a postponement.

EDWARD. Colin Campbell-Johnson.

KATHERINE. Oh, he's OK.
She gives up on this number and finds CAMPBELL-JOHNSON's
number instead and rings that.
The room is full and chaotic.

TOM. May I ask when you think you'll have time to defend this
woman if you postpone it, Miss Hughes?
She ignores him.
Are you aware that last week you asked us to try and have it
brought forward – which was accomplished with no small
difficulty?

KATHERINE. Oh shut up, Tom.
This causes some embarrassment in the room and it goes a bit quieter.

TOM (*sotto*). And she wonders why life doesn't run smoothly.
This is the last straw.

KATHERINE *leans across to* TOM, *still holding the telephone and still
waiting for a reply.*

KATHERINE (*quietly*). Listen. One more foolish puerile remark
from you, you ignorant, lazy, overpaid, overstuffed berk, and
I'll shove this telephone down your stupid throat. Hello? Colin
Campbell-Johnson? Katherine Hughes.

62. Interior. Judge's Chambers. Old Bailey. Day.

LANGTRY's *chambers.*
He sits, wigless, with an old cardigan over his robes, puffing a cigarette.
COLIN CAMPBELL-JOHNSON *and* KATHERINE.

LANGTRY. Mr Campbell-Johnson.
COLIN CAMPBELL-JOHNSON. There does appear to be a danger in
proceeding too quickly, Judge. There's a strong element of
doubt in my mind about the police evidence and I understand
the two detectives in question could even be the subject of an
internal police inquiry. There's a lot of concern about how
they came to be on hand.
LANGTRY *puffs and ponders and enjoys both but he clearly gets the
drift.*
LANGTRY. Yes. But I fail to see how any such doubts would
affect a case in which the defendant intends to plead guilty. Is
that still the intention, Miss Hughes?
KATHERINE. Even so, your Honour, I think we should all be
extremely worried about this whole case.
LANGTRY. Worry away, Miss Hughes; no doubt you are paid to
worry. However, I still see no proper reason to keep this
woman waiting. Surely the time approaches when the poor
creature must be put out of her misery?
KATHERINE *shoves* CAMPBELL-JOHNSON *with her eyeballs.*
COLIN CAMPBELL-JOHNSON. Yes. Judge, there is also a very clear
forensic difficulty which Miss Hughes has brought to my
attention only today.
LANGTRY. And what's that?
COLIN CAMPBELL-JOHNSON. Well . . . perhaps Miss Hughes would
prefer to explain it herself?
KATHERINE. Your Honour, it concerns my client's underwear.
LANGTRY. Oh, really?
KATHERINE. I asked for her pants to be examined by Home
Office forensic scientists and their findings make it clear that
the garment in question must have been tampered with in
some way after her arrest.
LANGTRY *does his Edith Evans impersonation.*
LANGTRY. Tampered with? In what way?
KATHERINE. Well the panties she was wearing when she was

searched by WPCs Kenton and Platt cannot really be the ones she wore on her journey from Bombay to Lewisham Police Station?

LANGTRY. Why not?

KATHERINE. Well, sir, how can I put it? The absence of debris strongly suggests this.

LANGTRY. I'm sorry, I don't follow you.

KATHERINE looks him straight in the eyes.

KATHERINE. To put it bluntly, your Honour, if you wore a pair of knickers from Bombay to Lewisham there'd be certain tell-tale signs. However microscopic.

He thinks.

LANGTRY. Oh, I see. Well why didn't you say so? Yes, that's a different matter. We'll take the case out for a week or two. I'm very impressed, Miss Hughes.

KATHERINE. Thank you, Judge.

LANGTRY. I must say: if *I'd* been caught red-handed in possession of a large amount of heroin the tell-tale signs in *my* underwear would be considerably more than microscopic.

He laughs.

63. Interior. Cubicles. Day.

FRANKLAND *and* KATHERINE *waiting.*

KATHERINE. Listen. I don't want to tell her about the fact she was going to be arrested anyway. Let's leave that out.

He's not happy. He consents.

They hear her approach under escort.

She comes into them.

CORA. Hello.

KATHERINE. Hello, Cora.

FRANKLAND. Hello, dear. Now. Did somebody let you know that your case was listed for Tuesday?

CORA. Was?

FRANKLAND. We've been given an adjournment.

CORA. I don't want an adjournment.

FRANKLAND. Let me finish, dear. Now, Miss Hughes has a few things to say to you and then you're going to have to make a decision, so listen carefully. And remember: the decision is yours.

He's talking to her as if she were senile.

KATHERINE. Cora. Pamela Hollis. Your friend Pamela, who asked you to go to India and bring back some heroin.

CORA eyes on the table.

Pamela Hollis is Sergeant McCabe's mistress.

CORA *looks incredulous.*

Pamela Hollis also works for her lover running messages into
and out of prisons to men waiting trial. Prisons like
Wormwood Scrubs where your son-in-law Dennis is
imprisoned.

CORA *starting to see it all.*

Where you met Pamela, didn't you? Sitting in the waiting
room.

CORA *nods.*

And she befriended you? And heard all your money problems.
And found a way to help you.

   CORA *can hardly bear this realisation.*

FRANKLAND. We don't possess corroborative evidence of any of
   this, Mrs Davis, and so there's no hope of having the case
   thrown out. However, that hardly matters. Since we've given
   fairly clear warning of our intention to expose McCabe and
   Mrs Hollis in court, the police solicitor is very likely to instruct
   counsel to offer no evidence rather than risk a complete fiasco.

CORA. I see. But I've pleaded guilty.

FRANKLAND. Not at all. None of your previous statements now
   matter. What matters is what you say in court on the day.

CORA. Well I shall be saying that I've always said, that I'm guilty.

FRANKLAND (*staggered*). Are you saying that you still intend to
   plead guilty?

CORA. Yes.

FRANKLAND. You're quite sure about that?

CORA. Yes. I'm guilty, remember.

FRANKLAND. Well.

   He doesn't get it.

KATHERINE. What's guilt got to do with anything? Guilty people
   go free all the time. Innocent people go to jail all the time.
   This is a lottery, not a confessional. You've been given a
   winning ticket. You mustn't get mixed up between the law and
   morality. What you did was wrong – but the judge won't give
   you absolution, just a meaningless prison sentence. What's *right*
   about you going to prison while Hollis and McCabe and
   whoever's behind *them* stay free? What good would be done?
   Will you be an example? Is anybody going to be put off from
   being a courier? No, of course not. The dealers will just have
   to pay more for the greater risks, because there'll always be
   people who need the money, like you did. It would be
   completely pointless, Cora. (*Pause.*) All you have to do is go
   along with it.

   Pause.

CORA. I won't say I'm not tempted. Thank you for all you've done, both of you.
She knocks on the door.
I wish you hadn't told me about Pam. How could the bloody cow do that to me?

KATHERINE. Why don't you ask her next time she pops in for a chat? Or has she already been in today?

CORA *feels sorry for* KATHERINE.

CORA (*softly*). It's a fantastic amount of money, Katherine.

A WPO *comes in and takes her away.*

64. Interior. An office. Night.

McCABE *sits, dishevelled and broken.*
HOLLAND *looks at him through a glass door.*

65. Interior. McCabe's house. Night.

McCABE'S WIFE *and* THREE KIDS *look on as* CUSTOMS *and* EXCISE MEN *tear the place apart in vain search for heroin.*
They give up.
They start tidying up.

MRS McCABE. Tell him not to bother coming back.

66. Interior. Office. Night.

HOLLAND *and* O'NEILL *look through window into car park as* McCABE *gets into a battered old Cortina.*
He has trouble getting it to start.

67. Interior. A pub. Night.

McCABE *is drowning his sorrows.*
Two men arrive looking for him. He makes a dash for it. They grab him and frogmarch him out the door.

68. Exterior. In a large Mercedes car. Night.

The two heavies, the ITALIAN *and* McCABE *sit in the parked car.*
The ITALIAN *is shaking his head sadly.*

ITALIAN. You see, my natural instinct is to want to help you in some way. A ticket to Miami.

McCABE. Yeh. I mean, I'm prepared to make myself useful in any way.

They laugh.

ITALIAN. I don't think useful is the word to describe you,
George. No. I think it would be better all round if you just
disappeared.

McCABE. Disappeared? In what sense?

ITALIAN. In the sense if you don't you'll be found dead under a
bush in Surrey.

They chuck him out and drive off.

69. Interior. Inner London Crown Court. Day.

Outside the courts.

HENRY *sits waiting with* ARNOLD FLOWERS.

The usual busy comings and goings. The usual anxiety and misery.
The usual crowds of POLICE, COURT OFFICIALS, SOLICITORS, *all*
earning a living.

FRANK *arrives in his gear. He joins them.*

FRANK. OK, Henry?

FLOWERS. Henry's thinking – I dunno – might he be better
pleading, looking for a bit of leniency, not wasting the court's
time . . .

FRANK. Is this your idea, Henry? I thought we were agreed to
fight it.

HENRY. Well, it's just Mr Flowers thinks I should be trying to get
the best I can for myself.

FRANK. I see.

CLERK (*approaching*). Mr Cartwright? Are you in Griffiths?

FRANK. Yeh.

CLERK. Is it contested?

FRANK. Let me come back to you.

CLERK *goes off.*

FRANK *looks around and spots the* PROSECUTING COUNSEL *and the*
POLICE SOLICITOR *in a huddle.*

They see him and wave him over.

FRANK. That's the Prosecution, wants to talk.

FLOWERS. If they're offering a deal I think we should bite their
hands off. Possession, yeh?

FRANK. Let's see.

He goes over.

PROSECUTING COUNSEL. Good morning, Cartwright.

FRANK. Good morning.

PROSECUTING COUNSEL. I was wondering how you saw this case?

FRANK. I'm looking forward to getting George McCabe into the
box.

PROSECUTING COUNSEL (*smiling*). We wondered whether it might not be in the general interest to drop the dealing charge.

FRANK. I think it would.

PROSECUTING COUNSEL. Well we'd need something from you of course.

FRANK. You want him to plead to possession?

PROSECUTING COUNSEL. I think that would allow us to proceed quickly.

FRANK looks across the throng to where HENRY and FLOWERS are looking at them anxiously.

He also scans the room for MCCABE.

Well perhaps you could put it to him. Time is rather short.

FRANK. No. I think we'll take it into court and give it a run.

He walks off back to HENRY and FLOWERS.

PROSECUTING COUNSEL and SOLICITOR look pissed off.

FLOWERS. What did they want?

FRANK. Just sit tight a minute. Henry, can you see McCabe anywhere?

HENRY has a good look about.

HENRY. No.

CLERK approaches again.

CLERK. Mr Cartwright? Is it contested?

FRANK. Yes.

They sit.

The previous case in their court comes out.

That's us next.

PROSECUTING COUNSEL waves him over.

PROSECUTING COUNSEL. Well, done, Cartwright. We won't offer any evidence. In the absence of our star witness.

70. Exterior. Inner London Crown Court. Day.

HENRY *in tears of joy hugging* FRANK.

71. Exterior. Motorway. Day.

McCABE *driving his banger mindlessly along. He doesn't know where he's going or why. It runs out of petrol and glides to a halt. He sits.*
A motorway patrol arrives. TWO COPS *get out and approach him.*

FIRST COP. What's the problem?

McCABE shrugs.

72. Exterior. Gray's Inn. Day.

KAREN *walking through grounds to the Bailey. Passes a marquee being erected for the Field Club Ball.*

73. Interior. Cell below court. Old Bailey. Day.

CORA *composed.*
KATHERINE *agitated.*
MIRANDA *biting her nails.*

PRISON OFFICER (*arriving*). He's ready for you, Miss Hughes. (*He goes.*)
KATHERINE. Are you sure about this? OK. This is what's happening. I'm going round to see the judge. I'm going to ask him for another adjournment. Don't worry, he won't allow it. It's just so I have something to bargain with. Assuming he refuses, and you then plead guilty, you'll be sentenced this morning. OK? Cora?
CORA *nods.*

74. Interior. Langtry's chambers. Old Bailey. Day.

LANGTRY *in his gear, without the cardigan.*
COLIN CAMPBELL-JOHNSON *and* KATHERINE.

KATHERINE. Judge, I think this is now a very clear case. The evidence is overwhelming – albeit circumstantial evidence – that those policemen entrapped my client.
LANGTRY. This may well be true – though you clearly cannot establish it or we wouldn't be sitting here – but entrapment is not in any case a legitimate defence. Presumably she knew what she was being asked to do and she jolly well went and did it.
KATHERINE. Perhaps so, your Honour. But you must admit: it's great mitigation. Another week or so might allow the full facts to emerge.
LANGTRY. But, Miss Hughes, these inquiries you wish me to await might go on a very long time and still never establish the exact role of the police in this affair. It is so often the case that the police are afterwards found to have behaved a little unwisely but without the criminal wickedness so frequently imputed to them by defence counsel. Besides which, your client still intends to plead *guilty*.
KATHERINE *decides to lie.*
KATHERINE. She is considering changing her plea, sir.
LANGTRY *is very miffed.*
After all, she's laying herself open to a very heavy sentence.
LANGTRY *sighs and lights a cigarette. He ponders and puffs angrily.*

LANGTRY. I see. Would your client be inclined to keep to her original intention if she knew I were minded to take the whole of the circumstances into account when fixing the sentence?

KATHERINE. She might. Can I give her some idea of what's in your mind as an appropriate sentence?

LANGTRY (*after a think*). You may indicate to her that I regard this as a unique case.

KATHERINE *accepts that this is the best she's going to get.*

75. Interior. Cell below court. Day.

CORA, KATHERINE, MIRANDA.

KATHERINE. He's determined to get the whole mess under the carpet as tidily as possible. He won't have anything to do with an adjournment. He doesn't want to sit in a case where there might eventually be hard evidence of police involvement in drug smuggling. He won't be precise about sentence. If this was anybody else, I'd be expecting maybe eighteen months. You've done six. With remission you'd be out in another six. But he won't say. I don't trust him. It's up to you, Cora.

CORA *is cracking a bit. She looks to* KATHERINE *hopefully.*

CORA. I expect he'll go easy on me, won't he, love? After all, I'm a granny.

She attempts a chuckle. There is now almost no similarity between this CORA *and the* CORA *who landed at Heathrow.*

76. Interior. Courtroom. Day.

KATHERINE *winds up her mitigation.*
CORA *sits in the dock watching* LANGTRY.
MIRANDA *sits beside* KATHERINE.
LANGTRY *is smiling benignly at* KATHERINE.
The public gallery has a few people in it, including HOLLAND *and* LEONI.

KATHERINE. And therefore, your Honour, I respectfully suggest that an enlightened view of the whole circumstances of my client's case, including the role of the police, her age, and her five and a half months in prison on remand, will have convinced your Honour that the severity of the crime has in this case been uniquely diminished. Thank you. (*She sits.*)

LANGTRY. Have you finished?

KATHERINE (*keeps her temper and stands briefly*). Yes, your Honour. Thank you. (*She sits.*)

LANGTRY. I must first of all dispose of one very distasteful aspect

of this affair. Matters have been raised with me concerning the
conduct of the police officers in this case. It would not be
appropriate for me to make any comment; their conduct has
not been a matter for this court. I intend to confine myself to
matters on which I've heard the facts.

He gazes on CORA *for the first time.*

Stand up.

She stands, her hands trembling as she grips the rail.

Cora Davis, you are a very stupid old woman. The crime
you've admitted committing is a disgraceful and despicable
one. Despite this, however, I have been asked to show leniency
and compassion. And I intend to show compassion.

He smiles.

CORA *smiles nervously and nods gratefully.*

KATHERINE *sees what's coming and closes her eyes.*

Compassion, that is, for the community that you have
polluted. I'm sending you to prison for three years.

CORA. Thank you.

LANGTRY. What?

CORA. Thank you, sir.

LANGTRY. You're very welcome. Take her down, will you?

CORA *is led away.*

KATHERINE *looks miserable.*

77. Interior. Old Bailey concourse. Day.

KATHERINE *comes out of court and sits collecting her papers and her
thoughts.*

HOLLAND *approaches her. The concourse is thronging with cases. She
eyes it tiredly.*

HOLLAND. Pleased with your day's work?

KATHERINE. Are you going to charge McCabe?

HOLLAND. With what? You had the only witness. At least we got
her.

KATHERINE *is angry and frustrated again.*

KATHERINE. Well for Christ's sake, it's just an old woman on her
way to Styal Prison in the back of a van. I mean: what good's
that doing anybody?

HOLLAND. She'll be out in eighteen months.

KATHERINE. That really annoys you.

HOLLAND *very close and very vehement.*

HOLLAND. I'd *hang* people who bring in heroin. It's our only
chance of stopping it.

KATHERINE. You're talking to the wrong person.

HOLLAND. Yeh? Have you ever seen a twelve-year-old strung out on heroin?

KATHERINE. No.

HOLLAND. Want to see some photos?

KATHERINE. No thanks.

He presses a photo into her hand which she takes but ignores. She keeps walking for the exit.

HOLLAND. Look at it, go on. Put it on your desk. Look at it next time you get asked to help out a heroin dealer.

KATHERINE. She wasn't a dealer.

HOLLAND (*relentless*). You know what twelve-year-olds do to get hold of the money to buy it? Twelve-year-old girls.

KATHERINE. Talk to the people responsible. Talk to the people who made the world where twelve-year-olds want heroin. Talk to the people who protect the big dealers. Get them into court for a change.

HOLLAND. Why? So somebody like you can do a deal with a bent judge and get them a fortnight in a holiday camp?

KATHERINE. You do your job, I'll do mine.

HOLLAND. You're bent, dear. Completely bent.

They're approaching a door to a non-public area. A SECURITY MAN *approaches to stop* HOLLAND.

SECURITY GUARD. Is there a problem, Miss Hughes?

KATHERINE. He's got a problem, not me.

She goes through.

78. Interior. Corridor, Old Bailey. Day.

On the other side of the door.

KATHERINE *tears up the photo without looking at it. She gets her breath back.*

79. Exterior. Gray's Inn. Night.

In the grounds. The summer ball is in full swing. Music and revelry.

80. Interior. Grimshaw's. Night.

KATHERINE's *room. She's there with* FRANK.

FRANK. How's Richard?

KATHERINE. Richard who?

FRANK. Robert, sorry.

KATHERINE. Packed his bags and gone home to mother.

FRANK. Sorry. I thought this was working out.

KATHERINE. He said living with me was like being stuck in a lift with the Bride of Lammermoor. Can't say I blame him.

FRANK. You need the support of people who believe the same things as you do about this job.

KATHERINE. Which is what, Frank?

FRANK. That the law's a bulldozer being driven by vested interests. We can pull a few people clear of it. We can pull a few great strokes like you did for Cora Davis. But we can't make it make sense. If she'd got off it wouldn't have made sense. It isn't supposed to make sense. It's supposed to stop people at the bottom thieving from people at the top, that's all. Any justice that gets dished out on the way is purely accidental.

She's at the window listening to the band.

KATHERINE. How does lefties huddling together in Fetter Court change that?

FRANK. It doesn't, in the short term. But it says something. It says 'We have little faith in the system we're locked into, but we have a bit of faith in ourselves. We do what we can while the band plays on.' Care to dance?

EPISODE TWO

White Man Listen

Cast

KATHERINE HUGHES	Jane Lapotaire
FRANK CARTWRIGHT	Jack Shepherd
JAMES BINGHAM	Julian Wadham

The Marshall Inquest

ALTON PHILLIPS	Clarke Peters
MRS MARSHALL	Carmen Munroe
MR MARSHALL	Tommy Eytle
CORONER	Robert Gillespie
COLLINS	Alan Devlin
PC TURNELL	Daniel Hill
PC MILNES	Gary Powell
DR TAYLOR	Anthony Douse
MR BARNES	John Barrard
NOLA MARSHALL	Corinne Skinner-Carter
JURY FOREMAN	Christopher Whittingham
YEW TREE ROAD SERGEANT	Christopher Leaver

The Blinkho Case

GAVIN BLINKHO	Ewan Stewart
MICHAEL FEINGOLD	Milo Sperber
MIKE FINDLAY	Peter Sproule
CLIVE CURRAN	Michael Feast
MILLIGAN	Philip Lowrie
COLIN BLINKHO	Colin Dudley
BOYS ON TRAIN	Gary Beadle
	Jason Campbell
	Martin Multon
TRAIN PASSENGERS	Harry Beety
	Oscar Peck

MAGISTRATES CHAIRMAN	Michael Wisher
1ST CLERK TO THE MAGISTRATES	Ninka Scott
SOLICITOR	Carmina de Gale

Fetter Court

LORRAINE	Caroline Hutchison
TESSA PARKS	Joanne Campbell
HUGH	Eamonn Walker
MICHAEL KHAN	Raad Rawi
KEN GORDON	Tom Marshall
ROBERT HOLMES	Michael Fitzgerald
STIPENDARY MAGISTRATE	Tamara Hinchco
2ND CLERK TO THE MAGISTRATES	Debbie Manship
CROWN PROSECUTOR	Peter Blacker
ANTROBUS' SOLICITOR	Nigel Nevinson
BISAKHA PATEL	Sheila Chitnis
PAUL WATSON	Norman Tipton
SIR CHARLES BINGHAM	Wensley Pithey

Grimshaws

ALEX GRIMSHAW	Ernest Clark
TOM	Sam Cox
EDWARD	Duncan Bell
ALAN ACKROYD	Toby Salaman
MRS WELSH	Celia Imrie
PROSECUTING COUNSEL	John Tallents
MR JUSTICE MERRICK	John Baker

1. Exterior. A busy street outside a pub. Day.

Passers-by are rather enjoying the spectacle of NOLA MARSHALL, *a thirty-eight-year-old black woman who is very drunk and singing. She knows who she is and where she is and is enjoying herself, clapping her hands more or less rhythmically.*

The owner of the small newsagent next door to the pub, MR BARNES, *is making a telephone call.*

NOLA *is not a bad singer. She is singing 'Bye Bye Blackbird'. She's offering to dance, but there are no takers. She's very merry and nobody's really offended. The reactions range from ignoring her, through pity for her, to enjoyment of her.*

BARNES *is now looking on and waiting for the police.*

BARNES. Nola. Go away. I've called the police.

   NOLA (*continues singing 'Bye bye blackbird'*).

2. Exterior. A stopping train in South London. Night.

The train is heading through South East London towards Brighton.

On board one of the carriages is a sprinkling of passengers. Singles and couples, all ages, mostly white, they all sit in deathly silence wishing they were somewhere else.

FOUR BLACK LADS *aged about sixteen are drunk and making a big nuisance of themselves. They are holding a jousting tournament. Two of them are being horses and two of them are being riders. The narrow aisle down the centre of the carriage is their lists.*

Screaming and swearing they run at each other repeatedly and exchange punches.

People are being stood on, shoved against and abused. People are very angry but doing nothing about it.

Staring straight ahead of him is GAVIN BLINKHO, *a thirty-year-old white man. He has a big rucksack by his side and a ten-day growth of beard on his face. He's wearing combat gear.*

WINSTON. Charge!

   The other team isn't ready, the rider shouts as he tries to mount his horse.

PAUL. Hang on, hang on! Oh, sorry darling.

   His horse tramples on a WOMAN's *foot. The* MAN *she's with mutters; he's angry but frightened.*

FIRST MAN. Bloody nuisance.

   Everybody's looking out of the window and wishing somebody else would stand up and kill the bastards.

BLINKHO *is rolling himself a cigarette. He looks across the aisle to an* ELDERLY MAN *who is seething with frustration.*

WINSTON. What? You don't mind our fun. Do you? Oi! Mate? Do you?

FIRST MAN. No.

WINSTON'S HORSE. 'Course you don't, cos you know you'll get your head kicked in, don't you?

They shriek with laughter as PAUL *and his horse join them at their end of the carriage.*

PAUL. Where, where, where? Who wants his head kicked in? Are you the one looking for trouble? What's your room number?

He laughs.

They all laugh.

It should be apparent by now that PAUL *is ESN as well as aggressive and drunk.*

They are crowding round the FIRST MAN, *pushing him.*

FIRST MAN. Just leave me alone, all right? I've told you. Get off me.

Other PASSENGERS *are letting their curiosity get the upper hand and are peeping over the tops of seats.*

FIRST MAN *is almost in tears.*

The ELDERLY MAN *is standing up.*

ELDERLY MAN. Let him alone you, mental bastards!

He sits.

The mood of the lads, especially PAUL, *changes suddenly. He is more menacing.*

PAUL. Who said that? Who called me a mental bastard?

Nobody wants to know. They reach the ELDERLY MAN.

ELDERLY MAN. I'm warning you lot, I've got a pacemaker here.

He taps his heart.

PAUL. You shouldn't call me a mental bastard then, should you? Eh?

PAUL *knocks the man's cap on to the floor.*

The ELDERLY MAN *bends forward to pick up his cap and* PAUL *pushes down on his back, bending him double.*

The OLD MAN *is gasping for breath.*

You're sorry, are you?

A WOMAN *nearby bursts into tears.*

The FIRST MAN *is on his feet. He shouts through tears.*

FIRST MAN. For God's sake, he's an old man.

This sends PAUL *over the edge.*

He leaves the ELDERLY MAN *and dashes to the* FIRST MAN *at the end of the carriage.*

PAUL. Right! I'll have you then. You've had it mate! What did you call me?

The FIRST MAN *is petrified.*

They all surround him.

He tries to be calm and rational.

FIRST MAN. I didn't call you anything.

PAUL. Oh you've bloody had it mate, you call me names, you've bloody had it.

THE WOMAN HE'S WITH. For God's sake somebody do something to help him.

BLINKHO *looks on.*

PAUL *grabs the* FIRST MAN's *tie and pulls him along the aisle.*

WINSTON *jumps on the* FIRST MAN's *back.*

The other two lads watch, cheering them on.

Everybody else is watching or still trying to pretend they aren't there.

PAUL. Come on, horsey, giddy up.

The FIRST MAN *falls to his knees and cries.*

WINSTON *dismounts.*

ANOTHER WOMAN *is in tears.*

PAUL. Sit down! Everybody sit down and shut up unless you want the same.

Some people comply.

The lads shriek with laughter.

Hands on heads. Hands on heads. It's time you learned some discipline.

BLINKHO *stands up and steps into the aisle.*

PAUL *sees him.*

Oh yeh? What do you want? You can have it.

BLINKHO *takes a sheath knife from his pocket. It's a lethal-looking weapon.*

WINSTON *and the two horses immediately back off. Fear flickers across* PAUL's *face.*

I ain't scared.

WINSTON. Paul, come on. All over now, right?

PAUL. No I ain't scared.

PAUL *approaches* BLINKHO *slowly.*

ELDERLY MAN. Stick it in the bastard.

PAUL *is confident* BLINKHO *will back away.*

He walks quickly towards him and gets a knife buried in his stomach.
He realises what's happening and he groans. He looks down at the blood on his stomach.

3. Exterior. Fetter Court. Day.

FRANK CARTWRIGHT *is arriving on foot. He passes* TESSA PARKS. *They exchange a few words as they move in opposite directions.*

FRANK. Tessa.

TESSA. Frank.

FRANK. How did your affray go?

TESSA. He got eighteen months.

FRANK. Great.

TESSA. He was thrilled. His wife was crying. She gave me a box of chocolates. They're on Lorraine's desk.

FRANK *nods and smiles as he goes. He remembers something.*

FRANK. Tessa.

They reconverge.

Talk to me sometime about the Nola Marshall inquest.

TESSA (*lying*). What's to say? She's dancing in the street. She's drunk, she falls over and bangs her head. Now she's in a fridge with her name on her toe.

FRANK. Yeh, but I mean about me and Bingham being briefed in it.

TESSA. The Marshalls hired Alton Phillips to do the job. He's briefed you and Bingham.

FRANK. No, come on. Michael Khan is angry about it. You're angry about it.

TESSA. What's Michael said?

FRANK. Michael Khan says there should be a black on it. You don't say but I think you think there should be no whites on it. Is this happening in our chambers?

TESSA. I mean it's one of those issues Frank, sensible people go mad. It pushes people's buttons.

FRANK. Are your buttons being pushed?

TESSA. If Alton Phillips wants to brief you and James, why not? I mean, it's great, it's heavyweight, it shows we mean business about this.

This isn't entirely convincing, she isn't doing eye contact.

FRANK. Bingham's doing it for free, you know.

TESSA. I know. I know. You're heroes.

FRANK. But Michael Khan should have been briefed?

TESSA. There's pros and cons. Whoever does it is in a war with the police. If it was two black barristers the press would use it. If it's two white barristers Alton gets called Uncle Tom, if he gets one of each it's the black and white minstrel show. You're not going to win that argument. Don't try. Just get on with it. Win the case. Get that result. 'Unlawful killing'. Because Nola Marshall was . . .

She's suddenly on the verge of tears. She breathes deeply.

Lorraine showed me the photographs.

FRANK *is angry.* TESSA *is distressed.*

It's not Lorraine's fault. She didn't know Nola and me were friends.

FRANK *comforts her. She has to go. She pats him on the chest, sniffing back the last of her tears.*

Just nail them Frank?

FRANK *nods.*

Because they can't be allowed to keep on getting away with this, OK? See you, pal.

She goes quickly. He watches. He goes into Fetter Court.

4. Interior. Fetter Court. Day.

The clerks' area.

LORRAINE *and* HUGH.

The telephone is ringing as FRANK CARTWRIGHT *enters.*

HUGH *answers it.*

HUGH (*into the telephone*). Fetter Court. Yes he is, you're speaking to him.

HUGH *has a quiet talk with somebody on the telephone, referring to a large diary on the desk in front of him.*

FRANK CARTWRIGHT *picks up his mail.*

LORRAINE (*saying hello*). Frank.

FRANK *smiles at her.*

FRANK. Messages?

LORRAINE. Katherine Hughes rang. 12.30 is OK.

FRANK *looks at his watch.*

FRANK. Is James in?

LORRAINE. He's in a con. He's got this most gorgeous rent boy on a theft charge. I'm seriously in love with this boy. If James doesn't get him off I don't know what I'll do.

FRANK. How long will he be?

5. Interior. A Conference Room. Day.

JAMES BINGHAM, ROBERT HOLMES *and* PAUL WATSON *sit.*

ROBERT *is a young white boy from Manchester.*

WATSON *is his solicitor.*

ROBERT. That bloke who used to read the news was there as well. Fantastic frock he had on. Must have been up all night with the hems. This dozy old sodomite I'm with says to him 'I know you. Didn't you keep a shop in Dulwich?' That's right, that. 'Didn't you keep a shop in Dulwich.' I wept laughing.

FRANK *knocks and pokes his head round the door.*

FRANK. Sorry James. Are you joining us?

JAMES. I'll have to catch you up.

FRANK *looks miffed.*

BINGHAM *joins him at the door in a huddle.*

FRANK. The whole point of this is for you to talk to her.

BINGHAM. I'll be there, but look . . .

FRANK accepts situation.

With an acknowledging look at ROBERT *and a nod at* WATSON, *FRANK goes.*

ROBERT *picks up where he left off.*

ROBERT. He took a shine to me anyway. I'd often wondered what was behind the news. It's not a pretty sight.

He laughs.

JAMES *has enjoyed this enormously.*

6.   Interior. Fetter Court. Day.

Coming out of the Conference Room, FRANK *meets* MICHAEL KHAN *with* BISAKHA PATEL – *an Indian woman solicitor* – *and an Indian couple who are her clients.*

KHAN *is about to check on the room.*

FRANK. James is in there.

KHAN. Ah, we'll have to use my desk, I'm afraid. If it's free.

FRANK. Use mine. If it's free.

HUGH. Frank Cartwright, Bisakha Patel.

BISAKHA. I'm determined to brief you down at Harmondsworth. It's appalling down there. We need the best like you and Michael.

FRANK. Look forward to it. Nice to meet you. Hello.

He nods to the clients as BISAKHA *ushers them towards* KHAN's *desk.*

KHAN. How would you like to have to stand up in court in front of some ex-colonial David Niven lookalike and have to prove you married your wife because you loved her and not because of her passport? And not any old kind of love but some concept of pure, Romantic Love only found in nineteenth-century novels?

FRANK. It would be tricky for me. I'd have to brief you – you're the expert.

KHAN. I'm the expert because these are the only briefs I get.

He goes. FRANK *winces. He walked into that.*

7.   Interior. Clerk's area. Day.

FRANK *comes back.*

FRANK (*to* LORRAINE). I'll be out till about two. Lorraine. Where are the photos?

LORRAINE. In a sealed envelope on your desk. I'm sorry.

FRANK. It's OK.

    FRANK goes, taking a chocolate.

    HUGH *slaps his wrist and smiles at* LORRAINE.

HUGH. Is he having lunch with Katherine Hughes?

LORRAINE. Looks like it.

HUGH. Oh, no.

LORRAINE (*who shares his doubts*). You don't know her Hugh.

HUGH. I'm telling you. I know the junior there. And I'll tell you
    what she is, shall I? (*He bangs his head on the desk.*) We don't
    need her. We're doing all right.

LORRAINE. Yours is not to reason why.

HUGH. My what isn't to reason why?

LORRAINE. I dunno.

HUGH. Talk proper English then.

8. Interior. Fetter Court. On the stairs.

FRANK *is descending the stairs and meets* KEN GORDON *ascending with
a* SOLICITOR'S CLERK *and a* CLIENT, *a middle-aged woman.*

KEN. Hello, Frank.

FRANK. Ken. How did your hockey stick case go?

KEN. Go up to the clerk's room, Oliver. Lorraine'll get some tea
    going.

    The SOLICITOR'S CLERK *and the* CLIENT *go up.*

    KEN *talks as he backs up the stairs.*

KEN. Fiasco. Bindhra Surinder, my man, sits like a dummy in
    Burton's window all week, only with a turban on. Finally I'm
    so exasperated, I've no idea what his defence is, and nor has
    anybody else, the Prosecution's running away with it, so I bung
    him in the box. 'Mr Bindhra Surinder, did you have any cause
    to attack this man as the prosecution alleges?'

    He mimes BINDHRA *smiling and shrugging.*

    'Well I think that means "No", your Honour'. 'Well I don't
    know about that', says the Judge. Prosecution's already
    uncorking the champagne. I'm desperate. 'Mr Bindhra
    Surinder, would it not be fair to say that this man drew his
    hockey stick before you drew yours?' Prosecution on his feet.
    Judge looking daggers at me. But at last I've got my client to
    open his trap. He goes 'I really cannot remember'. He thinks
    amnesia's a defence to Actual Bodily Harm. Four years. Got to
    go.

    He goes up. FRANK *goes down.*

9. Interior. Brixton Prison remand cell. Day.

GAVIN BLINKHO *lies on his bunk, reading. Calm and self-contained. A key turns in the lock.* BLINKHO *closes his book. The book is called 'Hard Core Survival'.*
The door opens.
A PRISON OFFICER *appears.*
BLINKHO *gets to his feet quickly.*

10. Interior. Brixton Prison. Day.

GAVIN BLINKHO *is being escorted from his cell to an interview cell.*

11. Interior. Brixton Prison. Day.

GAVIN BLINKHO *is shown into an interview cell.*
This is his first sight of his solicitor, a venerable man called MICHAEL FEINGOLD.
FEINGOLD *stands and smiles openly.*
BLINKHO *looks him over.*
He smiles thinly.
FEINGOLD. Michael Feingold. Mr Blinkho I presume.
  He offers his hand, BLINKHO *shakes it.*

12. Interior. Grimshaw's. Day.

In KATHERINE's *shared office. She's working at her desk on a brief. She sees the time. She collects things to take out with her.*

13. Interior. Grimshaw's. Clerks' Room. Day.

EDWARD *and* TOM *are working and chatting.*
They go silent as KATHERINE *comes in.*

KATHERINE. Edward, can you arrange a conference with Rod Connor for late tomorrow? Five-ish.
EDWARD. Can do.
  He makes a note.
  The telephone rings.
  TOM *answers it.*
KATHERINE. I'm going out for lunch, then I'm in court, so unless Rod Connor needs to talk to me . . .
  EDWARD *understands.*
TOM (*into the telephone*). Hello? Hello Derek. I think she may be able to. I can ask her now. Can you do a rape for Derek Harrison next week? You seem to be free – it looks like

Wednesday/Thursday. It's straightforward he says.

KATHERINE. Ask him: what's the defence?

TOM. Derek? She'd like a word.

TOM puts the telephone down on the desk.

KATHERINE picks it up.

KATHERINE (*into the telephone*). Derek. Hi.

She listens briefly.

Um. Is he admitting the sex? He is? OK. Well, I don't do that Derek, OK? I don't do consent rapes, OK? Sorry. (*Lying.*) Oh I'm fine. How are you? OK. Sorry. Bye.

TOM is signalling to her.

Hang on. Tom would like you back.

KATHERINE puts the telephone down on the desk.

TOM picks it up.

KATHERINE notices some messages for her on the board. She reads them through.

EDWARD sees this.

EDWARD. Oh, sorry, Miss Hughes.

TOM. Derek, can I offer you Alan Ackroyd?

KATHERINE raises her eyes to the ceiling.

I'll have a word with him this afternoon. Haven't you? He's a very very good brief. A rising star. And I'm sure he'd love to do it. OK? I will. Bye.

TOM puts down the telephone.

Silence.

KATHERINE is writing a note to somebody in response to one she has just read.

TOM. I take it you have no objection to other barristers earning a living even if you don't wish to?

KATHERINE. No. Nor to earning one myself. And I don't want to argue with you, Tom, because we both know from experience you will not understand what I'm saying.

EDWARD. But surely the man has a right to a barrister?

KATHERINE. Tom's fixing him up with one. Alan Ackroyd will no doubt do what's required in these cases. I wouldn't be able to. I do not attack rape victims.

KATHERINE gets on with her note.

TOM thinks.

TOM. Perhaps one day we might get a case where somebody had raped a policeman. Or a judge.

He winks at EDWARD.

KATHERINE ignores him and seals her letter.

TOM. No? So in future then: no more rape cases for you?

KATHERINE. If the defence is 'I didn't do it' or 'it wasn't me' I can do that.

TOM. Well it's outrageous, that's all. And it's asking for trouble.
Because it's a denial of one of the pillars of the legal system.

KATHERINE. Oh don't give me pillars of the system. Where was
your concern about everybody's right to a barrister when Alex
Grimshaw – the head of this chambers – turned down brief
after brief during the miner's strike?

TOM. No, no, no. He didn't turn down a single brief.

KATHERINE. He did.

TOM. He didn't.

KATHERINE. He did. If you say to a striking miner on remand in
Armley prison on some trumped-up charge of obstruction 'yes
I'll defend you but it'll cost you 500 a day' and he says 'all I've
got is legal aid', then you're turning him down. Why is it all
right to turn down a brief out of financial greed but not out of
political conviction?

EDWARD (*baffled*). Politics?

KATHERINE. Yes, politics.

EDWARD. Well answer me this: why is it all right to get an
acquittal for a nutcase who bottles people when you know he's
guilty, but not to try and do the same for a rapist?
There is a pause.

KATHERINE. The answer is simple but hard to understand. It's to
do with power.
EDWARD *is unconvinced.*

KATHERINE. Edward, let's have lunch one day. I'm late.
KATHERINE *goes.*

TOM. Is this or is this not the most appalling hypocrite at the
English bar?

EDWARD. She's mental.

TOM. You know who she's lunching with, don't you?
EDWARD *nods.*
TOM *grins and rubs his hands with glee.*

14. Interior. Cavernous cellar of a wine bar. Day.

The place is crammed. FRANK *and* KATHERINE *sit at a table eating
plates of nosh. She's eating heartily but drinking only mineral water.*
FRANK *has a glass of wine.*

FRANK. Erm . . . It doesn't look as if James will be coming. I'm
sorry.
She isn't crying.
Well I mean the important thing is: he's very keen for you to
come in.

KATHERINE. Uh-huh? Frank, don't be ridiculous. It's the last thing he wants. He knows you want it, that's all.

FRANK. You underestimate him. He's very much his own man.

KATHERINE. He's an opportunist. He's never done anything that wasn't calculated to get him one step closer to taking silk. His politics are a joke really. He thinks you can still get away with being a radical toff. You can't. Except in places like this. Or the bar mess. This is where he's at home, where you can hear the authentic sound of timid careerists quacking like nervous ducks worried they might have offended somebody in the Lord Chancellor's office. It's that particular combination that drives me round the bend: cowardice and ambition.

There is a silence.

FRANK. It drives you round the bend but you seem happy to stay in a chambers built on precisely those virtues.

KATHERINE. I didn't say I was happy.

FRANK. I think perhaps you are. Living in your corner. Pretending you're the only show in town. The only one with any real politics.

Now they're both pissed off with each other.

Come on, there's a job to do. You can't go on being their pet monster. You make yourself look foolish.

Silence.

Well, look: Margaret Wharton has been asking me out to lunch. I can't hang around waiting for you. If you change your mind in the next few days let me know, will you?

Silence.

BINGHAM *joins* KATHERINE *and* FRANK, *looking chirpy. He has a plate of food.*

Silence.

FRANK *and* KATHERINE *nod at him and push the remains of their lunches around their plates.*

BINGHAM. I've got a client who claims to have slept with a former Home Secretary, a former Foreign Secretary, a BBC Newsreader and a High Court Judge who gave him a solid silver cigarette case with his name on it. And your time starts now.

15. Interior. Fetter Court. Frank's desk. Evening.

BINGHAM *and* FRANK *are looking at photographs of* NOLA MARSHALL. *They show horrific facial and body bruising.*

Silence.

Three extra chairs have been set out.

BINGHAM. She still says no then?

FRANK. Yes.

BINGHAM. What do we have to do – get down on our hands and knees?

FRANK looks at him. He's unsure of BINGHAM's *true feelings.*

FRANK. She's a great advocate and she gets people going. But I think she may be settling for a quiet life.

They hear footsteps on the stairs.

BINGHAM *goes to the open door to greet* ALTON PHILLIPS *while* FRANK *collects up the photos and puts them in a drawer in his desk.* ALTON *arrives at the open door with* IVANHOE MARSHALL *and his wife* JO MARSHALL.

16. Interior. Fetter Court. Frank's desk. Evening.

The same, later that evening.

They are all sipping tea.

MRS MARSHALL, *sixty, looks withdrawn and suspicious, studying both* FRANK *and* ALTON.

MR MARSHALL, *is speaking, a sad and bewildered man of sixty-two.*

IVANHOE MARSHALL. Nola was our only child. When we came here, we didn't expect it to be easy. Ten hours a night stacking boxes in them walk-in fridges. I'm still there – despite I've lost four of my toes. We pushed Nola through all the classes. She became a nurse, to our pride. She could have gone anywhere. But she stayed where she was needed. She was the perfect daughter, Frank . . .

JO MARSHALL *looks askance at him.*

Will this inquest tell me the point of this? I put up with all the talk about coons and about rivers of blood. Twenty-seven years I put up with it. Twenty-seven years later where am I? And twenty-seven years after we come to start a new life my lovely daughter Nola is kicked to death by –

He chokes back his despair.

JO *looks at* IVANHOE *sympathetically.*

She touches him.

JO. Ivan.

She looks back to FRANK *and to* BINGHAM, *waiting for their reaction.*

FRANK. It's important from the outset that we are able to speak plainly among our ourselves. Because if we don't, they'll bury us.

JO. Nola was an alcoholic. We know that. Everybody knew that.

IVANHOE. I don't want her name dragged through the mud.

JO. Ivan. Listen to me. It would be better if you sat in Alton's car.

IVANHOE *nods.*

BINGHAM. There's a waiting room. I'll get you some more tea.
BINGHAM and IVANHOE leave.

JO. Mr Cartwright, you ask for plain speaking. Here's mine.
Nothing will come of this. No Home Office action. No action
at all by anybody. This is just another black person dead. If
this had been a white nurse the papers would be full of it
every day.

There is a pause.

ALTON. That's true. But when the inquest starts –

JO. Let me finish, Alton. We've been fools. Our generation was
used to doing what it was told. Nola's generation won't do
that, they're going to stand up for their rights. You've seen
some photographs.

FRANK nods.

So you know what they did to her, and you know why. How
many times, Alton, did Nola give statements about police
brutality on blacks? She was marked down for this.

They are all silent.

*BINGHAM has come back and listened from the door. Now he comes
back into the room and takes his seat.*

It would be better if I sat with Ivan. Alton knows all the facts.
He says you're good lawyers and good men. He says you'll do
your best.

FRANK. Mrs Marshall, just give me a second. If we can force the
coroner's court to establish that what happened to Nola while
she was in police custody amounted to unlawful killing then
the police will be under severe pressure to open their own
criminal investigation.

JO MARSHALL doesn't look very convinced.

JO. Mr Cartwright, I think the police already know what
happened to Nola.

ALTON. Jo, when we get a chance to show the world exactly what
kind of shit is coming down here, we've got to take it. We can't
shrug our shoulders and say 'you win, all right: it is your
world'. The whole black community is looking to the outcome
of this case.

JO MARSHALL studies him.

JO. The Association of Black Families is paying all your fees, not
me. I'll shut my mouth. But if the day comes when blacks
need real leaders, they better be careful who they choose.

ALTON is gobsmacked.

17. Interior. Grimshaw's. Katherine's room. Day.

KATHERINE *is working at briefs at her desk.*
ALAN ACKROYD *is also working at his nearby desk.*
TOM *comes in.*

TOM. Michael Feingold has come on about an attempted murder.
KATHERINE. Fine.
TOM. The thing is: am I to get you the brief or issue a
    questionnaire or . . .?
KATHERINE. Well what is it?
TOM. A stabbing on a train at Lewisham.
KATHERINE. I read about it. They were black, and he was white,
    yeh?
TOM (*sighing*). I've no idea. His name is Bilko or something.
    KATHERINE *is thinking.*
    TOM *is exasperated in a quiet way.*
TOM. I think if you want to vet every brief for every political
    nuance there's really not a great deal of assistance I can be to
    you. You have Feingold's number. If you decide to take the
    brief, perhaps you could let me know.
    He leaves.
    KATHERINE *rings the number. She looks up to see* ALAN ACKROYD
    gazing at her.
    He looks away then back again.
ALAN. I'm doing that rape.
KATHERINE. Good luck.
ALAN. It was actually a pretty tepid thing. He didn't knock her
    about or anything.
KATHERINE. I expect he'll get a medal then. (*Into the telephone.*)
    Hello. Katherine Hughes. Can I have Michael Feingold?

18. Interior. A pub in Chancery Lane. Early evening.

MICHAEL FEINGOLD *and* KATHERINE *sit in the busy pub.*
KATHERINE *is drinking orange juice.*
FEINGOLD *is drinking scotch.*
FEINGOLD. I've met him three times since he was arrested, taken
    long statements from him, and looked meticulously at the way
    the police are handling it and it's all above board: it's really
    very interesting in fact, Katherine, because it's law and order.
    He's saying 'I couldn't stand it any longer and I went for him
    with a knife' which he was carrying because he's been on a
    camping holiday and not because he's a psycho or anything.
KATHERINE. What is he then?
FEINGOLD. He's a very buttoned-up man. Lives alone. Steady job

in a library. No nasty habits except voting Conservative. He's a
man who reads all about the law and order crisis, he believes
there's a mugger round every corner, you put him in a
situation where he's threatened and he's got a weapon and
bam!

KATHERINE. Is this what he says?

FEINGOLD. Well, he doesn't say much, to be fair – you'll need all
your famous skills of rapport with your clients.

KATHERINE *acknowledges this bullshit.*

But the witnesses are all saying it loud and clear. And I think
if Blinkho's got any sense – which undoubtedly he has – he'll
go along with it. I mean, it's a field day for you: you can
blame anybody you like as far as I'm concerned: *The Sun, News
of the World*, Thatcher, Tebbit.

KATHERINE. Can I call them?

FEINGOLD. I think we may have a bit of trouble on that one.

KATHERINE. OK.

FEINGOLD. Great. There's no money in it. He's on legal aid.

KATHERINE. Why can't I defend rich psychos?

FEINGOLD. Because they don't get caught.

19. Interior. A Magistrate's Court. Day.

On the bench are THREE MAGISTRATES, *two of whom are white women
and one of whom is a black man.*

GAVIN BLINKHO *is brought into court. He looks immediately to the
public benches.*

Five or six men, including MIKE FINDLAY, *give him a cheer. There are
one or two people in the press box including* CLIVE CURRAN *of 'The
Scorcher'.*

FIRST MAN. Good on you, Gavin.

FINDLAY. Chin up Gavin. Your dad says hello.

BLINKHO *smiles and nods.*

The bench is not happy though.

CHAIRWOMAN. Be quiet.

*The public benches are quiet but they continue to give him the thumbs
up and gestures of encouragement.*

CLERK TO THE JUSTICES. Your Worships, there's a renewed
application for bail.

CHAIRWOMAN. Does the police objection remain?

POLICE SERGEANT. Yes, Your Worship. This is a very serious
crime and we have reason to suspect the prisoner might
abscond.

A VOICE ON THE PUBLIC BENCHES. Rubbish.

CHAIRWOMAN. Bail is refused then.

There is a low rumble of discontent from the public benches.

THIRD VOICE. Fix. Fix.

FOURTH VOICE. Never mind, Gavin, chin up.

CHAIRWOMAN. Look, be quiet.

There is more muttering on the public benches. Somebody makes a monkey noise. The CHAIRWOMAN *is getting narked.*

CHAIRWOMAN. Be quiet. If there are any further disturbances the benches will be cleared. Is the defendant represented?

JUNIOR BARRISTER, *a young woman, stands.*

JUNIOR BARRISTER. I am representing the defendant today, Your Worship.

CHAIRWOMAN. Who are these men? Are they related to your client?

JUNIOR BARRISTER *has no idea.*

JUNIOR BARRISTER. I'm afraid I don't know, Your Worship.

The benches are quiet.

The CHAIRWOMAN *pushes on.*

CHAIRWOMAN. The prisoner is remanded in custody for a further eight days. You'll come before us again then. You can take him down.

FIRST MAN. Don't worry, Gav. Chin up son.

FINDLAY. Chin up, Gavin.

They applaud him as he's led away.

On the press bench CURRAN *is intrigued.*

20. Exterior. The Temple grounds. Day.

ROBERT HOLMES *and his solicitor,* PAUL WATSON, *are walking through the Temple grounds towards Fetter Court.*

ROBERT *is giving him a cod conducted tour of the Temple.*

ROBERT. And on my right the oldest building in London. Built by Edward the Confessor as the capital's first Thornton's Chocolate Cabin. Soon to be demolished and not before time. On my left the very house in which Charles Dickens wrote his number one best seller 'Another Hundred Things to do With a Young Boy'.

A pin-striped clerk hurries past them.

Hello, darling. Don't speak then; but I still have the photographs.

ROBERT *spots a portly bencher heading up some steps fifty yards away.*

I'd know that bum anywhere.

ROBERT HOLMES *puts his fingers between his teeth and whistles. More than one head is turned by this unseemly behaviour.*

WATSON *gives* ROBERT *a stiff warning as they go on their way and* ROBERT *protests that it was only a joke. They disappear towards Fetter Court.*

21. Interior. Fetter Court. The clerks' area. Day.

ROBERT HOLMES *is gazing into* LORRAINE's *eyes.*
HUGH *is book-keeping.*

ROBERT. Oh those eyes, Lorraine. You've been here before, haven't you? Have you ever had an 'out of your body' experience?

LORRAINE *recognises the bullshit but is captivated by him.*
LORRAINE. No, not really.

HUGH. She's had a few out of her mind experiences at the Three Tuns.

ROBERT. You couldn't lend me a fiver, could you, Hugh, till I get to the bank?

HUGH. No.
  BINGHAM *inserts his head busily.*
BINGHAM. Robert.

22. Interior. Fetter Court. Day.

ROBERT HOLMES *and* BINGHAM *go from the clerks' area towards a conference room.*

ROBERT. James, did you see *Private Eye*?
  He reads the cutting which he takes from his wallet.
  Can we make this quick – I'm having lunch with my agent?

23. Interior. Fetter Court. Conference room. Day.

ROBERT *and* BINGHAM *enter the room and join* PAUL WATSON.

BINGHAM *looks at* ROBERT HOLMES *sternly.*
BINGHAM. Take my advice, Robert. Cool it, Robert, considerably.

ROBERT. He isn't really my agent, he's this bloke I met in Strangeways – (*He has a brilliant idea.*) 'Strange ways' – that's the title for my book. 'Strange Ways: A Film by Robert Holmes and Derek Jarman'.

PAUL WATSON. The Crown Prosecutor's offering us a deal. They're offering not to bring any evidence if you'll agree to being bound over.

ROBERT. No thanks, I've been bound over, it was very painful.

BINGHAM. Robert. I usually advise people to accept this.
  ROBERT *realises they're at least half-serious. He's astonished.*

ROBERT. James, I'm so disappointed in you.

BINGHAM. If we lose –

ROBERT. No, no, no, no, no, no, James. We're not going to lose. Antrobus gave me that cigarette case and I'm going to tell everybody why. We're going to win.

24. Interior. Grimshaw's. Clerks' Room. Day.

KATHERINE *enters in a hurry. She goes into the clerks' room.*
EDWARD *and* TOM *are there with a couple of other* BARRISTERS *from the set.*
Silence.

KATHERINE. I got a message – ?
Something has happened.
ALEX'*s door opens and* DICK SMITH *comes out.*
ALEX *comes out too. He sees* KATHERINE.
ALEX. Ah, Katherine, come in.

25. Interior. Alex Grimshaw's room. Day.

ALEX *and* KATHERINE *sit.*

ALEX. There's been a terrible accident. Alan Ackroyd was taken to hospital last night having unfortunately taken an overdose of sleeping pills.

KATHERINE. You mean he tried killing himself?
ALEX *doesn't reply.*
TOM *comes in with the court diary. He sits.*
Shit. How's his family? Is he OK?

ALEX. Well, he's going to survive. Things had rather been building up. I was aware of it but not of the extent. The important thing is that we all rally round.

KATHERINE. Yes of course.

ALEX. Now Tom thinks you're free on Thursday and there's a rape case at the Bailey you could take over.

KATHERINE. Ah. Well. It would be better if someone else . . .

ALEX. Katherine, there is nobody else. We're all doing things we don't want to do. I'm the only one free to go to Swansea for three days next week to defend some appalling football fan, but there we are. We have to pull together. Everyone's mucking in.

KATHERINE. Yes. Of course.

26. Interior. Law Centre. Day.

Crowded with people waiting to be seen.
ANGIE *at her desk.*
ALTON *comes in from the street. People look hopeful when they see him.*
He smiles at familiar faces and leans across ANGIE's *desk to talk quietly.*

ALTON. Did you get that list?
ANGIE (*not believing it for one moment*). They're far too busy to deal
  with trivia like this on the phone. Somebody has to go down to
  the station.
ALTON. Right. We'll do it the hard way.

27. Interior. Yew Tree Road Police Station. Day.

ALTON *near the counter. He's been waiting a long time.*
He approaches the SERGEANT *at the counter.*

ALTON. What's the hold up then?
SERGEANT. There's no hold up, sir. It's being attended to.
ALTON. I've been here ninety minutes. All I'm asking for is a
  piece of paper with the names of people you had in custody
  on a particular night. It's not a difficult thing to do.
SERGEANT. Don't lose your temper.
ALTON. I'm not losing my temper, I'm being very reasonable.
SERGEANT. You may think you're being reasonable, but in fact
  you're coming across as rather agitated and irate, which
  doesn't help you.
ALTON. OK, let me see the officer who commands this place.
SERGEANT. He's out, I'm afraid, sir.
ALTON. Is somebody doing it? It's a simple thing. Why can't one
  of these men do it. (*There are other officers sitting around.*)

28. Interior. Old Bailey Court Number Four. Day.

KATHERINE HUGHES *is about to cross-examine the main prosecution
witness. This is a thirty-five-year-old woman called* MRS WELSH.
*The press box is full. The public gallery is virtually empty. On the bench
is* MR JUSTICE MERRICK.
MRS WELSH *makes herself look briefly at the defendant in the dock. Then
she fixes her gaze on* KATHERINE.

KATHERINE. Mrs Welsh. You are aware, aren't you, of the
  seriousness of the charge you've brought against my client?

That what you are claiming happened that afternoon carries the possibility of grave consequences for him?

There is a silence.

Are you aware of that?

MRS WELSH. Yes.

KATHERINE. Could you please speak up so that everybody can hear you?

MRS WELSH *looks around the court self-consciously.*

MRS WELSH. Yes.

KATHERINE. Good. So you can see – can't you? – that all the relevant facts are bound to be made known to the Jury.

MRS WELSH. Yes.

KATHERINE. In fact you wouldn't want them to be concealed would you?

MRS WELSH *is not sure what all this is about.*

MRS WELSH. No.

KATHERINE. Good. Now. We've heard you earlier describe with enviable eloquence and great dramatic flair the events of that afternoon. We've all heard you tell how you met my client in a public house where you'd spent the afternoon drinking with friends. That my client and other men and women made their way back to your flat with you – though you do not now apparently remember issuing an invitation to any of them. That more drinking there ensued during which music was –

MRS WELSH. I didn't say that.

KATHERINE. I'm sorry?

MRS WELSH. I said I didn't say that. I didn't have anything else to drink.

KATHERINE. I didn't say you had. I said there was further drinking. Are you now denying that?

MRS WELSH. No.

KATHERINE. So there was drink. (*She pauses while everybody makes a note of this.*) There was music. There was dancing. By sometime around 4.30 – you can't remember when exactly, no doubt your head wasn't as clear as it might have been – the other guests left your impromptu party.

The PROSECUTING COUNSEL, *a middle-aged man, looks at the* JUDGE *who acknowledges the bad form but doesn't stop* KATHERINE.

MRS WELSH. It wasn't a party.

PROSECUTING COUNSEL *again looks to the* JUDGE *who again nods.*

KATHERINE. And you found yourself alone with my client. Which you claim was not something you welcomed.

MRS WELSH. Why should I welcome it? I hardly knew him.

KATHERINE. Mrs Welsh, you are of course a married woman?

MRS WELSH. Separated.

KATHERINE. How long is it since your husband left home?

MRS WELSH. Um . . . it's a bit less . . . nearly a year.

KATHERINE. Do you work?

MRS WELSH. No.

> KATHERINE *glances at the* JURY *of three men and nine women.*

KATHERINE. So then, for nearly a year you've lived alone in your apartment in Hampstead and you don't work.

> MRS WELSH *too glances at the* JURY.

Who pays the mortgage?

MRS WELSH. My husband. Well, actually the business. It's complicated because I was owed –

KATHERINE. Yes. Just answer please. The answer is your husband pays the mortgage.

MRS WELSH. Yes.

KATHERINE. Thank you.

> *She pauses while everybody writes this down.*

And so what do you do with yourself, Mrs Welsh?

MRS WELSH. Well . . . I'm sorry: you'll have to be more specific.

> MRS WELSH *glances to the prosecution for some support, but no joy.*

KATHERINE. Well what time do you get up in the morning?

MRS WELSH (*pondering*). Um . . .

KATHERINE. Usually.

MRS WELSH. About 10.

> KATHERINE *looks very taken aback.*

KATHERINE. 10 o'clock.

> KATHERINE *glances at the* JURY *and can see them thinking 'lazy cow'.*

MRS WELSH. There's not much point in me getting up early.

KATHERINE. And then what? Do you dress for breakfast?

MRS WELSH. No, I just sit and have a coffee.

KATHERINE. What time is it by the time you manage to dress?

MRS WELSH. About 11.30.

THE JUDGE. Miss Hughes, fascinating though all this is . . .

KATHERINE. I think my point is about to become clear, Your Honour.

> MERRICK *assents.*

KATHERINE. So at around 11.30 you dress – and then what?

MRS WELSH. Well . . . shopping, or . . .

KATHERINE. Or what? What other sorts of things.

> *There is a pause.*

Let me help you. How often would you say you went to the pub at lunchtime?

MRS WELSH. I didn't know it was a crime to go to the pub.

KATHERINE. Nobody's suggesting that.

MRS WELSH. Well . . .

KATHERINE. Not every day.

MRS WELSH. No.

KATHERINE. Once a month?

MRS WELSH. No.

KATHERINE. Shall we settle on two or three times a week?

MRS WELSH (*a bit more defiantly*). I really don't see the relevance of this.

KATHERINE *pauses knowing that the* JUDGE *will come in.*

THE JUDGE. You must answer counsel's questions.

KATHERINE. Would it be fair to suggest that things have gone on the slide a bit since your husband left?

PROSECUTING COUNSEL *is on his feet at last.*

PROSECUTING COUNSEL. Your Honour.

THE JUDGE. Miss Hughes, perhaps you could confine yourself more closely to the issue.

KATHERINE. Mrs Welsh, on the two or three occasions per week that you go drinking at lunchtime, how do you dress? As you are now?

MRS WELSH *is dressed very conservatively. She thinks and decides to tell the truth.*

MRS WELSH. No.

KATHERINE *looks slightly disappointed that* MRS WELSH *hasn't lied.*

KATHERINE. How then?

MRS WELSH. Casually.

KATHERINE. Does that mean skirts and cardigans?

MRS WELSH. No. Jeans and a shirt or . . .

KATHERINE. Is that what you were wearing on the day you met my client in the pub?

MRS WELSH. Yes.

KATHERINE. Jeans and a shirt. Tight jeans?

There is a pause.

MRS WELSH *is scrutinised by the predominantly male court.*

KATHERINE *is transfixed by this woman's misery.*

MRS WELSH. Yes. I suppose so.

She has now lost all trace of defiance. She no longer addresses her replies to KATHERINE *but to a space on the floor a few yards in front of her.*

KATHERINE. A heavy shirt? Or a thin one?

MRS WELSH. Not particularly thin.

KATHERINE. Not particularly thin. Do you normally wear a bra Mrs Welsh?

PROSECUTING COUNSEL. Your Honour.

THE JUDGE *ponders for a second.*

THE JUDGE. No. It's a reasonable question in the circumstances.

This is generally taken in the court to be a reference to Mrs Welsh's breasts. She shuffles.

KATHERINE *notices the tiny smiles playing on the lips of* THE JUDGE, *of the* DEFENDANT, *of* PROSECUTING COUNSEL *and some of the* JURY.

MRS WELSH. No. I don't.

KATHERINE. And you weren't wearing one on the day in question?

MRS WELSH. No. Nor do I think it would have made any difference. It wouldn't have made any difference if I'd been in a suit of armour.

She struggles to hold herself under control.

KATHERINE. Why this particular pub, Mrs Welsh?

MRS WELSH. There are sometimes people there that I know vaguely . . . well enough to have a conversation . . . you see: you lose your friends when your marriage goes . . .

She's tumbling into a collapse. KATHERINE *lets her go on.* PROSECUTING COUNSEL *looks like a man who's just lost his case.*

You get desperate . . . you want . . . you just want . . .

29. Interior. The Old Bailey. The concourse outside the courts. Day.

MRS WELSH *sits alone on one of the benches.*
The concourse is quiet as Court Number Four empties.
The DEFENDANT *and his* SOLICITOR *emerge, celebrating. The* PROSECUTING COUNSEL *looks pissed off.* PROSECUTING COUNSEL *goes to the* POLICE OFFICER *who has brought the action.*
MRS WELSH *overhears in the background.*

PROSECUTING COUNSEL. She's got him off, I'm afraid. I'm afraid it's been a bit of a waste of time for you.

POLICE OFFICER *shrugs shoulders.*

MRS WELSH *can't believe it. She watches the jubilant* DEFENDANT *congratulating* KATHERINE.

PROSECUTING COUNSEL. I'm afraid the jury got Miss Hughes' message.

PROSECUTING COUNSEL *approaches* KATHERINE.

Well done Miss Hughes.

KATHERINE *doesn't reply. She takes leave of the* DEFENDANT *as quickly as she can and of his* SOLICITOR *and walks away briskly. Without looking at* MRS WELSH.

MRS WELSH *is finding this very difficult to accept. She gets very angry. She starts shouting.*

KATHERINE *walks off the concourse upstairs towards the Robing Room without looking back.*

30. Interior. Old Bailey. Robing Room. Day.

KATHERINE *sits half out of her gear.*
She makes a decision.

31. Interior. A room in Gray's Inn. Day.

ALEX GRIMSHAW *drinking a sherry before lunch with half a dozen other benchers* — LAW LORDS, *senior* BARRISTERS, *a couple of* GUESTS.
A FLUNKEY *comes in and murmurs to him.*

32. Interior. A withdrawing room. Gray's Inn. Day.

GRIMSHAW *joins* KATHERINE *in a book-lined room.*
He sits.

KATHERINE. I'm sorry, Alex.
  He waves away her apology, it's only lunch with the boys.
  Well . . . I've decided to go.
GRIMSHAW. Any point in trying to persuade you to stay?
KATHERINE. No.
GRIMSHAW. Well, our loss is Cartwright's gain.
KATHERINE. Please: one thing: no 'do' of any kind.
  GRIMSHAW *nods.*

33. Exterior. Outside a Coroner's Court. Day.

FRANK CARTWRIGHT *and* JAMES BINGHAM *arrive in their cars.*
FRANK *drives a five year old Volkswagen,* BINGHAM *a BMW. They park near the mortuary and walk together towards the Coroner's Court building.*
There is a lot of activity outside the court building.
The MARSHALLS *and* ALTON PHILLIPS *are posing grimly for* PRESS PHOTOGRAPHERS *and* NEWS CAMERAMEN *and giving an impromptu press conference.*

ALTON PHILLIPS (*quietly*). . . . the whole black community will be
  looking to this inquest for justice and for the truth finally to
  begin to be established about the death of Nola Marshall . . .
  FRANK *is filmed entering the building through the throng.*
  Questions are thrown to him but he smiles and keeps quiet.
  A noisy but orderly demonstration by various anti-racist groups and by members and supporters of the Association of Black Families is taking place.
  POLICE *are heavily in evidence.*
  The MARSHALLS *and* ALTON PHILLIPS *now make their way into the building through the crowd and past people queuing to get into the Public Gallery.*

34. Interior. Coroner's Court building. Day.

The corridor is thronged with people including many POLICEMEN. *The*
MARSHALLS *both look anxious and disoriented. They meet up with*
FRANK *and* BINGHAM.
There is chaos and noise as they push their way past the office of the
CORONER's OFFICER, *towards the courtroom.*
Inside the office of the CORONER's OFFICER, *several* POLICEMEN *look on*
with distaste at the crowd and at FRANK CARTWRIGHT.

35. Interior. Coroner's Court. The courtroom. Day.

Silence.
Packed into the tiny, high-ceilinged courtroom are the CORONER, *his*
OFFICER, *lots of* POLICE, *the* MARSHALLS *and their* LAWYERS, MEDIA
REPRESENTATIVES, *and an almost wholly black Public Gallery.*
The CORONER's OFFICER *has just called for quiet.*

THE CORONER. Many of you will never have had cause to attend a
coroner's inquest before so let me begin by making one or two
things clear so that there is no subsequent confusion. Firstly, a
coroner is completely independent. Secondly, despite
similarities in the trappings, this is not a criminal court and I
am not a judge. Look, no wig.
This attempt at humour is completely out of character and equally out
of place. It raises a few supportive chuckles from the CORONER'S
OFFICER *and the* POLICEMEN *in court. No one else thinks it's funny.*
Nor is this a trial. No one is accused. It is not a crime which is
being investigated but a death. No blame will be apportioned.
Some people on the public benches don't like this.
But FRANK *is merely settling down for a long gruelling day, getting*
his bearings and having a look around the court.
I am here, along with the jury, charged with the task of
ascertaining as nearly as I can the cause of the death of Nola
Marshall. There are many witnesses to be heard and I
anticipate a lengthy hearing. We'll begin today by hearing Mr
Coleman, The Assistant Medical Officer, read the report of
the autopsy.
FRANK *stands.*
FRANK. Sir, will the jurors be given a sight of the photographs
taken at the post mortem?
THE CORONER. They are unnecessarily distressing. The autopsy
report is full and detailed.
FRANK. Sir, may I ask if the police officers we see here are to be
called as witnesses?
THE CORONER. Yes, they are.

FRANK. May I ask if you intend to allow them to remain in court throughout each other's evidence?

THE CORONER. That's for me to decide and I see no reason why not.

FRANK. May I ask, sir, why you think it appropriate for the police to have the benefit of hearing all the evidence but – ?

THE CORONER. No, I'd rather we got on with it actually.

FRANK. May I ask you, sir, to consider the idea that for some interested parties including the one I represent it may seem baffling that seventeen policemen are apparently required to give evidence and that such a heavy and constant police presence throughout the hearing might seem intimidatory?

The row of POLICE *witnesses looks pissed off.*

THE CORONER. No.

FRANK. Sir, is that 'no I won't consider the idea' or 'no I don't think it's true'?

THE CORONER. It's 'no, I'm not listening to any more of this nonsense'. Sit down, please.

FRANK *sits.*

The POLICE *are delighted.*

FRANK *is imperturbable. The* PRESS *are scribbling.*

THE CORONER *nods to his* OFFICER, *who brings in* MR COLEMAN.

MR COLEMAN *stands on the witness stand and takes out his report.*

ALTON *looks to* JO *and* IVAN *in support.*

They steel themselves to hear the autopsy report.

36. Interior. Alex Grimshaw's room. Day.

KATHERINE *enters the room to see the following:* ALEX GRIMSHAW *and the other available members and staff of the chambers (including* DICK, TOM *and* EDWARD) *stand ready to toast her departure in sherry. There is a grim silence.*

ALEX. Well I won't keep you all too long. It's a sad day indeed for our set to be losing such a distinguished and valued colleague as Katherine.

EDWARD *offers* KATHERINE *a sherry.*

She scrutinises it.

And at such short notice. But we hope she may be happier in her new home. Bon voyage.

They all raise their glasses and drink.

A few people mutter.

Voices saying 'Bon Voyage'.

There is a pause.

KATHERINE. I see you've given them your cheap South African

muck, Alex.

ALEX *chuckles.*

ALEX. Completely apposite of course that Katherine should choose to leave us with a taste of her sharp tongue.

KATHERINE. It won't taste as sharp as that rubbish. You might at least have opened a bottle of decent amontillado.

They don't know whether to laugh or spit.

KATHERINE. Well. Goodbye.

She goes.

37. Interior. Coroner's Court, Courtroom. Day.

COLEMAN *is on the witness stand.*

COLEMAN (*reading from his report*). '. . . severe contusions on the left knee; the insides of both thighs were covered with areas of contusions; the outside of the left thigh had a large contusion measuring four inches by three inches; the outside of the right thigh and the right buttock were covered in contusions; there were contusions on the genital area and the lower abdomen; there were seventeen small contusions on the chest and upper abdomen; there were eleven contusions on the back and shoulders; the upper arms had severe gripping contusions; the face and neck were very severely bruised; it was not possible to separate the number of contusions. In all I counted sixty-three separate external injuries, mainly abrasions and contusions, to the face, body and legs of the deceased. In addition to the brain haemorrhage which was the actual cause of death'.

A pause.

COLEMAN *folds his statement.*

CORONER. Thank you, Mr Coleman.

IVANHOE MARSHALL *looks washed out and broken.*

JO MARSHALL *is staring – as she does throughout the proceedings – at the line of* POLICEMEN.

CORONER. We will now adjourn for lunch.

Silence breaks up slowly into conversations and the noise of people getting to their feet and moving out.

The line of POLICE *stands and leaves by a side door in single file.*

The CORONER *leaves through his own door.*

JO's *face drains of tension. She looks old.*

ALTON PHILLIPS *pats her hand.*

38. Interior. Brixton Prison Interview Room. Day.

GAVIN BLINKHO *is brought in to meet the waiting* FEINGOLD *and* KATHERINE.

FEINGOLD. Hello, Gavin. How are you?

> BLINKHO *nods to them and sits. He squints at* KATHERINE *who smiles encouragingly.*

KATHERINE. How are they treating you?

BLINKHO. Not bad.

> KATHERINE *is sympathetic. She's looking at the papers.*

KATHERINE. Michael has talked to me already about what went through your mind on the night as you watched those boys doing what they did. And we've got a lot of good witnesses who also say you were all being subjected to a very frightening and intimidating ordeal. Now what I'm rather glad about in a way – and you will understand this, I think – is that two of those lads, including the lad you stabbed, are backward. I don't know if you knew that.

> BLINKHO *shrugs. He didn't know.* BLINKHO *stares blankly at* KATHERINE.

KATHERINE. Well, the reason I'm glad about it is this – it means that the jury doesn't have to decide who's wicked, you or him. They can sympathise with the lad and understand why you did what you did. We don't have to do 'the beast on the 10.40 to Peckham Rye' routine. OK?

> BLINKHO *doesn't respond. She takes this for assent.*

Are you always this quiet, Gavin?

BLINKHO. Yeh, I don't believe in a lot of talk.

> *The first alarm bell rings in the back of her head.*

KATHERINE. Well, I'm afraid I have to. You're pleading not guilty to attempted murder but we accept the stabbing took place. I understand from Michael that you wish to say that it was self-defence. Now, they will in all likelihood reduce the charge to grievous bodily harm so I take it you will still be saying you acted in self-defence. Is that right? Self-defence.

BLINKHO. Yeh, self-defence. He came at me.

KATHERINE. Only one of our witnesses says the lad touched you.

BLINKHO. So?

KATHERINE. So I wouldn't want to rely too heavily on that.

FEINGOLD. Luckily, Gavin, 'self-defence' can be broadened to include defending others. The man they were assaulting, for instance.

BLINKHO. Well right: I was defending other people.

KATHERINE (*looking at papers*). You say here that that's the point at which you drew the knife? Why then?

BLINKHO. They could've killed him.

KATHERINE (*pleased*). OK. Fair enough. Now as it turns out, the guy you were defending, the guy they were riding, didn't sustain any real injuries. It all seemed a bit worse at the time than it really was. But *at the time* you thought there was *real violence* happening, didn't you?

BLINKHO. Thought?

KATHERINE. I mean, you were presumably pretty terrified?

BLINKHO *considers this.*

Or . . . concerned anyway.

BLINKHO. Concerned, yeh.

KATHERINE (*whipping the mule along the track*). I think this is what we have to concentrate on: the whole *atmosphere* of violence that was there *at the time*. Now this is where our witnesses really do the business for us. I'll get them all to relive the nightmare in front of the jury and believe me, it'll be bingo – because if there's one thing we're all worried about – and juries are no different from anybody else – it's The Threat.

BLINKHO *not batting an eyelid. He's not impressed with this line of reasoning at all. She's worried. So's* FEINGOLD.

I just need to talk through some legal technicalities with Michael for a second. OK? Do you smoke, Gavin?

BLINKHO. No.

KATHERINE. Well, just bite your nails or something then, eh? Won't be a tick.

KATHERINE *and* FEINGOLD *step outside the room.*

BLINKHO *takes out his book 'Hardcore Survival' and finds his place.*

39. Interior. Brixton Prison, a corridor in the cell block. Day.

PRISON OFFICER *sees* KATHERINE *and* FEINGOLD *stepping out of the cell. They signal that it's temporary. They huddle together and whisper.*
PRISONERS *and* ESCORTS *are arriving and departing.*
SOLICITORS, CLERKS *and* BARRISTERS *are all walking through the corridor.*

KATHERINE. Am I seriously briefed to stand on my hind legs in front of twelve intelligent people and say 'my client was so threatened by this youth and by media images of the violent breakdown of urban society blah blah that he panicked and over-reacted'?

FEINGOLD. I know. I must admit, I hoped he might open a bit for you.

KATHERINE. Michael, this bloke wouldn't even notice if a herd of elephants got on at Penge and stampeded through the buffet car. I mean: is he in a coma or what? You know what I'm beginning to think don't you?

FEINGOLD. I'm sure he's just a straightforward psychopath.

KATHERINE. I hope so.

40. Interior. Brixton Prison, Interview Cell. Day.

FEINGOLD *and* KATHERINE *have rejoined* BLINKHO.

FEINGOLD. Gavin. Remember how we talked about how before the night of the attack you'd been thinking for some time about the possibility of something like that happening sooner or later?

BLINKHO. Yeh.

FEINGOLD. You said you felt a growing sense of panic.

BLINKHO. I think I said anger. I don't panic.

KATHERINE *is looking very worried and so is* FEINGOLD.

FEINGOLD. I recall a particular telling phrase: you said there was a sea of crime and it would reach your door one day.

BLINKHO. Well, I was right, wasn't I?

KATHERINE *is getting a bit fed up with this.*

KATHERINE. OK. Look. I have to look at this through the prosecution's eyes for a second. And I ask myself: how do I discredit this man Blinkho? How do I get rid of all his jury sympathy and transfer it to the victim?

BLINKHO *looks alert for the first time.*

BLINKHO. Victim?

KATHERINE. Yes. Victim. Gavin, you're on trial, not them. You knifed this lad. A black lad.

She decides to take the plunge.

They were all black in fact, weren't they?

BLINKHO *seems not to see the point. He waits. Then.*

BLINKHO. Black. Yes. So? They're black. I didn't go looking for blacks, they came looking for me.

KATHERINE. But you see I might say – the prosecution might say – 'OK. They're black and you're telling me that's irrelevant. But all this business about a sea of crime and a fear of walking down the street at night, this is all code for saying what you really want to say: that this was racial.'

BLINKHO. They came looking for me.

KATHERINE. Perhaps you don't understand. The prosecution is going to say 'what we have here – whether he knows it or not – is a white racist. The victim of his own prejudices. There never was an attack on him. It was just his warped imagination'.

There is a silence.

You see we have another problem. None of our witnesses is black. There were blacks on the train but they didn't come forward.

BLINKHO. Well they wouldn't, would they?

Pause.

KATHERINE *is now trying to control her inner panic.*

KATHERINE. Why were you carrying a knife?

BLINKHO. I'd been living rough. In the hills in Brecon. Ten days. I could have done longer, but I'd proved my point.

KATHERINE. Which is what? Why bother? Why see how long you can survive in the hills in Brecon?

There is a pause.

BLINKHO. Because one day we're all going to have to, aren't we?

KATHERINE. So you're worried about nuclear war, are you?

BLINKHO *smiles at the joke.*

What then?

There is no answer.

What is this sea of crime that's going to drive us all into the hills?

Pause.

BLINKHO *puts his fingers into his armpits and pushes out his lips.*

BLINKHO. Oo, oo, oo, oo, oo, oo.

41. Interior. Coroner's Court. Courtroom. Day

After lunch.

PC TURNELL *is in the witness box.*

CORONER. Now, PC Turnell, you were the arresting officer.

TURNELL. Yes sir.

CORONER. Please tell the court about that and about subsequent events which may help shed some light on the affair.

TURNELL (*referring to written notes*). Sir. I went to Fooleigh Road to a public house called the Cock Inn on Friday the 15th of August last year in response to a telephone request for police assistance. When I got there I discovered the deceased woman in a drunken state sitting on the pavement. It was obvious to me that she was very drunk, she was too drunk to stand and her speech was very slurred and also that she had had a recent fall.

CORONER. This is important. How did you know this?

TURNELL. She had a swelling on the side of her face, on the right cheek. Also I asked two members of the public who were standing nearby who confirmed to me that the drunken woman had fallen heavily against the wall some minutes previous to our arrival.

CORONER. And did you recognise her?

TURNELL. Yes, sir, she was known to me because of her previous convictions for drunkenness. In fact I'd arrested her before in similar circumstances.

CORONER. Carry on.

TURNELL. PC Milnes and myself took her to Yew Tree Road Police Station where she was charged with being drunk and disorderly and put in a cell. When she was sober enough to stand unaided she was then taken to Willesden Magistrates Court where she was remanded in custody to Holloway Prison. Because of industrial action at the Prison due to overcrowding they were not accepting any more prisoners so we took her back to Yew Tree Road for the night. This would be about 6.45.

CORONER. And in what kind of state was she by then?

TURNELL. Her speech was still slurred, sir, but she could walk upright without assistance.

CORONER. What sort of thing was she saying?

TURNELL. As far as I could make out, sir, just general abuse directed towards the police. I couldn't really make it out.

CORONER. Was she complaining about her injury?

TURNELL. No, sir.

CORONER. You're quite sure she didn't complain of a headache?

TURNELL. She did complain of a headache, sir.

There is public bench annoyance at this rigmarole.

FRANK *is scribbling. And shaking his head.*

CORONER. She did. Thank you.

TURNELL. I believe that's why Doctor Taylor was called, sir, but I'm not sure. At this point – my shift having ended at six o'clock – I went off duty.

DOCTOR TAYLOR *is sitting there getting the message.*

CORONER. We'll come to Doctor Taylor later. When did you see the deceased woman next?

TURNELL. Sir, at noon the next day when it was my duty to look into her cell.

CORONER. And in what state was she then?

TURNELL. Well, frankly appalling, sir.

CORONER. In what way?

TURNELL. She had been sick in the night, she had also – how can I put it? Been ill in the night, so that her underwear was heavily soiled, and both her underwear and well – practically everything – was totally saturated with her urine.

CORONER. I see. So this couldn't have been very pleasant?

TURNELL. No, sir. It's just part of the job the public don't see much of.

CORONER. Can you describe it for us?

TURNELL. Well, sir, we carried her into another cell. The main problem as you can imagine, sir – and I don't mean to give any offence to anybody – was the appalling smell.

CORONER. But once again this was not the end of it for you?

TURNELL. No, sir, I had to clean out the cell.

This remark causes outrage on the public benches.

CORONER'S OFFICER. Quiet.

There is quiet on the public benches.

CORONER. No, I mean you saw her again.

TURNELL. Sorry, sir, I hope I haven't offended anybody, I misunderstood. I saw her again in her cell before going off duty. As I understand it she unfortunately went into a coma shortly after that, but again it was the end of my shift, sir.

CORONER. Thank you, constable. Mr Cartwright, do you have any questions for this witness?

BINGHAM stands.

Mr Bingham.

BINGHAM. Yes, sir. Constable, as you know we are not allowed a sight of police statements from witnesses so we're a little bit in the dark over here. You say you spoke to two members of the public who said they witnessed Nola Marshall having a heavy fall a few minutes before you arrived to arrest her. Did you take statements from them?

TURNELL. No, sir.

BINGHAM. Why not?

TURNELL. At that point we had no reason to think it would be important.

BINGHAM. I see. So we have no way of checking this? I mean except with your colleague who was with you whose memory will no doubt coincide with your own. We can't hear from those witnesses to this alleged fall?

TURNELL. No, sir.

CORONER. But they were in no doubt about it?

TURNELL. No, sir.

BINGHAM. Constable, you say you recognised Nola Marshall because you'd arrested her before. Was she known to you apart from that?

TURNELL. In what way, sir?

BINGHAM. As a qualified nurse who had twice given evidence against police in criminal cases involving alleged police brutality and as a person who was involved in black community work.

TURNELL. No, I only knew her as a person with previous convictions for drunkenness, sir.

BINGHAM. I see. Constable, of her behaviour on the evening of her arrest, you say: one that her speech was too slurred to make out anything but general abusiveness; two: that she made no complaint about any injury; three: that she complained about a headache. Which of these is true? As I see it you can have one, but then not two or three. Or you can have two, but not one or three. Or you can have three, but not one or two. Which are you plumping for?

CORONER. I think we will proceed better without sarcasm, Mr Bingham.

BINGHAM. Sir, either she complained of a headache – in which case she was speaking intelligibly – or she didn't because she had no headache.

CORONER. The officer has made himself plain. Do you wish to ask anything else?

BINGHAM. No, sir.

42. The same. Later

PC MILNER *now on the stand.*

FRANK. Constable, you say that at noon on Saturday 16th August you and other officers carried Nola Marshall bodily into another cell. This is now nearly twenty-four hours after her arrest. So she presumably had shaken off the effects of her drinking. Why did you need to carry her?

MILNER. She wouldn't walk.

FRANK. Wouldn't or couldn't? Why do you say she wouldn't?

MILNER *looks blank.*

Could she stand?

MILNER. No, sir.

FRANK. Was she conscious?

MILNER. Yes, sir.

FRANK. I see. Was she warm or cold?

MILNER. Cold, sir.

FRANK. I see. So. Here was a woman whom we've already heard had had a lot to drink and a heavy fall less than twenty-four hours before. She'd vomited and been ill during the night and she was saturated with urine. She was incapable of standing and her body, as you say, was cold. And four of you picked her up bodily and put her in the cell? On the floor?

MILNER. Yes.

FRANK. Handcuffs?

MILNER. Yes. She was thrashing out at police officers and had to be restrained. She was handcuffed to a seat.

FRANK. So she was lying on the floor handcuffed to a seat. Did you put her in the three-quarters prone position as you are required to do by your own regulations?

MILNER. Well . . .

FRANK. Remembering that she was handcuffed at the time.

MILNER. No.

FRANK. Why not?

There is a blank again.

Your rules require, do they not, that this is the procedure when dealing with drunks?

MILNER *does not answer again.*

But she wasn't drunk, was she? She can't have been. Not twenty-two hours after her last drink?

MILNER. No. Obviously it was the blow on the head. Beginning to take effect.

FRANK. So you were very conscious of the fact of an injury to her head?

MILNER. Yes.

FRANK. That's why you dumped her on the floor of the cell and handcuffed her to the seat?

CORONER. Mr Cartwright, only you are using this unpleasant word 'dumped'. Please be more careful. Nothing that has been said so far suggests she was treated with anything but due care and attention by these officers.

There is outrage on the public benches.

CORONER'S OFFICER. Quiet.

There is quiet on the public benches.

CORONER. I do hope you've finished, Mr Cartwright?

FRANK. No, sir.

CORONER. Well I must warn you, my patience is wearing thin.

CORONER *allows* FRANK *to go on.*

FRANK. Constable Wilson, yourself, Constables Pearson and Turner were all present with Nola Marshall.

MILNER. Yes sir.

FRANK. What happened?

MILNER. I'm sorry?

FRANK. Did anything happen which accounts for the fact that when Nola Marshall was eventually examined at a hospital at least one member of staff said she'd never seen such injuries on a drunk?

This is a fast one and FRANK *knows it and the* CORONER *is angry.*

CORONER. Mr Cartwright, I hope you're not just making speculative accusations. You know very well no such evidence has been heard by this court.

FRANK. I intend to ask your leave to introduce exactly this evidence, sir. Will you on my application recall P.C. Milner after you've heard from the witness from the hospital?

CORONER. As you well know that is a matter for my own discretion.

There is outrage on the public benches.

CORONER'S OFFICER. Quiet.

There is quiet on the public benches.

The CORONER *addresses the public bench.*

CORONER. I did not invent the rules of a coroner's inquest. All civilised societies have rules and they must be obeyed. That's what civilisation is.

People on the public benches are amazed.

Mr Cartwright, have you finished?

FRANK. No, sir. Constable, what head injuries did Nola Marshall have already when she was moved?

By now MILNER *has had time to sort his head out and time to look to his mates for support.*

MILNER'*s going to brazen it out and to hell with* CARTWRIGHT'*s witness.*

MILNER. She had some very bad bruising on her face from the fall.

FRANK. So bruising under her right eye on her cheek where you say she'd fallen in the street? But no other bruises elsewhere on her face or body?

MILNER. No. Not that I'm aware of.

FRANK. And she sustained no further injuries during the move?

The CORONER *is looking very angry about this question.*

I'm merely asking the officer whether or not Nola Marshall may have hurt herself or accidentally hit herself. She may for instance have had a convulsion?

MILNER *is very tempted. He looks at his mates.*

MILNER. No.

FRANK. Thank you. So whatever her injuries were when she reached hospital eventually, she had sustained them in Yew Tree Road Police Station – with the exception of the bruising under her right eye caused by a fall in the street to which we have no witness. What is your answer?

MILNER. I don't know.

FRANK. Thank you.

FRANK *sits down.*

CORONER. Thank you, Constable.

MILNER *steps down from the stand puffing out his cheeks.*

I think we'll adjourn at this point until Thursday.

CORONER'S OFFICER. All stand.

The CORONER *disappears into his door in the wall.*

The POLICE *leave quickly through their side door,* MILNER *being patted on the back.*

ALTON. Good, Frank.

BINGHAM. Well done, Frank.

43. Exterior. A taxi. Evening.

FEINGOLD. I think . . . If we talk him through it very carefully we can probably stop him from talking himself into a life sentence.

KATHERINE. He's a head case. I can't believe this is happening. The Crown'll drop 'attempted murder' and offer us 'grievous bodily harm'. Blinkho will plead guilty. And I'll be standing there making a mitigation speech. What are the mitigating circumstances? Defending himself against four attackers? There isn't a mark on him. No. His mitigation is that they were black. I'm sorry, Michael. I've made a mistake. I can't defend him. It would be better if I returned the brief to you.

FEINGOLD. OK, he's a prick. But somebody's got to defend him, Katherine.

She closes her eyes. Not this line again.

KATHERINE. Not me.

KATHERINE *and* FEINGOLD *are in profound disagreement.*

44. Interior. The Garrick Club. Day.

BINGHAM *enters from the street and makes his way towards the luncheon room.*

BINGHAM. Hello, Dad.

SIR CHARLES. James. I've ordered you a chop and some jam roly poly, all right?

BINGHAM. Yes, good. Mother well?

He scans his father's Daily Telegraph while they talk.

SIR CHARLES. Yes. Gloria?

BINGHAM. Yes.

SIR CHARLES. Busy?

BINGHAM. Frantic. As usual.

SIR CHARLES. Anything good?

BINGHAM *casts aside the Daily Telegraph and looks at his father.*

BINGHAM. You only buy me lunch when someone's told you I need to be talked to. So let's get it over with, shall we?

Their chops arrive. They eat.

BINGHAM *senior is very discomfited.*

Well in that case it's obviously the rent boy. I didn't think you'd allow yourself to be used like this. I really resent it.

SIR CHARLES. The man's on his last legs, James. And he has been a tremendous public servant. Look, I couldn't care less about scruffy politicians and TV personalities – let all the shit in creation fall on their heads – or whether some tart does or doesn't get a silver cigarette case for his trouble, but Billy

Antrobus deserves better than this.

BINGHAM. It's not my problem. He gave my client a gift for services rendered. Suddenly he's arrested and charged with theft. Antrobus is a fool. All he had to do was admit it was a gift when they checked Robert's story.

SIR CHARLES. But what purpose is served by letting this repulsive creature drag decent people through the courts?

BINGHAM. It's my client who's being dragged through the courts.

SIR CHARLES. Oh, balls to that. It's common knowledge you were offered a bind-over.

BINGHAM. Oh, is it? This is disgraceful. If you say one more word about this, I'll leave.

They eat in silence, both red-faced and munching.

SIR CHARLES. Did the harpy duly drop into the nest?

BINGHAM. Yes.

SIR CHARLES. And you're still maintaining you're in favour, are you?

BINGHAM. Fully. She's extremely able, extremely clever and very, very charming. She'll have an enormous impact on the chambers.

SIR CHARLES *fingers his glass of wine.*

SIR CHARLES. Still going to the meetings, is she?

BINGHAM. I'm warning you, Dad.

SIR CHARLES. She's a notorious whore, you know.

BINGHAM. Father, she may or may not be a dipsomaniac, a nymphomaniac, or a crypto communist, for all I know or care. All I know is: in a world governed by crooks and paederasts – some of whose sons I went to school with – many of whom are members of this club – Katherine Hughes is a good, honest lawyer.

45. Interior. Fetter Court. Evening.

KATHERINE *and* FRANK *are at their desks waiting.*
FEINGOLD *comes slowly up the stairs towards the open door.*
He knocks on the open door.
He comes in.

KATHERINE. Come in, Michael.

FEINGOLD. May I? Hello, Frank. Are you going to win in that inquest?

FRANK. How do you win in an inquest?

FEINGOLD. By not letting the coroner screw you. You'll do it. You have to. You have to.

He sits.

There is silence.

KATHERINE. Well?

FEINGOLD. If only life could be simple. Your friend Mr Blinkho
has confided in me – oh, what a lucky man I am – that he's a
member of the National Front. Which particular version of the
one and only true National Front, he doesn't specify. I
understand a press release along these lines has been prepared
just in time for tomorrow's committal. We now have a full-
blown legal nightmare on our hands.

KATHERINE. We?

She shakes her head.

No, no, no, Michael.

FEINGOLD. Hear this: Blinkho insists you are still his brief.

KATHERINE. Oh no I'm not.

FEINGOLD. And if you refuse he'll drag you in front of the Bar
Council. I keep on underestimating this man. He's not stupid,
believe me. Whatever else he is, he's not stupid.

KATHERINE. I've returned the brief and that's all there is to say.

FEINGOLD. I've told him you'd say that. I've told him I can get
him a better barrister than you. He's not interested. You've got
a monkey on your back.

KATHERINE. Why don't you tell him to find a new solicitor as
well?

FEINGOLD. This is the acid test of whether my job is a sham: you
must defend the rights of your opponents. Besides, that's what
he's hoping I'll do. Why else did he come to me? Michael
Feingold. Cheerio for now.

He gets up to go.

KATHERINE. You lost your family to these Nazi pigs.

There is a pause.

FEINGOLD. Precisely. But they weren't able to build the camps
until they'd destroyed the law.

KATHERINE. Before they destroyed it they hijacked it. I'm sorry.
I won't lift a finger to help Blinkho, or his kind. Or do
anything that'll help get him a platform for his filthy ideas.

FEINGOLD. I think you'll find you've already done that. I wish
you well, Katherine. This could be the one they've been
waiting for.

FEINGOLD *goes.*

KATHERINE. Who's been waiting for? They're nobodys. They
don't exist. Michael's crazy to let them use him. Complete
stupidity. For a man like him to help them attack black people
in court . . .

FRANK. We could cobble together a story about a clash of dates.
Lorraine could do a bit of creative diary entering.

KATHERINE. Frank, I could have stayed at Grimshaw's and done
  that.

46. Interior. Magistrate's Court. Day.

BLINKHO's *committal proceedings.*
The public benches are full with a small band of BLINKHO
SUPPORTERS. *And many more supporters of Anti-racist Groups.*
The press benches are full too, including CURRAN.
A POLICE *presence too.*
It's a different magistrate from the last time.
Applause and boos as BLINKHO *is brought into the dock.*

CLERK TO THE JUSTICES. Your Worships, with your consent the
  Crown has withdrawn the charge of attempted murder.
  Applause from BLINKHO'S SUPPORTERS.
  Boos from others.
  Be quiet. The defendant is charged with causing grievous
  bodily harm and possession of an offensive weapon.
CHAIRMAN. Mr Feingold, is your client electing trial by jury and
  agreeing to a short committal?
FEINGOLD. Yes, indeed he is.
  There's more noise from the benches.
FIRST VOICE. Where's his barrister?
CHAIRMAN. Gavin Blinkho, I'm committing you for trial on these
  charges at the Central Criminal Court. Is there an application
  for bail?
FEINGOLD. No, your Worships.
SECOND VOICE. Where's his barrister?
CHAIRMAN. Take him down.
BLINKHO. Where's my barrister? Ask him that. I'm being
  victimised. It's a conspiracy.
  He is being taken down to the cells.

47. Exterior. Magistrate's Court Building. Day.

The POLICE *escort* FRONT MEMBERS *down the steps and through a*
CROWD *of chanting anti-racists.*

THE CROWD. Fascists, fascists, fascists.
  FINDLAY *and his* FOUR FRIENDS *and the* POLICE *are covered in spit*
  and there are scuffles but no big punch-up.
  There are camera CREWS *and* PHOTOGRAPHERS *and* CURRAN *is in*
  the thick of it.

48. Interior. A quiet pub. Day.

CURRAN, FINDLAY, COLIN BLINKHO, GAVIN's *ancient father.*
CURRAN *reading the press release.*

FINDLAY. What about a photo of Colin?

CURRAN. I'm not interested in all that happy families stuff. I
can't really use any of this. But I might be interested in the
woman. What's her name?

FINDLAY. Katherine Hughes. Some left wing slag, very good at
shooting her mouth off apparently. She could do with a bit of
attention. All this so-called radical lawyers' rubbish. Alternative
barristers.

CURRAN *is scribbling.*

You're going to cover the fact he's been charged and get over
the background, aren't you?

CURRAN. Yeh, I will, but you have to be so careful these days.
There's always some bastard in Parliament waiting to jump on
you and call you a racist. It's usually some bastard with a wife
and six kids in Sheffield and a bit of black pussy in Victoria.
He's looking at his notes.

So she's very left wing, is she? Know anything else about her?
What was it? Radical what?

FINDLAY. Alternative Bar. All the lefties grouping together.

CURRAN. Oh, we might be interested in that, I suppose.

FINDLAY. Communists, lesbians, wogs. Would any one of them
defend a white man who sticks up for himself?

CURRAN. It would be interesting to find out, wouldn't it?

49. Interior. Fetter Court. Clerk's area. Day.

It's busy.

LORRAINE, HUGH, KEN, MICHAEL KHAN, *and* BINGHAM.
BINGHAM *is reading 'The Scorcher' and is groaning.*

KEN. All she has to do is say she was double booked, surely?

HUGH. Why should she?

LORRAINE. Michael, can you sit somewhere else?

MICHAEL KHAN *gets off her desk.*

Ken, your Aylesbury shoplifting's been taken out.

KEN. Well it's too late now – she's left herself wide open.

BINGHAM. And everybody else.

HUGH. Rubbish.

LORRAINE. You've changed your tune.

The telephone rings, HUGH *answers it.*

HUGH (*into the telephone*). Fetter Court.

Enter KATHERINE, TESSA PARKS *and* JOANNA DAVIS.

There is silence.

LORRAINE. How did your man in the jockstrap do?

KATHERINE. He got three months. Can you imagine it for him? He's so pathetic. Little weedy fella. They were all laughing at him. All this stuff about him poking his little winkle through a hole in the cubicle wall and . . . ugh, it was humiliating for him, wasn't it, Tessa?

TESSA. Revolting.

KATHERINE. Pointless, spiteful waste of time catching, trying and imprisoning a man like that.

She shakes her head.

KHAN. Still it's a job, isn't it?

KATHERINE *chuckles too. She looks at* JAMES BINGHAM.

KATHERINE. James you shouldn't read that, you'll go blind.

LORRAINE. *The Guardian* rang.

KATHERINE. Saying?

LORRAINE. 'Can we have a comment on the Blinkho case?'

KATHERINE. I have nothing to say that won't get me into more trouble.

LORRAINE. That's what I thought.

BINGHAM. You could say you were double booked on Blinkho.

KATHERINE. I could.

HUGH. Why should she? The guy's a racist.

KATHERINE *is dumping circulars into a bin and looking at her letters.*

KHAN. What about the man in the jockstrap? Might he not have been a racist?

KATHERINE. For all I know, I didn't ask.

KEN. What about rape? I mean, nobody likes rapists either.

KATHERINE. I don't do consent rape cases. If I can avoid it.

KEN. Why not? Don't women sometimes consent to sex? I mean they don't with me, but some men occasionally get lucky, I hear.

KATHERINE. Yes, we do consent occasionally to sex. We sometimes even initiate it. But we don't consent to rape. And we never initiate that. Despite what some judges may think.

BINGHAM. But that's the point at issue: it isn't rape if it's consented to.

KATHERINE. You can't consent to rape. It's self evident.

BINGHAM. No, but you can consent to sex and then change your mind.

KATHERINE. Then you're not consenting. Do you do consent rapes then? Willingly?

BINGHAM. I have done, yes. Willingly.

KATHERINE (*to* MICHAEL KHAN). Do you?

KHAN. I've never been sent that kind of brief. But I would do it.

KATHERINE (*to* KEN GORDON). Do you?

KEN. Yes. Why not?

KATHERINE *sighs*.

KATHERINE. You know, I have to say this Mr Bingham, Mr Khan and Mr Gordon, you've got your heads up your arses about this. But I accept it. I accept your right to have your heads wherever you want them. Fetter Court is in the grip of libertarian democracy.

HUGH *laughs out loud*.

LORRAINE. Hugh, nearly four o'clock.

KATHERINE *is on her way out of the door*.

BINGHAM. Why do you accept my right to be wrong but not Blinkho's?

KATHERINE. James, because you're not asking me to mouth your opinions in a serious criminal trial.

BINGHAM. But that's your job.

This halts her in her tracks. She comes back. The mood is changing.

TESSA. Hey, get your hand off it, James.

BINGHAM. Well, isn't it?

KATHERINE. Criticise me, but don't tell me what my job is.

HUGH. Can you see anything up there, James? Want a torch?

BINGHAM. Thank you, Hugh, that'll do.

LORRAINE. Hugh, go over to the list office now.

HUGH. Yes, boss.

BINGHAM (*to* HUGH). What does that mean? I don't want that rubbish from you.

HUGH. OK, Bwana.

LORRAINE. Hugh!

KHAN. Hugh, you're out of order.

FRANK is arriving unnoticed in the doorway.

TESSA. He isn't out of order. Let's have a straight answer. (*To* BINGHAM.) Would you defend Blinkho if they asked you to? Knowing that he's National Front?

BINGHAM. Yes, and I'd try my hardest to get him off. Of course. There is no other answer to that question.

TESSA. Well, there's a word for that, isn't there?

KATHERINE. Whoa, whoa, hold it. Everybody. Please.

They all take a step back from it.

They notice FRANK watching in the doorway.

BINGHAM (*quietly, gently*). Katherine. All I'm really trying to say is that we as a chambers are heading for trouble on this. If it hadn't become public, OK, fair enough, but it has. Politically, it would be clever to bite the bullet and help Blinkho to his day in court.

KATHERINE. For the sake of the chambers?

BINGHAM. If for no other reason.

KATHERINE. We must all muck in.

BINGHAM. We're a team.

Silence. She thinks.

KATHERINE. I will not defend Blinkho.

She goes.

They look to FRANK.

LORRAINE. She's had a warning from the Bar Council. Blinkho's made a complaint.

50. Exterior. The Temple. Day.

MICHAEL FEINGOLD *and* FRANK CARTWRIGHT *are buying a sandwich and a coffee at an open air stall. They find a bench to sit on. They eat and drink.*

FEINGOLD. My client, Gavin Blinkho, instructs me to offer you my brief. If you turn me down he wishes me to offer it in turn to each of your colleagues.

FRANK. Oh, God.

FEINGOLD. You must persuade Katherine to take back this brief. Once you start picking and choosing there's no way out of the mess.

FRANK. She won't. She's only doing what most of us do. None of us in Fetter Court ever prosecutes, whatever the case.

FEINGOLD. Nobody asks you to.

FRANK. Because they know we won't do it. None of us will help put people in prison. The state prosecutes, we defend. All unofficial, all against the rules, everybody knows about it, nobody bothers us. We all pick and choose. She's just being honest about it.

FEINGOLD. She can't afford to be honest.

FEINGOLD takes out his copy of 'The Scorcher' and shows him the small story headed 'Court rumpus in race train case'.

FRANK nods, he's already seen it.

You think I like doing this? Take my advice: persuade her. Somebody has to defend this maniac before we turn him into a celebrity. You people aren't taking your responsibilities seriously. It isn't enough to be right. Who does she think she is?

He's getting loud, FRANK's *getting nervous.*

This is public and FEINGOLD *has a notoriously bad temper.*

FRANK. That's not fair, Michael. She's taken a lot of stick on these issues: she did the Islington fire bomb case and had real threats to her life.

FEINGOLD stands up. He's gone over the edge.

FEINGOLD. Threats? Threats? I walked out of Buchenwald. I ate
my own shit to stay alive. How dare this woman talk to me in
your office about losing my family? How dare she say that! Or
lecture me about people hijacking the law. (*He gathers himself
slowly*). My client wants an answer.

FRANK. Can't it wait till after the Marshall inquest? Blinkho's case
isn't even listed. Can't you baffle him with science, tell him he
has to wait – ?

FEINGOLD. Frank, be clever. I can wait. I can wait forever, but
what is this all about, do you think? Who is running this man
Blinkho? Not me. It's that child molester Findlay. And who
runs him? Who has what Findlay needs to spread the good
word?

FEINGOLD *waves his copy of 'The Scorcher' in the air.*

Ask *them* to wait. You think they're going to be nice about this?
You think these animals are going to wait now that Katherine
has offered them her throat? Does she even know what she's
done?

51. Interior. A Newspaper Office.

CURRAN *is talking with his Scottish editor,* MILLIGAN, *in* MILLIGAN's
office.

CURRAN. The black guy's family has started up a committee for
justice, claiming he was a bit backward and he was only having
a bit of fun.

MILLIGAN. Aren't they all? Who's on the committee? Any mad
buggers?

CURRAN. Not really.

MILLIGAN. Stuff it then. Ignore it.

CURRAN *has a think.*

CURRAN. I want to do something on the Front. Well, Blinkho
Action Committee.

MILLIGAN *is already shaking his head.*

MILLIGAN. No.

CURRAN. At least they're trying to do something. Nobody else
mentions the blacks unless there's an election or a riot.

MILLIGAN. Listen, shut your face, Clive, and live in the real
world. We are not allowed to say nice things about the Front.
They've been found out time and time again. Mickey Mouse
wears a National Front watch.

CURRAN. Findlay's not stupid, actually.

MILLIGAN. Findlay interferes with little girls. I've seen the police
file, and so has every other editor, end of story. I'm not
interested in parcels of jobbies going through Pakis'

letterboxes. It's charmless. (*He's reading some notes.*)

CURRAN. No, it's different these days. They haven't been organised but there's different people getting involved now. Younger blokes. Brighter blokes. They're into survivalism.

MILLIGAN. Still gay boys and nutters.

CURRAN. No, I wouldn't say so.

MILLIGAN. Is Blinkho gay?

CURRAN *shrugs.*

Has he got a girlfriend?

CURRAN *shakes his head.*

He's bloody gay then, isn't he? If that comes out. I mean this Blinkho has to look the part if he wants to be our Vigilante Of The Year, you know.

CURRAN *is getting pissed off at this.*

CURRAN. That's what I'm talking about: he's a little story about survivalism. I mean, it's Rambo and that.

MILLIGAN. But what is it? Survivalism? They all go off into the woods and camp out together. Is this the white backlash or the girl guides? What is he, Conan the Librarian?

CURRAN. They do it alone. They don't go together.

MILLIGAN. There's a great slogan for election '92, 'National Fronters do it alone'.

CURRAN *concedes defeat. They sigh. It's hard work this.*

What about this woman?

CURRAN. Oh, she's a cow. I've done some homework.

MILLIGAN. If you can start something that'll run, fair enough. But you can't go making it all up, Clive. She's a lawyer.

CURRAN. I don't have to make it up. Listen, you name the whacky committee, she's been on it; mention any loony cause – women's rights, free school milk for gay one-parent families, she was there. In it. Giving it that. And she's a total, total hypocrite. She refused to defend men charged with rape just because they're men. Who else is gonna rape a woman? I ask you. She's in a loony left chambers. Chambers. That's what they call a group of barristers.

MILLIGAN. Is that right, Clive?

CURRAN. It's run by a bloke called Frank Cartwright who's a police hater – and boy do they hate him. I can tell you, I've been having a few drinks under the blue lamp. This place, Fetter Court, it's called: full of blacks, queers, lesers, it's got at least one BMW owner, bloke called Bingham who lives in Chelsea and does very nicely thank you out of the oppressed masses. They are ripe for rolling over. Him and Cartwright are doing the Nola Marshall inquest.

MILLIGAN *perks up.*

MILLIGAN. Oh, well that could be interesting. Does Findlay know that?

CURRAN. I don't know.

MILLIGAN. Well he should. If he's clever he should put the two together. Then we've got a real story. What about the woman though?

CURRAN. Well. She's been a soak, that's for sure. She's had a succession of live-in boyfriends – at least one of whom was black.

MILLIGAN. Likes a bit of tar brush. Drugs?

CURRAN. Not that I know of. Or not for certain, I mean . . .

MILLIGAN. No, no, no, it's good enough. Stick to what we can basically prove if necessary. Any gay affairs?

CURRAN. No. Too fond of men.

MILLIGAN. Not married?

CURRAN *is very pleased about the next bit. His pièce de résistance.*

CURRAN. Married at nineteen to a teacher. Married bliss lasted exactly eighteen months. He divorced her in '73 citing her adultery with – get this – Bobby Russell.

MILLIGAN *looks blank.*

MILLIGAN. Never heard of him.

CURRAN. No well I hadn't, but it turns out he's a 6'4" negro lawyer from Detroit who made his living defending the Black Panthers.

MILLIGAN. Say that again.

CURRAN. You must remember the Black Panthers.

MILLIGAN. No, no.

CURRAN *gets it.*

CURRAN. A 6'4" negro.

MILLIGAN. Bingo.

52. Interior. Alton Phillips' Law Centre. Night.

BINGHAM *and* FRANK *both looking very tired, are sitting in the reception.*

BINGHAM. Have you tried persuading her?

FRANK. No, it would be pointless now. If she or me or you or anybody from Fetter Court took the brief we'd just be making ourselves look ridiculous. We can't take orders from the gutter press about who we defend or don't.

BINGHAM. What now?

FRANK. We plough on. We ignore Blinkho. We say nothing to anybody ever again about Gavin bloody Blinkho and let's hope he eventually gets twenty years.

BINGHAM. Why are we having this meeting?

FRANK *shrugs, he doesn't know.*
Come on, Alton, for God's sake.
ALTON *comes out of the door to his office. He looks at them.*

53. Interior. The Law Centre. Night.

Inside ALTON's *office there is a committee meeting in progress of the Association for Black Families.*
JO MARSHALL *is there,* ALTON PHILLIPS *is there,* JOANNA DAVIS *from Fetter Court is also on the committee.*
FRANK *and* BINGHAM *have joined them. They are both looking rather surprised.*

BINGHAM. 'Why did I say I would defend a racist if asked to?'
There is a pause.
FRANK *glances accusingly at* ALTON *who wishes he wasn't here.*
Well. We have a rule at the Bar that anybody who needs a defence gets one. You may hate somebody, you may be certain he's guilty, it doesn't matter; you defend them. You do your best. That's the theory. Like everybody else, I go along with the hypocrisy that I'm a taxi cab, willing to go anywhere; when in fact I'm a London bus and I stick to the routes I like. I advertise that route as loudly as possible so that nobody will ask me to go somewhere different. However, the fact remains that I have said something which you feel damages my credibility as Frank's junior in this inquest. I have been asked what would I do if I found I had a fare paying passenger who wanted to go to Dartmoor for ten years in order to make some point to people who aren't listening anyway –
VOICES FROM THE COMMITTEE. 'Yes they are. They are'.
– about black racism on whites. And I have said honestly that I would take him where he wants to go. I wouldn't believe him. I wouldn't enjoy the trip. But I would have to take him where he wants to go. If I said no then he'd say – and quite rightly – 'Look. No justice here for me. No fair hearing for me'. And the racists at the Bar and in the Inns of Court – very nice racists for the most part – and other racists in the gutter press will say "Well now: that's the left for you. When they say 'justice and equality for everybody' what they really mean is 'justice and equality for everybody as long as we don't disagree with what they want to say'." Freedom is indivisible. Does that answer your question?
There is a long silence.
FRANK *wants to die.*
JO. It's all very clever. Very clever.
BINGHAM *is dismayed.*

The night Nola was murdered I tried to get a taxi cab to take me from my office cleaning in Covent Garden to go up to the hospital. They wouldn't stop for me. So I got a bus and Nola was dead when I got there. I listened to you carefully Mr Bingham, but it's just a lot of clever words.

BINGHAM *bows to the inevitable.*

54. Interior. Coroner's Court. Court room. Day.

DOCTOR TAYLOR *the police surgeon is on the stand.*

FRANK. Doctor Taylor, as I understand it you were first called to Yew Tree Road Station at four o'clock in the morning after Nola Marshall's arrest. Sixteen hours after her arrest. This was because she had apparently been found to be unable to stand. We therefore assume somebody had been asking her to stand although it was the middle of the night.

TAYLOR. Police regulations covering drunks require them to be observed every thirty minutes and in this case the officer in charge had obviously taken the wise precaution of requiring her to move around.

FRANK. I see. That's an assumption on your part?

TAYLOR. No, that's what I've been told by the senior officer.

FRANK. Right. And you say you found Nola Marshall unable to stand or speak. Was she injured?

TAYLOR. She'd had a fall.

FRANK. Yes, we've heard about this fall.

TAYLOR. No, she had apparently fallen in the cell during the night. *This is new to everybody. Disbelief on public benches.* POLICE *looking sheepish.*

FRANK. She'd had another fall? Well this is news to some of us, you see. PC Turnell was apparently unaware of this when he gave evidence last Tuesday.

TAYLOR. Well . . .

CORONER. Am I to understand, Doctor Taylor, that where your statement referred to 'the conditions caused by the recent fall' you mean this later fall, not the original fall?

TAYLOR. Yes, sir.

CORONER. Very well. When did this fall happen?

TAYLOR. I'm told at about 2.30 a.m. after she'd been roused to check on her condition. She'd fallen against the wall and struck her face on the concrete floor of the cell.
FRANK is conferring with ALTON PHILLIPS.

FRANK. So she was now heavily bruised and couldn't stand or speak? Was she conscious?

TAYLOR. Yes.

FRANK. This must have been a great concern to you?

TAYLOR. Well of course she was in a rather pitiful state but I felt given what the police had told me she was still getting over her drinking bout.

FRANK. Had she been sick at this point?

TAYLOR. No.

FRANK. What did you do?

TAYLOR. I advised that observation be kept on her and should her condition change she should be taken to hospital. I also said if accommodation was obtained at Holloway they should be fully informed of her history and condition.

FRANK. What did you do then?

TAYLOR. I went home to my bed whence I'd come.

FRANK. You next saw Nola Marshall another fourteen hours later at 6 p.m. that evening twenty-eight hours after her arrest. Why were you called to the station?

TAYLOR. She was in a coma.

FRANK. A coma. What did you do?

TAYLOR. I immediately arranged for her to be an emergency admission to the Royal Free Hospital.

FRANK. Where a surgeon operated to remove a brain haemorrhage. But in vain. Is that correct?

TAYLOR. Yes.

FRANK. Let's go back to the night you first saw her. You advised the police officers in whose care Nola Marshall was that she should be taken to hospital if necessary. In what circumstances did you advise them to do that?

TAYLOR. If she was repeatedly sick.

FRANK. You know she was never taken to a hospital?

TAYLOR. So I understand.

FRANK. You know she was sick repeatedly?

TAYLOR. So I understand.

FRANK. Would you expect that sickness, uncontrolled urinating and inability to speak might have alerted the police that something was wrong?

TAYLOR. Well I suppose it could be confused with drunkenness.

FRANK. Twenty hours after the event?

TAYLOR. I can't speak for the police.

FRANK. But they had certainly not followed your instructions?

TAYLOR. It would seem not.

There are cheers on the public benches.

FRANK. Thank you.

CORONER. Thank you, Doctor Taylor. The court is adjourned until ten tomorrow morning.

CORONER'S OFFICER. Quiet. All stand.
But a row is going on between POLICEMEN *and* PEOPLE *on the public benches who are shouting abuse at* OFFICERS.
The CORONER *disappears through his door as his* OFFICER *attempts to restore order.*

55. Interior. Magistrates Court. Court room. Day.

ROBERT HOLMES, BINGHAM, PAUL WATSON.
The prosecution is there. There are one or two in the public gallery. But more importantly for ROBERT, *the press benches are almost half empty.*

ROBERT. Not much of a turn out.
ROBERT is taken into the dock.
The Stipendiary MAGISTRATE *comes in.*
CLERK OF JUSTICES. Court will rise.
The Stipendiary MAGISTRATE *sits.*
They all sit.
The POLICE SOLICITOR *arrives and goes into a huddle with the* CROWN PROSECUTOR.
Your Worship, this is police versus Robert Holmes. The defendant is charged with theft of a silver cigarette case valued at a hundred and twenty pounds. Defendant has already entered a plea of not guilty.
MAGISTRATE. Mr French.
CROWN PROSECUTOR (*stands*). Your Worship. The prosecution offers no evidence.
MAGISTRATE. I see.
He writes.
BINGHAM *collects his papers.*
ROBERT *is baffled.*
The case is dismissed.

56. Exterior. The Magistrates Court. Court building. Day.

ANTROBUS' SOLICITOR *is addressing half a dozen* PRESS MEN *on the steps of the court building.*

SOLICITOR (*reading*). 'My client wishes me to make the following statement. "I met Robert Holmes when he hitched a ride in my car on the M1 Motorway in August 1986. Because he seemed hungry and destitute I offered him a meal at my flat in London. He had a meal and a bath and left. It was only some days later I noticed the disappearance of a solid silver cigarette case . . ."'

ANTROBUS *is sitting in a car, turning his face away from two or three*
PHOTOGRAPHERS.
WATSON, BINGHAM *and* ROBERT *walk past.*
ROBERT *has the cigarette case in his hand.* BINGHAM *shakes his*
hand. ROBERT *is very depressed.*

BINGHAM. What's the plan?

ROBERT. Well funnily enough I haven't been inundated with
media offers for my kiss'n'tell memoirs. At least we didn't lose.
Didn't fancy trying to earn a living in Wormwood Scrubs.
Well . . . Keep your pecker up, James, old boy. Things could
be worse, remember the Alamo.
He goes, smiling at a man entering the building.
BINGHAM *shakes his head.*

57. Exterior. Coroner's Court building. Day.

The usual large media and public presence but no sign of disorder.
Plenty of POLICE *around.*
CURRAN *is highly visible among the throng.*
FRANK *and* ALTON PHILLIPS *and* MARSHALL *are coming out of the*
court building. They're being filmed by news crews as they pass their
supporters.
There is a sudden commotion. A little old man has walked through the
cameramen and grasped IVANHOE MARSHALL's *hand in his. It's* COLIN
BLINKHO, *wearing his World War Two campaign medals.*

COLIN. Mr Marshall, I'm Gavin Blinkho's father.
As the others try to escape from him, cameras click and a rumpus
breaks out, but IVANHOE *allows his hand to be shaken.*

IVANHOE. Mr Blinkho. Your boy should have proper legal help.

COLIN. How come they can spare the time for your daughter but
Gavin still hasn't got a barrister? Can anybody say this is a fair
country? My son's the forgotten man in Brixton Prison! This
man admits it.

ALTON. Mr Marshall has nothing to say about the Blinkho case.
In the commotion, with ALTON *taking* IVANHOE *away as quickly as*
he can from the court building and from COLIN BLINKHO *the latter*
loses his footing and falls to the ground.
CAMERAMEN *take lots of photos of his pathetic figure looking old and*
frail and upset.
CURRAN *and his* PHOTOGRAPHER, *the only ones not apparently taken*
by surprise by this whole event, are particularly interested in getting a
good photograph of COLIN BLINKHO *on the ground.*

COLIN. Is this why we gave our lives in the war? For England?
This isn't England.

He weeps for the cameras.

58. Interior. Fetter Court. Morning.

FRANK *is at his desk looking at 'The Scorcher'. The front page story. The headline is 'Is this England' over a picture of* BLINKHO's *dad falling to the floor in a sea of angry black faces.*
BINGHAM *looks on as* FRANK *reads.*

BINGHAM. 'See page 14'.
    FRANK *turns to centre pages to read 'Loony Left at the Bar'.*
FRANK. Shit a brick.
    They read.
BINGHAM. 'The head of this set of Bar misfits is Frank
    Cartwright, one-time member of the Communist Party of
    Great Britain who has never publicly renounced his Soviet
    style beliefs – '
FRANK. I'm late.
    He takes his stuff and goes.

59. Montage.

READING. 'Cartwright's speciality is attacking the police in court
    and in print. He has never been known to pass up an
    opportunity to accuse the police of racism, sexism, brutality
    and all the other smeers of the loony left. But the undoubted
    star of the Bar when it comes to the radicals is Katherine
    Hughes who mixes her similar brand of far left politics with a
    raunchy lifestyle of blokes and booze. Attractive Katherine is
    the lady who breaks all the rules of her profession: she: won't
    defend men on rape charges: won't defend white people
    accused of offences against black people; speaks out publicly
    about senile judges and the immorality of prison. We ask 'who
    does she think she is?' This holier than thou attitude rings as
    phoney as a crocodile's tears coming from a woman who has
    had a succession of live-in lovers since her marriage to teacher
    Eric Dewar ended in divorce when he could no longer tolerate
    her lengthy and public affair with black American Civil Rights
    lawyer Bobby Russell during his two year stint as visiting
    lecturer at the London School of Economics. Unfortunately
    for Ms Hughes, no sooner had the divorce come through than
    6'4" Russell promptly returned to his wife and children in
    Detroit leaving the Raunchy Radical older but apparently not
    wiser.'
    Montage. This piece is shared by:

60.

IVANHOE *and* JO *at home.*

61.

SIR CHARLES *at the Garrick.*

62.

LORRAINE, HUGH, TESSA, MICHAEL *and* KEN *at chambers.*

63.

TOM *and* EDWARD *at Grimshaw's.*

64. Interior. Fetter Court. On the stairs. Day.

KATHERINE *is coming in from the court. She passes* MICHAEL KHAN *on the stairs.*

KATHERINE. Michael. How did your primary purpose go?
MICHAEL KHAN. We lost. The guy's already back in Pakistan.
KATHERINE. Something's got to be done. It's absurd.
MICHAEL KHAN. Yes, well . . . we do our best. Immigration isn't sexy.
He keeps going. He wasn't rude, but he wasn't friendly either. She has been hoping to discuss the case. She goes upstairs into the Clerks' area.

65. Interior. Fetter Court. Day.

LORRAINE *is alone as* KATHERINE *joins her.*

KATHERINE. Hello.
LORRAINE smiles and works.
KATHERINE picks up her letters.
Quiet. Everybody in court. A sign of a good clerk.
LORRAINE smiles again.
LORRAINE. I'm glad somebody thinks so. (*But she's uneasy with* KATHERINE.)
KATHERINE. You're probably wishing I'd stayed at Grimshaws.
LORRAINE (*genuinely*). No.
She's about to continue to explain why she thinks KATHERINE *should defend* BLINKHO *when* KEN *sweeps in off the street.*
KEN. Sorry, can I interrupt girl-talk for just one second? Why was I not told my Aylesbury shop-lifting case had been taken out?

LORRAINE. You were told, Ken.

KEN. Oh yeh. When?

KATHERINE *moves off towards her desk.*

LORRAINE. You were standing exactly where you are now when I told you.

66. Interior. Fetter Court. Day.

KATHERINE *waves at* TESSA *who's working, and waves back.*
KATHERINE *sits at her desk.*
TESSA *comes over.*

TESSA. You're very strong, aren't you? They're all waiting for you to say you were wrong and you're sorry James got thrown off the inquest. I'm very glad you came here. Has Frank asked you to climb down?

KATHERINE. No. But then he hasn't said anything to me. None of this is actually doing Frank any harm.

67. Exterior. Outside Coroner's Court building. Morning.

FRANK *arrives in his car. He parks. He gets out. He's surrounded by cameras. He goes inside past a large anti-racist demonstration who cheer him and boo the police.*

68. Interior. Coroner's Court building. Morning.

FRANK *is a bit late.*
He's only just going to make it into court in time.
Every POLICEMAN *he passes has a smirk on his face and the office of the* CORONER'S OFFICER *with several* POLICEMEN *working in it, has the centrefold spread complete with photographs of* FRANK *and* KATHERINE *sellotaped onto the door.*

69. Interior. Coroner's Court. The court room. Morning.

FRANK *takes his seat to a buzz of excitement and support from the public benches.*
The POLICE *file in and each of them is carrying a copy of 'The Scorcher'. They sit down, take them out and read them studiously.*
FRANK *looks at* JO *and* IVAN. *They smile at him, looking drained.*
CORONER'S OFFICER. All stand.
   They all stand.
   The CORONER *comes in and sits.*
   They all sit.

70. Interior. Coroner's Court. The court room. Morning.

BARNES *is in the* WITNESS *stand.*

FRANK. Mr Barnes, you in fact are the person who called the police to come and do something about Nola Marshall on the afternoon of the 15th of August last year.

BARNES. Yes, sir.

FRANK. You wanted her to be moved.

BARNES. Yes, sir, well . . .

FRANK. A not unreasonable wish. You kept your eye on her until the police arrived.

BARNES. Yes, because she was right in front of my shop, you see.

FRANK. Did she have a fall?

BARNES. No.

FRANK. You're sure about that?

BARNES. Yes.

FRANK. Did you see her face before she was taken away?

BARNES. Oh, yes.

FRANK. And did you see any injuries on it?

BARNES. No. None at all.

FRANK. Thank you.

CORONER. Mr Barnes. Can you explain how it can possibly be that no fewer than eleven policemen have stated that they saw clearly the evidence of this fall either at the time of the arrest or very soon afterwards?

BARNES. No, sir.

CORONER. Thank you.

71. Interior. A bedsitting room. Day.

FINDLAY *is in his room.*

The walls are covered with Nazi memorabilia. There are posters of young children. On the table in front of him is a copy of 'The Scorcher' showing the photograph of KATHERINE.

FINDLAY *is typing. We see as much as possible of the letter that he is typing.*

'Katherine Hughes, This is to inform you that we have been watching you. You are a filthy traitorous bitch whose only concern is the welfare of wogs who attack decent white people.'

FINDLAY *thinks.*

He's twisted. 'You are a whore. The whole world knows that you have been going with blacks. You must have had a' – *and we cut away at this point.*

We see FINDLAY's *face, his throat is dry. He swallows.*

We go back to the letter.

*'For this you will pay the price. We will get you when you least expect it.
Probably a razor blade across your face. Brigato Blanco.'*

72. Interior. Coroner's Court. The court room. Day.

CORONER. Before I call this final witness I feel bound to point
out that the man you're about to hear evidence from is himself
an habitual drunkard and this indeed is why he occupied a
nearby cell on the night in question. I'm not suggesting he
would deliberately mislead you, but his credibility must be
weighed against his record as an offender.
He nods.
The CORONER'S OFFICER *brings in* COLLINS.
COLLINS *takes the stand. He's a middle-aged Irishman, shabbily
dressed.*
Mr Collins, you've seen enough court rooms to know that
perjury is a crime.

COLLINS. Yes, sir.

CORONER. When did you last have an alcoholic drink?

COLLINS. Two days ago, sir.

CORONER. Very well.
FRANK stands.

FRANK. Mr Collins, you were in a cell next door to Nola
Marshall.

COLLINS. Yes, sir.

FRANK. Because you were drunk yourself.

COLLINS. Yes, sir.

FRANK. How long had you been in the cell when Nola Marshall
was brought in?

COLLINS. Five hours, sir.

FRANK. So you were sobering up. What time was this?

COLLINS. About seven o'clock, sir.

FRANK. How did you know it was Nola Marshall?

COLLINS. She talked to me, sir, through the walls. If you raise
your voice, you can talk. It's a regular thing. She said 'I'm
Nola Marshall, who's that?' I said 'I'm David Collins.' She was
very merry. We sang two or three songs together. She was
calling out to the police telling them to come and sing and
come and dance.

FRANK. She was inviting policemen to sing and dance?

COLLINS. Yes, sir. She sang 'Bye bye blackbird'.

FRANK. What else did she sing?

COLLINS. Well now, sir, I . . .
COLLINS is looking uneasy, glancing at the MARSHALLS.

FRANK. You can speak freely. We realise Nola was very drunk

and that she was in high spirits.
There is a pause.

COLLINS. Well, sir. She shouted out that she was feeling randy.
And could anybody oblige her.

FRANK. What happened then?

COLLINS *doesn't want to tell, but.*

COLLINS. Well, sir. This went on for a while. She was telling
these fellas they weren't real men and what have you. Then all
of a sudden a group of I should say four or five of them came
into the cell block from the stairs and they went into her cell.
He pauses.

And there was a lot of shocking abuse and she was screaming.

FRANK. Why was she screaming?

COLLINS. Well they was giving her a terrible battering, sir.
Kicking and punching her. And calling out 'black slut' and
'black slag' and 'black whore'. I would say they lost control of
themselves.

73. Interior. Coroner's Court. Court room. Later that day.

A hushed silence as the JURY FOREMAN *stands.*

JURY FOREMAN. We find that Nola Marshall was unlawfully killed.
Pandemonium in the court. Half celebration, half abuse at the
POLICE, *already filing out of court.*

74. Interior. Fetter Court. Night.

*A big sprawling party is going on throughout the chambers and on the
stairs and all over to celebrate* FRANK's *victory. Everybody from
chambers is there along with friends and colleagues.*
FRANK *and* KATHERINE *are missing though. Hubbub, music, drinking.
Especially drinking.*
BINGHAM *is looking puzzled. He finds* LORRAINE.

BINGHAM. Where's Frank? You give a man a party and he
disappears. Fetter Court's first big win.

LORRAINE. Where's Katherine?

They put two and two together.

75. Interior. Grimshaw's. Grimshaw's room. Night.

ALEX GRIMSHAW, *waistcoat unbuttoned, sits back in his chair with a
cigar and a brandy.*
FRANK *stands looking tired in his overcoat.*

FRANK. You owe her something, Alex. Help her. Take the

Blinkho brief. Get this monkey off her back.
GRIMSHAW *thinks*.
ALEX. If Feingold offers it, I'll take it. But he'll get ten years
whoever defends him.
FRANK. Thank you.
ALEX. Well done, by the way. Very pleasing to see that coroner
with both tits in the mangle.

76. Interior. Fetter Court. Night.

The party.
TESSA *joins* LORRAINE.

TESSA. I just called her. She's waiting for a taxi.

77. Interior. Katherine's flat. Night.

KATHERINE *is sitting thinking. She's alone, ready to go out. She's
reading the newspaper report of the inquest hearing. The headline says
'Marshall "unlawfully killed"'.*
KATHERINE *is fed up with waiting for her taxi. She picks up her bag to
go out.*

78. Interior. Fetter Court. Night.

The party. FRANK *enters to cheers and congratulations.*
He joins BINGHAM *and has a drink thrust into his hand.*

FRANK. Where's Katherine?
BINGHAM *shrugs*.
BINGHAM. Licking her wounds I should imagine or getting some
slim-hipped youth to lick them for her.
FRANK *not liking this.*
Only joking, Frank.
FRANK. You believe what you read in the papers, do you?
BINGHAM. Look, they weren't exactly flattering about me either,
but there was a grain of truth in it.
FRANK. The attack on her was different.
BINGHAM. Quite. Well that's all I'm saying: no doubt if I was
Katherine I wouldn't feel like a party either.
FRANK. I think there's something you still haven't grasped about
Katherine, James. She's fearless.
He moves on to other people. BINGHAM *drinks.*

79. Interior. The house in which Katherine has a flat. Night.

KATHERINE *arrives downstairs to find* FINDLAY's *letter sticking through the letter box. She opens it and reads it. She screws it up and puts it in a waste paper bin. She steels herself to open the door to the street. She can't quite manage it.*
She sings to herself.

KATHERINE (*singing*). Pack up all your cares and woe. Here I go.
  She pulls the door to the street open. She holds it. She steps out and pulls it shut.

80. Exterior. The path outside Katherine's house. Night.

It's dark.
KATHERINE *walks slowly down the path towards the street.*

KATHERINE (*singing*). Singing low. Bye bye blackbird. Where somebody waits for me.
  She's at the end of the path. She hesitates.
  She steps out into the street. She's out of sight and gone.
  Fade out.

EPISODE THREE

The One about the Irishman

Cast

FRANK CARTWRIGHT	Jack Shepherd
JAMES BINGHAM	Julian Wadham
RUARI McFADDEN	Frank Grimes
FREDDIE HUNTER	Robert Stephens
EAMONN HAND	Colum Convey
PETER STEINSSON	James Villiers
HARRY OLLERTON	Tony Haygarth
GEORGE VINER	Bill Wallis
DEPUTY TO THE DPP	Charles Lewsen
LORRAINE	Caroline Hutchison
TESSA PARKS	Joanne Campbell
HUGH	Eamonn Walker
ANNIE CARTWRIGHT	Anna Mottram
SIR CHARLES BINGHAM	Wensley Pithey
LADY MARGARET BINGHAM	Faith Kent
GLORIA BINGHAM	Ruth Hudson
PATRICK O'BRIEN	John Keegan
MARGARET GRADY	Rynagh O'Grady
NICK WILSON	Robert Bathurst
SPECIAL BRANCH OFFICER	Trevor Nichols
EDWARD LATHAM	Raymond Brody
MR KELLY	Timothy Kightley
TV NEWSREADER	Gordon Honeycombe
LAVINIA DALYRIMPLE	Annie Irving
HAMILTON KNOX	Robert Demeger
MP ON NEWS	Ken Morley
RICHARD	John Atterbury
HEATHER	Rosemary McVie
DELIA	Elaine Banham
CONRAD	David Brierley
JOHN	Donald Hoath

1. Exterior. London Streets. Winters Day.

January 1987.
With sirens screaming, a convoy of police cars and bikes escorts an armoured prison van at high speed.

2. Interior. Courtroom in Lambeth Magistrates Court. Day.

COURT OFFICIALS *prepare the court for the hearing.*
Armed POLICE *search the court.*
Sniffer dogs hunt for hidden explosives.

3. Exterior. Outside Lambeth Magistrates Court. Day.

A sizeable crowd of PHOTOGRAPHERS, CAMERA CREW, JOURNALISTS, SUPPORTERS, POLICE, *reacts as the* CONVOY *arrives and disappears through gates.*

4. Interior. Inside the building. Day.

Armed POLICE *watch as other* OFFICERS *thoroughly search the belongings of anybody being passed into the courtroom.*
JOURNALISTS, MEMBERS OF PUBLIC, SOLICITORS, CLERKS, *all are required to pass through a metal detector.*
Among those going in are HARRY OLLERTON, *fifty, a pressman; and* NICK WILSON, *thirty, a TV journalist.*

5. Interior. Cells below court. Day.

The seven DEFENDANTS *enter the cell area through the heavy street door. Each of them is handcuffed to two* PRISON OFFICERS. ARMED POLICE *march them quickly into a large cell immediately below the courtroom.* RUARI McFADDEN, PATRICK O'BRIEN, SEORAS DUNDAS *and* DESMOND HAGUE *look reasonably composed.* EAMONN HAND *looks apprehensive.* MARGARET GRADY *and her daughter* DEIDRA *look as if they are in shock.*

6. Interior. The Courtroom. Day.

The public gallery and the press benches are packed and noisy.
COURT OFFICIALS *look warily and with some hostility on the Irish* SUPPORTERS *on the public benches.*
POLICEMEN *are placed strategically around the room.*

On the press benches, HARRY OLLERTON *scans the public benches for familiar faces. He spots a* MAN *sitting quietly watching the others around him. He catches his eye and winks.*

The MAN, *(a special branch officer) doesn't respond visibly.*

Sitting beside OLLERTON *is* NICK WILSON. *He has observed this little exchange.*

WILSON. Friend of yours, Harry?

OLLERTON. Nick, how are you, my boy?

> *A* PRISON OFFICER *comes up from the cells and passes through the dock into the well of the court. His appearance causes the buzz of expectation to rise. He speaks to the Magistrates'* CLERK *who in turn makes his way to the door in the corner which leads into the Magistrates' retiring room.*
>
> *This door is guarded by a* POLICEMAN.
>
> The CLERK *knocks once and goes in. Some laughter from the* PUBLIC.

OLLERTON. The natives are getting restless.

> WILSON *ignores him.*
>
> OLLERTON *leans into him.*

OLLERTON. Knock, knock. Knock, knock.

WILSON (*sighing*). Who's there?

OLLERTON. Irish stew.

WILSON. Go on.

OLLERTON. Irish stew in the name of the law.

> WILSON *nods and looks bored.*

WILSON. How about some background? Is it true they were under surveillance from start to finish?

OLLERTON. Buy a newspaper.

> *The* CLERK *emerges from the retiring room, leaving the door ajar. He nods to the* PRISON OFFICER *who then goes back down to the cells. The buzz intensifies.*

WILSON. Here we go.

OLLERTON. Heard the one about the Irishman with athlete's foot? Doctor tells him to put a clean pair of socks on every day. By Friday he can't get his shoes on.

> *He chuckles.*

WILSON. You know your problem, Harry? You're a racist.

OLLERTON. You'll still have to read my copy to find out what's happening.

CLERK. All stand.

> EVERYBODY *stands as the stipendiary* MAGISTRATE, *a man of fifty walks briskly to his seat on the bench. He sits. Everybody sits. He surveys the court with a no-nonsense look.*

MAGISTRATE. Let me make one thing clear at the outset. If these committal proceedings are interrupted at all in any way I'll have the public benches cleared immediately. I hope that's understood.

The public benches look suitably subdued. He nods to the PRISON OFFICER *who is standing at the top of the stairs in the dock.*

The OFFICER *opens a door and the* DEFENDANTS *are led up into the dock, still handcuffed to two* GUARDS *each.*

Shouts and applause greet them.

The DEFENDANTS' *names are called by friends and relatives.*

McFADDEN, O'BRIEN, DUNDAS *and* HAGUE *smile, wink or nod; The* GRADYS *look anxiously for friendly faces and find them with a mixture of relief and despair;* DEIDRA *instinctively goes to wave her hand and has it pulled down;* EAMONN *has located his family and exchanged nods and smiles, but he seems to be looking for somebody else. Whoever it was he was hoping for, evidently isn't there.*

The MAGISTRATE *decides he's been kind enough.*

MAGISTRATE. Be quiet.

CLERK. Be quiet.

An uneasy quiet falls.

The Prosecuting counsel, PETER STEINSSON QC, *a portly sixty-year-old, bides his time patiently. The* MAGISTRATE *nods to him.*

MAGISTRATE. Counsel for Prosecution.

STEINSSON *stands.*

STEINSSON. Sir, I appear with my learned junior to represent the Crown. The Defendants are represented as follows: Ruari McFadden by Mr Hunter; Patrick O'Brien by Mr Gillard; Eamonn Hand by Mr Cartwright.

The MAGISTRATE *is looking at the* DEFENDANTS *as they are named and at their* BARRISTERS. *And so are we probably.*

SOLICITORS LATHAM, VINER, POOLE *and* CONNABOY *are all there too.*

STEINSSON. Syaw Sw – I beg your pardon – Seoras Dundas by Mr Roland; Desmond Hague by Mr Bevan; Mrs Grady by Mr Burgess and Miss Grady by Mr Salter. The Defendants are all charged with conspiracy to contravene the Explosive Substances Act in that between August 8th, 1986 and November 7th, 1986 they conspired together and with others to cause an explosion or explosions at or near the Cenotaph in Whitehall.

VOICE FROM PUBLIC BENCHES. Good on you, Irish patriots.

This causes cheers and applause.

DUNDAS *attempts to raise his fist in salute. He's roughly prevented.*

This causes unrest on public benches.

MAGISTRATE. Look, I have given you all fair warning.

ANOTHER VOICE. Get your hands off him, you pigs.

More shouts.

CLERK. Be quiet.

DUNDAS and his GUARDS stop struggling.

The noise subsides.

The MAGISTRATE is trying not to look ruffled. He nods to STEINSSON who had sat down. He stands.

MAGISTRATE. Please continue, Mr Steinsson.

STEINSSON. Sir, the Crown will show that this conspiracy was the most atrocious act of criminal terrorism –

Again vocal unrest on public benches.

CLERK. Be quiet.

The MAGISTRATE is now running out of patience.

STEINSSON. The most atrocious act of criminal terrorism yet contemplated on the mainland –

This word is the match to the fuse. The public benches erupt in outrage.

MAGISTRATE. Clear the public benches, please, will you? The Press can remain.

Pandemonium as the COURT USHERS and POLICE move in to clear the public benches.

7. Interior. A corridor in the Magistrates Court. Day.

POLICEMEN, COURT OFFICIALS, PRESSMEN, LAWYERS, *are talking in groups. Nearby are public telephones.*

PRESSMEN *are phoning in their copy. One of them is* HARRY OLLERTON.

OLLERTON. With armed soldiers guarding the building and police thronging the courtroom itself, comma, the defendants, dash, all seemingly unconcerned by the unprecedented gravity of the charges against them, dash, turned their backs on the court and attempted to shout Republican slogans as Counsel for the Crown, capital c, capital c, Mr Peter Steinsson outlined the case against them. Full stop.

LATHAM passes by, heading for the street with his CLERK.

OLLERTON. Hold it a minute. Mr Latham? Any chance of a word off the record?

LATHAM just smiles and shakes his head as he goes.

OLLERTON. Hello? New sentence. After the public benches had been cleared of the cheering, comma, slogan-chanting relatives and fanatical political supporters of the accused, comma, all seven were eventually committed for trial at the Old Bailey later this year, full stop. Paragraph. The case of the so-called Cenotaph Seven, capital c, capital s, in which the defendants are accused of conspiring to mount a daring rocket attack on

the Cenotaph, capital c, on Remembrance Sunday, capital r,
capital s, last November could well last several months and is
already being called the Trial of the Century, capital t, capital
c. Full stop. Last sentence. The trial is expected to show that
only through thorough police intelligence work was a plot
foiled which would have taken the lives of several members of
the Royal Family, capital r, capital f, comma, the government,
comma, opposition parties, comma, and senior military
commanders, full stop.

8. Exterior. Street outside Lambeth Magistrates Court. Day.

NICK WILSON *talking to camera*.

WILSON. After scenes of near pandemonium, the seven were
  eventually convicted for trial on a charge of conspiring to
  launch a rocket attack on the Cenotaph which might have
  wiped out a whole upper echelon of – Did I say 'convicted'?
  He sighs.
CAMERAMAN. Sorry, I wasn't listening.
WILSON. I'll just go back. Committed. Committed. Committed.
  Committed.
  He pauses and then relaunches his speech.
  After scenes of near bedlam the seven were eventually
  committed for trial charged with an offence of almost
  unprecedented gravity. The implications for British public life
  of a successful rocket attack on the Cenotaph on
  Remembrance Day are only now beginning to come home.
  This is Nick Wick Nick Wilson, oh Christ. They *will* be bloody
  convicted by the time I get this sodding thing right.
  CAMERAMAN *laughs.*
WILSON. Right. Try again. OK. Straight faces. Ready?

9. Interior. Bingham's bedroom/Frank's front room. Night.

BINGHAM *is in bed with* GLORIA. *He's watching late night news. She's
dozing, face buried in her pillows.*

TV. This is Nick Wilson for the BBC News outside Lambeth
  Magistrates Court.
LAVINIA DALYRIMPLE (*on TV*). And here with some of the
  background to the case of the Cenotaph Seven is Hamilton
  Knox.
KNOX (*on TV. His voice-over police photos of the seven in which they
  look like sub-human desperadoes*). The Cenotaph Seven – five men

and two women – have already been in custody for nine weeks
since their arrests at addresses in West London and in
Manchester.

BINGHAM. Would you let a police photographer do *your*
wedding?

KNOX (*on TV*). But today for the first time police revealed just
how close the nation may have come to a devastating blow.
The four rocket launchers – which some sources are now
suggesting may have been supplied specially for the attempt by
Libya's Colonel Gadaffi –

BINGHAM. I don't believe it.

KNOX (*on TV*). – had apparently already been mounted on the
back of a lorry when police swooped.

BINGHAM *remote-controls it off*.

BINGHAM. They'll have Hitler lighting the blue touch paper next.
Or Yasser Arafat. Or Tony Benn.

GLORIA (*gone*). Mmm.

BINGHAM *picks up the newspaper from by his side and reads Harry
Ollerton's story headlined 'The day they said "Let's go for Britain's
Throat"'.*

BINGHAM. Harry Ollerton. Unbelievable. (*He shakes his head in
disbelief.*) I must've been on another planet on Remembrance
Day. I saw no rocket attack on the Cenotaph. Did you? The
entire ruling class wiped out? Country crashing out of control
like a headless chicken? I didn't.

GLORIA (*slowly into her pillow*). We were in Tuscany.

BINGHAM. They're behaving as though the seven are accused of
an actual attack. And there's an absolute presumption – I
mean: no *question* – that they're guilty. I mean: they've all got
suspicious names like Paddy and Seoras and Ruari – who even
spell their names in a guilty way. Questions have to be asked.
Because the appalling thing is that somewhere out there twelve
people are watching this drivel and reading this crap and
they're going to be the jury!

GLORIA (*same*). We went with whatsisname and his new
girlfriend.

BINGHAM. God, I'd love to be in this.

He sighs. He puts out the light.

GLORIA (*same*). Then after that we drove down to Nice and went
on the Motorail.

He switches the light back on and TV, soundless.

BINGHAM *dials a number and gets* FRANK *who is sitting watching TV
in his front room – which looks even more than usual like a bombsite.
He turns sound off but goes on watching* HARRY OLLERTON *being
interviewed as an expert on security matters.*

FRANK. Frank Cartwright.

BINGHAM. Frank, James. Are you watching? Amazing, isn't it?

FRANK. Hello, James. Yes. Very bad.

BINGHAM. Are those people going to get a fair trial?

FRANK. Well that's the sixty-four thousand dollar question. If my client was one of the big fish I'd be thinking in terms of trying to show how the burden of proof gets altered in Irish cases.

BINGHAM (*envious*). I'd love to run a defence like that. I'd love it.

FRANK. But I'm not sure that would be the best thing for Eamonn Hand as it happens.

BINGHAM. Who is Eamonn Hand anyway?

FRANK (*tutting*). That's what everybody says. He's the one from Manchester. The gofor. I'd rather've had O'Brien. Or McFadden. McFadden's really interesting. I saw him speak in London – oh, ten years ago – he was very powerful. He must be on the Army Council now, or close. I'm amazed they've got their hands on him in an active service unit over here. All will no doubt not be revealed.

BINGHAM. God, I envy you. The Trial of the Year. You decided on Tessa as your junior?

FRANK. Yes.

BINGHAM. Good choice. Very good choice.

FRANK (*smiling*). Thank you, James.

A terrific slamming of the street door.

ANNIE *storms around the house looking for* FRANK. *She tracks him down and glowers at him.*

FRANK. I have to go now, James. (*He puts down the telephone.*)

ANNIE (*raging*). You were supposed to pick up Alethea from school this afternoon. We agreed. Look at this place.

10. Exterior. Chancery Lane. A taxi driving south. Day.

BINGHAM *and* HUNTER *flag a taxi in Chancery Lane. They get in.*

BINGHAM. Brixton, please.

CABBIE. What?

BINGHAM. The Prison.

CABBIE *gives them a filthy look.*

HUNTER *glares at him. He drives on with bad grace.*

BINGHAM *reads his paper: Harry Ollerton's latest piece headlined 'A Very Special Breed'.*

HUNTER *has the same paper and is reading.*

BINGHAM. Is he going to keep this up till the whole lot of them gets the CBE?

HUNTER. He obviously believes the nation owes them a great debt.

BINGHAM. Harry Ollerton has a fully furnished flat up Special
    Branch's backside.

HUNTER. I can't say working in Nelson Mandela Chambers has
    done a great deal for your use of English.

BINGHAM. He's a mouthpiece, Freddie. He prints black
    propaganda over his byeline. In return he gets a lot of free
    background with which to astound his gullible readership. He
    probably knows more about this case than we ever will.

HUNTER (*enjoying baiting him*). Well I never knew I was so
    gullible. Thanks for putting me straight.

BINGHAM. Welcome. And by the way, 'Nelson Mandela
    Chambers' isn't actually very funny if you think about it.

HUNTER. I knew this would happen. I told everyone who'd listen.
    I said 'Leaving Pump Court to work for Zircon Chambers will
    have no effect whatever on James's career. James is destined
    for greatness at the Bar. But mark my words: he'll eventually
    become as grey and humourless as the rest of them. It'll be
    Cuban holidays and Solidarity badges' and by God I was right.

    JAMES *smiles and shakes his head.*

    HUNTER *chuckles.*

HUNTER. Oh. I'm delighted you're my junior on this. We'll run
    the defence together, eh? Just like old times.

BINGHAM (*sceptical*). Oh yes?

HUNTER. I see your friend Cartwright's briefed. He's a very
    clever barrister, no doubt about it.

BINGHAM. Yes.

HUNTER. Though even clever men have to eat. Surely he can't
    afford to do quite as much legal aid work as he seems to? How
    does he pay to have all those children educated?

BINGHAM. His three children go to state schools.

HUNTER. Ah. So the taxpayer shoulders the burden. I might've
    known. Speaking of legal aid – which I only normally do when
    with consenting adults – I do think it's a bit rich, you know,
    Provisional IRA holding out the begging bowl. I mean: let's
    have a bit of integrity with our terrorism. The old Officials
    would've gone out and robbed a bank to pay their legal bills.
    Not this lot. And they had better songs. I defended a chap in
    the fifties who insisted on standing outside Lambeth Palace all
    day shouting 'Up the long ladder and down the short rope!
    To hell with King Billy and God bless the Pope!' (*He laughs.*)

11. Interior. C-Wing. Brixton Prison. Day.

HUNTER *and* BINGHAM *are escorted on to the cold and grim C-Wing
passage – a separate block, a prison within a prison. Its solid rooms are*

guarded by men in the corridor and outside the windows.
BINGHAM *and* HUNTER *are eventually shown into a room. Waiting there for them are* RUARI McFADDEN *and* EDWARD LATHAM. *The escort leaves.* McFADDEN *and* LATHAM *stand.*

HUNTER. Good morning, Edward. Good morning, Mr McFadden.

McFADDEN. Mr Hunter.

LATHAM. Ruari, this is Mr Bingham, Mr Hunter's junior.

McFADDEN. Mr Bingham.

BINGHAM. Mr McFadden.

They all sit.

BINGHAM. I hope you're being treated well.

McFADDEN. Apart from the cold. We had a little problem when we arrived. They were keeping a child molester on the wing which obviously we couldn't tolerate. The governor refused to move him. But it all got sorted out amicably. We had a quiet word with the feller and he asked to go into solitary.

He smiles broadly. HUNTER *not sure how to respond.* BINGHAM *has to smile.*

HUNTER. Good. Well now. Shall we make a start? I don't know whether you need me to . . .?

McFADDEN. I'm pretty familiar with the British legal system, Mr Hunter.

HUNTER. I see, good, well let's start by looking at the evidence contained in the police depositions. This falls broadly into two categories. Evidence obtained by police observation – which does seem to have begun at a very early stage, does it not? – and then forensic evidence in the form of fingerprints found on documents taken at the scene –

McFADDEN. Mr Hunter?

HUNTER. Yes, of course.

McFADDEN. There's no reason for this to be more than a formality. You've got a very busy practice. You don't want to waste a lot of time on legal aid cases.

HUNTER (*poo-pooing this idea*). No, no. Doesn't enter into it. Private or NHS – it's all the same to me.

He smiles amiably. McFADDEN *smiles back at him.*

HUNTER *thinks he's really broken the ice.* BINGHAM *can see that* McFADDEN *thinks* HUNTER *is a prize charlie.*

HUNTER. What I want is to reach a point today where we agree the basic thrust of the case against you.

McFADDEN. The basic thrust is that the British government has instructed its police force and its legal officers to have me charged with conspiracy to cause explosions. I'll be pleading not guilty. First of all: to cause as much aggravation as possible. And secondly – though I agree this is virtually irrelevant – because I'm innocent of the charge. In fact I'm not even sure what the charge means. (*Rhetorically*.) What is a conspiracy?

HUNTER. A conspiracy is simply an agreement. You're charged with agreeing with others to cause explosions.

McFADDEN. Did I write a letter to the Anti-Terrorist Squad telling them I'd agreed or did they observe me winking and nodding at people or what?

HUNTER. Well the Prosecution doesn't claim to have a letter from you saying 'Dear Mr. O'Brien, let's go and shoot some rockets at the Cenotaph!'

McFADDEN. That's something anyway. So what I'm actually charged with is agreeing something in my head? (*He looks at the ceiling with a smile*.) Are the Thought Police listening now, you think?

BINGHAM *smiles. He likes* McFADDEN.

McFADDEN. Mr Bingham has a very subversive smile on his face. If I were you I'd make strenuous enquiries into his mental activities.

BINGHAM. I've no doubt they already have.

HUNTER. I'm not sure this is getting us very far. I think we all know perfectly well what's meant by the charge.

McFADDEN. I beg your pardon, Mr Hunter, I'll try not to be facetious. I don't want to make life difficult for you. You want to know what my defence is, don't you? I have no defence. There is no defence against conspiracy – that's why the charge is used against people like us. So that we can be put away for what we *are*, rather than for anything we might've done. Or *thought* of doing in an unguarded moment. Mr Bingham's smiling again.

HUNTER. A conspiracy charge is something of a legal strait-jacket, I admit. But if this is your way of telling me that you intend to offer no defence, I strongly advise you to think again.

McFADDEN. Do you really? What's your opinion, Mr Bingham?

BINGHAM. Mr Hunter's right. There was always Houdini.

McFADDEN. He wasn't Irish, though.

BINGHAM. On his mother's side. You should fight it. Sooner or later one of you is going to fight it head on and win.

McFADDEN. You're very naive.

BINGHAM. That's what junior counsel are for. Nevertheless. Your alternative only throws the case to the State. 'He isn't defending himself because he's guilty'. (*He stops smiling*.)

McFADDEN. Thank you for your opinion, old chap.

HUNTER. You see, Mr McFadden, the charge against you –

McFADDEN. – is a politically motivated legal fiction. This will be a
show trial, Mr Hunter, I accept that. And I'm sure in your
heart you do too. In fact that's why you're here. The Army
Council asked for you to be briefed because you're part of the
political establishment and my defence – such as it will be –
might sound more convincing to British ears coming from
your lips.

HUNTER *is not enjoying this and* BINGHAM *observes this wryly.*

McFADDEN. I'm not sure about that, but I will be asking you to
put one or two things to the court and the press box on my
behalf which might help put this pig circus into its proper
political context.

HUNTER. Aren't you forgetting the Jury? Or am I to address
myself entirely to the Press Box?

McFADDEN. Oh yeh, I nearly forgot, you still have some of the
trappings of justice over here – not like in occupied Ireland.
But the jury doesn't matter, Mr Hunter, they're hand-picked
and they'll be under round-the-clock police surveillance and
constant attack from the media, to make sure they get well-
and-truly scared shitless in plenty of time to find us all guilty
as charged – no matter how ridiculous the evidence may
appear to any rational mind that may stray into the
courtroom. Am I right, Mr Bingham?

BINGHAM *silent because of* HUNTER.

McFADDEN. I will be found guilty. I don't want any of us to waste
time trying to stop that. I'll be given a punitive sentence –
which, incidentally, I don't expect to serve out. In case that
remark worries the Thought Police: it doesn't mean I'm
planning an escape – though could you ask the Governor
where Gerry Tuite left his shovel? – no, it means that we all
know there will be an amnesty once the war's over and the
British Army is out of Ireland. If it makes you feel any better,
Mr Hunter, I have a soft spot for Britain. I hope to come back
one day as Irish Ambassador to the Court of St James.

McFADDEN'*s smiling.* BINGHAM *chuckles.*

McFADDEN. You think I'm joking?

BINGHAM *shakes his head.*

McFADDEN. Look at Menachem Begin. Or Robert Mugabe.

BINGHAM. Or Benjamin Franklin.

HUNTER. So. To put it bluntly, Mr McFadden, you intend to
treat your trial as a farce.

McFADDEN. Yes. But I want you to take it seriously. It'll look
better for the Jury.

HUNTER. Well, of course, this is entirely your business. But I

think you're unwise; courts aren't at all impressed by
flippancy, and if what little you've told Mr Latham is true,
then you do indeed have the beginnings of a defence.

McFADDEN. '*If* what I say is true'?

HUNTER (*caught out*). I beg your pardon if –

McFADDEN. No 'ifs'. You're paid to believe me. The British
taxpayer's shelling out good money for you to believe every
word I say.

HUNTER *is very pissed off by now.*

HUNTER. I think you misunderstand what's required of me. I
don't have to believe you. I have to *behave as though* I believed
you.

McFADDEN (*laughing out loud*). And you're telling me that's not a
farce? Tell me, Mr Hunter, do you support this government?
Do you support British policy in Ireland? Do you have any
friends or relatives in the government, the opposition, the
SDP, the Royal Family, the Church, the Army, the Navy, the
Air Force, or any of the War Veterans organisations?

HUNTER *doesn't reply. He looks daggers at* LATHAM.

McFADDEN. Are you seriously telling me, Mr Hunter, that you
believe I'm going to get a fair trial? Or do you only have to
behave as though you believe I'll get a fair trial? Where are they
going to find a jury of twelve unbiased people to decide my
case when I can't even find *one* to *defend* me?

McFADDEN *grins, but there's no mistaking his anger at* HUNTER's
bland charm.

12. Interior. Hunter's room at Pump Court. Temple. Day.

HUNTER *has a scotch.* BINGHAM *shakes his head to one.*

HUNTER. To be lectured on justice and fair play by a murdering
fanatic . . . unbearable.

BINGHAM. We don't know that.

HUNTER. Do you doubt it?

BINGHAM. In the absence of any evidence.

HUNTER. If ever I saw a hard-line IRA activist, he's it.

BINGHAM. He may be or he may not be, that's not really the
point, is it? The point is: there's no decent evidence against
him, on this charge.

HUNTER. Which I would forcefully point out in his defence, if
he'd *let* me. But he's not interested.

BINGHAM. Because he knows the case won't be decided on
evidence.

HUNTER. Well that's his opinion.

BINGHAM. If this were an armed robbery charge and the police were putting up this sort of case, what would you be thinking?

HUNTER *drinks and refuses the bait.*

BINGHAM. You'd be thinking of an acquittal. And what will McFadden get?

HUNTER. Well we don't know, do we?

BINGHAM *a bit pissed off that* HUNTER *isn't coming clean.*

HUNTER. James. This *isn't* armed robbery. This is . . . different.

BINGHAM. Why? Why does it matter what the charge is? Where is it written that the burden of proof is different in terrorist cases? But we know it. I'm saying it's about time somebody said so.

HUNTER. We don't know any such thing.

BINGHAM. Irish cases are being tried by different rules.

HUNTER. No, nonsense.

BINGHAM. You just admitted as much yourself. 'This isn't armed robbery – this is different'. Be honest.

HUNTER *studies him.*

HUNTER. Have you ever seen someone who was standing next to a nailbomb, James?

BINGHAM. Ah. And therefore we have to get them behind bars – even if it means inventing the evidence or bending the rules? Or using torture? Occasionally? Just a little bit?

HUNTER. You're going much too far. That isn't happening.

BINGHAM. Freddie. The Maguire Family. The Birmingham pub bombers. The Guildford pub bombers. Are you happy about those convictions?

HUNTER. I don't have to be happy or unhappy.

BINGHAM. You're proving McFadden's point. For people like you the courts are a political tool when it comes to Irish cases.

HUNTER (*quietly*). My God, you really have gone over the edge, haven't you? Perhaps I was wrong about your glittering career.

BINGHAM. Well if you don't mind me saying so, Freddie, that's very cheap of you.

HUNTER (*coldly*). You think so? Well, Well.

A JUNIOR CLERK *knocks and comes in.*

JUNIOR CLERK. Edward Latham's arrived.

JUNIOR CLERK *goes out.*

BINGHAM. If you think you should ask Edward to brief another junior, I'll go quietly.

HUNTER (*back from the brink*). That's not the way we do things, James, you know that. You're my junior. Unless you insist otherwise. Which I strongly advise against.

BINGHAM. You're right, Freddie. I'm sorry.

LATHAM *comes in.*

13. Exterior. Temple. Day.

BINGHAM *walks thoughtfully through the Temple, towards Fetter Court.*
Slowly, a smile lights up his face until he has to let out a laugh.

14. Interior. The Big Room. Fetter Court. Day.

HUGH *and* LORRAINE *were working,* FRANK *was getting ready to leave,*
when BINGHAM *arrived with his news.*
They are stunned for a moment.

FRANK. McFadden sacked Freddie Hunter? Who's leading then?
LORRAINE. Frank, do you want me to try and get you on it?
BINGHAM. He's asked for me.
  Silence.
FRANK. Bloody hell.
LORRAINE. Congratulations!
HUGH. You? Why?
  The commotion attracts TESSA *from across her desk.*
BINGHAM. Not everyone thinks I'm a total wally, Hugh. Maybe
  he thinks I can get him twenty instead of thirty.
HUGH. It's amazing, James. It's brilliant.
BINGHAM. Thank you.
FRANK. You think you've got a chance?
BINGHAM. Of an acquittal? Oh, I don't know about that . . .
FRANK. Of getting him twenty.
BINGHAM. It's a runner. There's not a lot of good evidence. A lot
  of surveillance that anybody could make up. A little bit of
  forensic.
FRANK. If you know a way of overcoming police evidence in an
  Irish case, you should patent it.
TESSA. James, it's fantastic, hey!
BINGHAM. Thank you, Tessa. What about your man? The gofor?
FRANK We're on our way to see him. He's a bar-room
  sympathizer who didn't know what he was getting into. That's
  our story anyway. But say I prove it – people've got fifteen for
  less . . .
BINGHAM. I'll talk to McFadden. Maybe the big boys can come
  up with something to help you.
FRANK. Thanks.
  FRANK *and* TESSA *go.*
  BINGHAM *makes a call.*
BINGHAM (*into telephone*). Gloria? Wonderful news!

15. Interior. C-Wing Passage. Night.

It's late in the day and already dark as EAMONN HAND *sits opposite*
FRANK CARTWRIGHT, TESSA PARKS *and* GEORGE VINER, *his solicitor.*
He sizes up FRANK, *who is reading notes.*

FRANK. Mr Hand.

EAMONN. Eamonn.

FRANK. Eamonn. It's worth remembering that we're probably not
alone. So if you have anything to say in confidence.
He pushes a paper and pencil into the middle of the table. EAMONN
nods, but it seems irrelevant to him. He's uneasy and troubled, FRANK
notices, but who wouldn't be?

FRANK. Eamonn, I've had a look at the evidence and at what
you've told George. Now in order to convict you on a
conspiracy charge the Prosecution has to prove that you were
part of the preparations to the crime and that you knew what
was going on. First of all they'll attempt guilt by association:
they'll drag in everything they know about your politics, about
your background, your friends, family, where you were born,
what you eat for breakfast, you name it. This is allowed in a
conspiracy trial – they can drag in all sorts of evidence that's
normally ruled out. We'll come back to that later, because
there's actually not much I can do about it, OK? Let's
concentrate now on the part they say you played. They say
first of all that it was you who made two telephone calls to
Ireland containing coded messages about rocket launchers and
you were used, they'll no doubt say, because of your English
accent. Now I've listened to this tape and the quality is dodgy.
My guess it that the man who's prosecuting is too shrewd to
risk this in court. I'll try and find out what his real intentions
are, but let's put that aside for now. Which brings us to the
business of a) you finding accommodation at the women's
house for O'Brien, McFadden, Hague and Dundas and b) you
hiring a flat-back lorry on to which rocket launchers were later
attached by other people. Allegedly. And you freely admit you
did these things.

EAMONN. Yes. I fixed them up at Margaret and Deirdra's. They
didn't know who they were. Why have they been charged? It's
unbelievable.

FRANK. How could they have known? You didn't know yourself
who the four men were.

EAMONN. No.

FRANK. Because you had been led to believe that the
accommodation and the lorry were for a gang of lump
workers, yes? Irish building trade workers.

EAMONN. Yeh.

FRANK. Perfectly reasonable thing to believe. So you thought
Patrick and Ruari and the others were . . .?

EAMONN *unconvincingly and reluctantly.*

EAMONN. Well. Just what you said. That's fine.

FRANK. Well it's what *you* say that matters. (*Whipping this old horse
along the road.*) You did these things to help them out. Not
because – as the prosecution will say – because you knew full
well they were intending to launch a rocket attack on a large
number of VIPs.

EAMONN. No. I didn't know anything about any rockets. I didn't
know anything about anything.

He's hopelessly unconvincing. He lights a cigarette as FRANK *and*
GEORGE VINER *exchange worried glances.*

FRANK. Margaret Grady is your mother's cousin.

EAMONN (*wincing*). Yeh.

FRANK. And you'd hardly be likely to involve her in an act of
criminal terrorism.

EAMONN *doesn't respond.*

FRANK. In fact, what could be more natural than helping out a
friend of a friend from across the water by asking your
mother's cousin to put up four Irish lads from the building
trade at her house for a week or two till they got on their feet?
That's what you told her, isn't it?

EAMONN *takes a while.*

EAMONN. More or less, yeh.

A GUARD *passes outside the window.* EAMONN *is staring at his hands
and smoking his cigarette.* FRANK *and* GEORGE VINER *look worried.
Except when he's talking about the Gradys,* EAMONN *seems to be
detached from his answers.*

FRANK. Let's go through that again in detail, shall we?

EAMONN *sighs heavily.*

FRANK. Eamonn, it's a reasonable story, but bear in mind, you're
going to have to stand up in the witness box and be cross-
examined about this.

EAMONN. I just can't understand how Margaret and Deirdra
could be charged with conspiracy to blow up the Cenotaph.
How could anybody take that seriously? They didn't know who
Pat or Dessie or Seoras were.

FRANK. Or Ruari McFadden presumably.

EAMONN. Leave Ruari out of it – he wasn't even here.

FRANK. Are you saying you fixed up accommodation for the
other three – but not McFadden?

EAMONN (*puts his head in his hands and rethinks*). The point is: the

Gradys' had no idea who any of them were, as God's my
witness.

FRANK. How could they have – since you yourself didn't?

EAMONN *sighs again. He seems to have no energy.*

FRANK. Eamonn?

EAMONN *lights another cigarette and looks out of the window.* FRANK
looks at VINER.

VINER. Eamonn . . .

EAMONN. Look, this is a waste of time. Nobody would believe this
load of shit in a million years.

VINER. Whoa: hold it, Eamonn. Just be careful and –

EAMONN. Look, it's bloody obvious I was in it, but the Gradys
didn't know anything –

VINER. Eamonn –

EAMONN. A bloody blind man could see I was in it. It's an insult
to Mr Cartwright's intelligence . . .

FRANK (*pissed off*). You see, Eamonn, if you're telling me you're
guilty, I can't help you to persuade the court that you're not.
So unless what you're saying is that your changing your
plea . . . ?

VINER. Hang on, I think there's a misunderstanding here.
Eamonn, you've got to choose your words more carefully. Let's
think about what's actually been said, shall we?

EAMONN *silent, rebarbative.* FRANK *thinks it's gone on too far.*

VINER (*determined to try and retrieve the situation*). You're not saying
you're guilty of the charge, are you?

EAMONN. No, I'm not guilty. (*This is said very definitely, almost
offended at the suggestion.*)

FRANK (*confused*). You're *not*?

EAMONN. No.

FRANK. You were *not* part of this conspiracy?

EAMONN. No.

FRANK. Right. But. You said you were 'in it', you see. You have
to be very careful with words, or you put me in a very difficult –

EAMONN. I *was* in it.

VINER *and* FRANK *are exasperated.*

VINER. Look, Eamonn, let's all take a deep breath –

EAMONN. It doesn't make any difference. He won't have to
defend me.

They stare at him uncomprehendingly.

The charge is going to be dropped anyway. I thought it would
happen before committal proceedings, but . . . there's
obviously a hold up.

They stare. They look at one another.

Well it must be dawning on you by now . . . ? I was working for Special Branch.

They are both stunned.

FRANK (*hoping against hope it's not true*). Special Branch.

EAMONN (*not wanting to offer details*). We've got an arrangement. In return for certain useful information I've been able to give them, they're going to drop the conspiracy charge against me and replace it with something littler.

FRANK. Such as?

EAMONN. They said it would most likely be Failure To Provide Information. Which only carries a maximum of two years, you see.

FRANK. Yes, I know. So. In exchange for providing information, you will have your charge reduced to Failure to Provide Information?

EAMONN. Yeh, I know it sounds Irish, but that's it.

FRANK. What information are you going to be charged with failing to provide?

EAMONN. Erm, I dunno, they haven't told me, yet. Probably some crap about Dessie Hague and the wagon. Obviously I'll have to deny it anyway, to keep up the show.

FRANK. I see. No I don't. You *have* provided information? But not the information you're going to deny having not provided?

EAMONN (*thinks*). Yeh.

FRANK. And what was it?

EAMONN. What was what?

FRANK. The information you really did provide?

EAMONN. Oh, I can't get into that. You needn't know anything about that. That's irrelevant.

FRANK. But it was to do with this alleged conspiracy?

EAMONN. Mr Cartwright, you needn't bother about that, OK? Ask me no questions, I'll tell you no lies.

16. Interior. Brixton Prison. Night.

VINER *and* FRANK *are passed off C-Wing and out to the main gates.* FRANK *is bursting with anger, but neither dares speak yet.*

17. Interior. C-Wing. Brixton. Cell. Night.

EAMONN *is returned under* GUARD *to the cell where* McFADDEN *is studying the chessboard.*

DUNDAS *and* HAGUE *sit talking.*

McFADDEN. How's your feller, Eamonn? Is he gunna do the business for you?

EAMONN. Oh, very good. Brilliant bloke.

18. Exterior. In Viner's car outside Brixton. Night.

FRANK. He's grassed the other six, hasn't he?
   VINER *shrugs helplessly and looks anxiously at* FRANK.

19. Interior. Communal cell. Night.

O'BRIEN *rejoins* McFADDEN *at the chessboard.* EAMONN *still standing near.*

McFADDEN. Cartwright thinks Eamonn might get reduced. I've
   told him: our briefs are instructed to co-operate with his briefs
   to do whatever's best for him.
O'BRIEN. That would be great, Eamonn. Fingers crossed for you,
   son. Don't bake a cake though: these fellers can be full of shit,
   you know.

20. Exterior. Viner's car still parked outside. Night.

VINER. I swear I had no idea.
FRANK. That doesn't help me. I'm defending a police informer.
VINER. I'm sorry, Frank, but I have to say: everything you've
   heard has been told to you in strictest confidence by my client.
FRANK. Oh, holy shit.

21. Exterior. Temple grounds. Evening.

PETER STEINSSON QC *is taking the evening air before going into dinner.
He's strolling round a patch of green. In the background,* FRANK
approaches and is directed to STEINSSON *by a* FLUNKEY *on the steps
leading into the inn.*

FRANK *joins* STEINSSON.
STEINSSON. Cartwright.
FRANK. I'm sorry to disturb you.
STEINSSON. I can't talk long, I'm afraid. I'm taking guests into
   dinner.
FRANK. It's about the Cenotaph case.
STEINSSON. Yes.
FRANK. I'm leading Eamonn Hand's defence.
STEINSSON. Hand is the one from Manchester.
FRANK. Correct.
   FRANK *waits a beat. Nothing.*
STEINSSON. Well? What can I do for you?
FRANK. He gives me to believe that the conspiracy charge is

going to be dropped in his case.

STEINSSON. Does he? I'm sure that's an enormous relief to you both. But I'm afraid no one's remembered to tell the Prosecution.

FRANK. He thinks he has a deal.

STEINSSON. I'm afraid he's pulling your leg, Cartwright.

FRANK. He seems very sure.

STEINSSON. If you don't want to take my word for it, you should posit the idea to the DPP. He prepared the briefs.

FRANK. It's not a question of not believing –

STEINSSON. No, no, of course not. But you want to be sure, don't you? Quite right. But if I were you I'd tell Mr Hand to get on with the business of preparing a defence. And from what I've seen of the evidence, he'd better make it good.

A taxi rolls up.

STEINSSON. Ah.

22. Interior. DPP's Offices in Queen Anne's Gate. Day.

The Deputy's Office.
FRANK *and* VINER *sit waiting.*
The DEPUTY *to the* DPP *rejoins them from another room, affable, detached, forty-five.*

DEPUTY. Sorry to keep you hanging on, but I thought it best to have the matter cleared up immediately. I've been in with the Director and made him aware of your client's claim to – erm – immunity in this affair, and –

VINER. No, he's not claiming *immunity*. He's claiming he was offered a *deal*.

DEPUTY (*agreeing*). I'm sorry, I beg your pardon: His claim to have been offered a *deal*. The Director made immediate inquiries in my presence to the appropriate sources and I have now to tell you quite positively and categorically: no such deal was ever offered. No deal of any kind has ever been offered or contemplated by the officer you have named or by any officer working on this case.

FRANK. The charge against our client will stand.

DEPUTY. Absolutely.

VINER *looks pretty convinced.*

FRANK *doesn't.*

DEPUTY (*not unsympathetically*). I think that answers your question.

FRANK. Yes, it does. But. It doesn't answer the question 'Was Eamonn Hand working for Special Branch as an informer?'

DEPUTY. I thought it did, but let me be clear: as far as I'm aware he was not.

FRANK. As far as you're aware. Well how far's that?

DEPUTY. My information is that he was not.

FRANK. How good is your information?

DEPUTY. I think I've answered your questions as fairly and as openly as I possibly can.

Silence.

The DEPUTY *has resented* FRANK's *impertinence.*

VINER *is ready to go.*

FRANK *is holding his ground.*

VINER. Well . . .

FRANK. I'm sorry . . . Has Special Branch ever had any kind of contact with my client? Before he became involved in this case?

To their surprise, the DEPUTY *has to think about this.*

FRANK. You see, I'm asking myself 'If Eamonn Hand has never worked for Special Branch how is it he can name and describe a particular officer?'

DEPUTY. I can see I'm going to have to be completely open with you and hope that you won't choose to abuse this information.

FRANK *gets ready to hear a pack of lies.*

DEPUTY. This is where there are one or two red faces in the Branch. Apparently your client did once offer his services as a police informer in the wake of the Birmingham outrage. The Special Branch officer he named to you in fact considered his offer and turned him down.

FRANK. Why?

DEPUTY. He considered that your client knew nothing and nobody and was simply a fantasist. With hindsight this is now seen to have been in Special Branch jargon a 'cock-up'.

23. Interior. Stairs in DPP building. Day.

FRANK *and* VINER *are leaving.*

VINER. Did you believe any of that?

FRANK. Absolute garbage. Nevertheless. Our Eamonn is what's known in legal jargon as 'up shit creek without a paddle'.

VINER. You're not tempted to share any of this with your colleagues, I hope, Frank.

FRANK. Tempted? Yes, I'm tempted. But no.

VINER. How's the young Turk doing?

FRANK. James . . . appears to think you can play this crowd at their own game and win.

24. Interior. C-Wing. Brixton. Day.

McFADDEN *being escorted briskly by* GUARDS *towards interview cell. He's whistling* 'The Colonel Bogie March'. *The* PRISON OFFICERS *don't like him. As they approach the door:*

McFADDEN. Not The Box, you yellow devils. Anything but The Box.

A PRISON OFFICER *opens the door.* McFADDEN *has to squeeze past him to enter the room. Their eyes meet.* McFADDEN *smiles.*

25. Interior. C-Wing. Interview room. Day.

McFADDEN. Mr Bingham's pulling our legs, Edward.

BINGHAM *shakes his head.*

BINGHAM. I want you to go into the witness box.

McFADDEN. Out of the question.

BINGHAM. If you really think this is such a lost cause, why bother to brief me?

McFADDEN. Don't get the wrong idea, James. You were the Army Council's idea. I told them you seemed very gullible. They like that in an Englishman. We've got one or two racists on the Council, you know? So don't get carried away. Let's just have a nice quiet time, eh?

BINGHAM. The first thing I have to explain to the court is what you were doing in London at the time of your arrest.

McFADDEN *smiles, he can't believe* BINGHAM's *real.*

BINGHAM. Well?

McFADDEN (*with a shrug*). I haven't been in London for eight years, James. I was arrested in Derry. I came over from Donegal on business and they jumped me and brought me over.

BINGHAM *surprised and intrigued.*

BINGHAM. So all this police evidence which says you were watched in London and Manchester in the weeks leading up to your arrest and you were seen with O'Brien at the Grady's house in Kilburn . . .

McFADDEN. Total crap. I've never been to Margaret's place in my life. Never met her. Never heard of her till I got to this place. You try proving it. You tell the jury half a dozen English policemen are lying to them.

BINGHAM. They do have your prints on a false passport allegedly found on O'Brien at the Gradys.'

McFADDEN. My prints are on a lot of false passports. That's my trade. It's probably one of a batch I made up in the Republic last year. I'm good at it, if you ever need one. Which you might, if you keep this up.

BINGHAM. I'll bear it in mind. Well?

McFADDEN. Well what?

BINGHAM's *face says 'You've got a case.'*

McFADDEN. I've told you it's out of the question.

BINGHAM. If you stand up in court and tell them exactly what you've told me – let Steinsson cross-examine you; let's give him all the details he wants about the actual facts of your arrest and about the prints – and I think you'll be setting them a real problem. Juries aren't stupid. Even heavily vetted juries know when they're being fed lies by the police if they have in front of their own senses a totally confident and truthful witness. Edward?

LATHAM. It's probably the only real chance you have, Ruari – short of the Prosecution ballsing up its own case.

McFADDEN. I've never heard anything so completely naive.

BINGHAM. What's your alternative?

McFADDEN. My alternative is to do what Pat O'Brien, Dessie Hague and Seoras Dundas will do. The women and Eamonn are different, they can and should defend themselves, this isn't their fight. But those of us from over the water will do the only thing we *can* do: deny everything and keep our mouths shut.

BINGHAM. And go to prison for thirty years.

McFADDEN. At least it means I didn't have to stand up in a foreign court and explain myself to my enemies. It means I didn't have to spend two weeks in a witness box with a British Government stooge questioning me about my politics, my past, and above all my comrades in the dock. I've known Pat O'Brien since we ran to school together. I stood beside him when they buried his father and then his two brothers. He stood with me – and so did Seoras Dundas – when I buried my sister, shot dead in cold blood by a British soldier. I was interned with Des Hague in '74 when we were both tortured by British officers – if you don't believe me ask Amnesty International. Do you seriously expect me to get up and allow them to question me about any of these men? Do you seriously expect *any* of us to stand up in a British court and ask for justice?

Silence.

McFADDEN *recovers most of his composure.*

BINGHAM. I find this very hard to accept –

McFADDEN. I don't care if you accept it. You see, you may be a critic of this system but you still belong to it. What's worrying you now – now that you've got this case – is how are you going to do something special with it, turn it into a victory of some kind. For you, not for me.

BINGHAM. That's not true actually. It's not the whole truth.

McFADDEN. It's true enough. I'm not complaining. No doubt you need to believe in this system on some level in order to go on from day to day.

BINGHAM. I believe you and too many others like you are being framed and it's making a mockery of the system. I believe somebody should stand up and say so.

McFADDEN. Well you stand up and say it, James. You say it. If it'll make you feel better. But there's only one thing I really want from you. When I've been sentenced, when the court doesn't need to see my unmarked face again, and I disappear down those steps for the last time: I'd like you to be right behind me, as close as you can get. Will you do that for me, James?

26. Interior. Drawing room of Bingham's dad's house. Night.

BINGHAM, GLORIA, SIR CHARLES BINGHAM, LADY MARGARET *having an aperitif.*

SIR CHARLES. Makes a very big change, I can tell you, from the usual 'James? Oh, he's defending a Pakistani shoplifter, very interesting case'. You see their eyes glazing over at the Club. But to be able to say 'James? Oh, he's defending the IRA's top man in the Cenotaph case' – they soon sit up, I can tell you.

Laughter and tutting from GLORIA *and* MARGARET.

MARGARET. I'm so pleased for you, James.

SIR CHARLES. I hope we're going to hear all about it.

BINGHAM. Well, it's just a case, you know.

His false modesty is hooted down.

MARGARET. I'd better check the kitchen. And I have a present for you.

She goes out.

SIR CHARLES. Just a case. Only the Provos' top feller, Gloria.

BINGHAM. He isn't actually.

SIR CHARLES. That's what it said in the Telegraph.

BINGHAM. Well there's a moral there for you.

GLORIA. James, stop being so other-worldly.

SIR CHARLES. He's *one* of the top men, though, isn't he?

BINGHAM. Yes. I suppose he probably is.

SIR CHARLES. What'll he get? As ringleader so to speak.

BINGHAM. He isn't the ringleader. O'Brien was probably commanding the unit. I don't know: thirty years if they're lucky.

SIR CHARLES *whistles.*

SIR CHARLES. Thirty years. Still, as long as you put up a decent
    show that doesn't really matter from your point of view.
    Nobody's expecting you to get him off.
BINGHAM. I'd never be forgiven. The problem is he's innocent.
SIR CHARLES. Innocent? In what sense?
BINGHAM. In the sense that he had nothing to do with it. I'm
    90 per cent sure he's being framed by the police.
SIR CHARLES. Oh.
    GLORIA *can't be doing with this.*
GLORIA. But he's done other things.
BINGHAM (*sharply*). He isn't being tried for other things.
    Silence.
SIR CHARLES. Well. Let the jury decide, eh?
    Enter MARGARET.
    MARGARET *gives him a box. He opens it to find silk hankies.*
MARGARET. Just some silk to be going on with.
BINGHAM. You're very sweet, mother.
    They kiss.
SIR CHARLES. A small token of things to come. Here's to you,
    James.
    They toast him.
    A ring at door. Guests are arriving.

27. Exterior. Entrance, Brixton Prison. Night.

VINER *and* FRANK *ringing the bell.*

28. Interior. C-Wing passage. Night.

EAMONN *is escorted by* GUARDS *through C-Wing.*
He's anxious.

29. Interior. Sir Charles' dining room. Night.

BINGHAM *is in his thoughts as the others at the table chat.*
SIR CHARLES, MARGARET, GLORIA, RICHARD, HEATHER, CONRAD,
DELIA, ELEANOR, JOHN.
MARGARET. James.
BINGHAM. Sorry?
MARGARET. Richard asked you something.
RICHARD. No, I was just wondering aloud really, James: what
    sort of people are they? I mean what sort of a man is
    McFadden? I mean the media make him out to be some sort
    of criminal superbrain.
HEATHER. My gut-feeling is that they're actually very ordinary

people. Not always all that bright perhaps, but certainly not the blood-crazed sub-humans you're led to imagine by the media.

RICHARD. No, I wasn't suggesting that. Obviously that's served up for public consumption. The State requires its people to hate and fear its enemies.

MARGARET (*over the chuckles*). Good heavens, Richard.

JOHN. This is the Open University for you.

CONRAD. Another of Harold Wilson's inventions.

Laughter.

CONRAD. Imagine having to get up at five o'clock in the morning to learn how to talk rubbish.

DELIA (CONRAD's *wife*). Comes naturally to some of us. No, I think Heather hit on it: they're perfectly ordinary people but not actually all that bright.

JOHN. Who – Labour Prime Ministers?

ELEANOR. Cunning though.

DELIA. Yes, *cunning*, but not particularly intelligent. There's a difference. I maintain that nobody with an *imagination* could ever plant a bomb.

This goes down well as an insight.

RICHARD. Yes, when you think about it, that's very true. Anyway what's your view, James?

All eyes on JAMES *who is about to speak reasonably.*

JOHN. Reminds me about the one about Paddy hitching a lift in Surrey. Bloke in a Range Rover picks him up and they tootle along. Bloke says 'You know, Paddy, I think my left indicator's not working. If I pull over, I don't suppose you'd be kind enough to get out and have a look for me?' Paddy says 'Sure begorrah, oi will that, surr'. So he pulls over and Paddy gets out and the bloke pushes his indicator and shouts 'There. Is it working, Paddy?' And Paddy says 'Yes. No. Yes. No. Yes.' . . .

The joke goes down fairly well considering its advanced years.

BINGHAM *grimaces.*

30. Interior. C-Wing. Night.

EAMONN *has just heard the news from* FRANK *and* VINER.

EAMONN. Is this a joke?

FRANK *shakes his head.*

FRANK. Nobody knows anything about a deal.

EAMONN. Well . . . they would say that, wouldn't they? They're not going to admit it to *you*, are they?

He gets no encouragement from their faces. He is visibly shaken.

VINER. I think you have to face your circumstances, Eamonn. Whatever they may have told you, there is no deal.

EAMONN *can hardly take it in. He is too stunned to speak.*

VINER. Which means: we must think about your defence.

EAMONN. Defence?! I haven't got a defence! I don't need a defence! I was working for the police!

FRANK. Well. One of your options is to say that to the court. Admit that you did what you did knowingly but you couldn't've been part of the conspiracy because you were a police spy.

EAMONN. Are you out of your mind? The Army Council would have me head torn off! Sweet Jesus Christ.

He's panicking. It's really sinking in.

FRANK. Another option is to seek a reduced sentence by pleading guilty and keeping quiet.

EAMONN. How can I plead guilty? Seven people accused of conspiracy. Six of them say there is no conspiracy. The seventh pleads guilty to it! Don't you think I've done enough to these people?

FRANK *and* VINER *are surprised at this.*

EAMONN. Don't you think I've betrayed them enough?

FRANK. But nothing you –

EAMONN. I've said enough. You two are in on this. I had a deal. I want my deal. You piss off and tell them now. Get that bastard in here. Get the top man in here. They can't do this to me. (*To the Thought Police.*) I've got things I could say about that lot – Special Branch. You tell them *now*. I want my deal.

31. The same. Later.

EAMONN. I was born in Derry. In twenty-four years I've been back twice. What am I? British or Irish? The British shouldn't be in Ireland. The only way that'll happen is when the IRA forces us out. So I support the IRA. Not everything they do. Birmingham was . . . nobody's in favour of that, only maniacs. Something went wrong there. I saw the pictures on the news and I thought 'if that's us I want no part of this, we haven't got the right to do that to human beings'. I mean all I'd ever done was collect a few quid in a jar and sing a few songs when I was pissed up. But next day I was arrested. Police went apeshit. They marched seven of us out of a pub in broad daylight. I don't think any of us had ever *been* to Birmingham. But we were photographed, fingerprinted, questioned. Knocked around a bit. The other six were let out after ten hours. I was kept for another night and a day. You see: I've got a sister called Brigid. She lives in Belfast with her husband. I was amazed when they showed me the stuff they had on her. I'd no idea she was in so deep with the Provos. She'd never told me. They said they'd have her interned if I didn't help them out. They kept talking to me about the Birmingham pubs. They were really fired up about it. They said all Irish shit should be loaded on to boats and blown up. They kept on about this head with no body and it was screaming for help to the fireman. Is that right? I still think about that a lot. Was it true that?

FRANK *shrugs*.

EAMONN. They say the blokes that set those bombs live quiet now in the South. What would you think about? Would you get any peace in your head? Anyway I was a waste of time. They used to take me for a drive and ask me has such-and-such-a-body been seen in Manchester this week? Does such-a-body drink with another bloke? Or another bloke go with this bloke's wife? I mean: how the fuck did I know? I just said 'yes' or 'no', whatever I thought would be most useless to them. Because I still thought of myself as a patriot. Do you understand that?

FRANK *nods*.

I still used to shout me mouth off in the pubs about what the Provos should be doing and what they shouldn't. And what was legitimate targets and what wasn't. It's like being two people. Last August. Seoras turned up in Manchester. He said it was time for me to do something more than talk. All he told me was it would be like Brighton, only bigger and all I'd have to do was hire a lorry and get some rooms. I felt really proud. But – he was being watched. My man had me in within half a day. He couldn't believe his luck. They told me to go all the way with it. They said if not they'd send my file to the Army Council.

FRANK. Did they tell you you'd have to be arrested?

EAMONN. No chance of that, they said. I'd be kept right out of the picture.

FRANK. But you were arrested.

EAMONN. They told me not to worry: I'd get a short sentence and a lump sum waiting for me when I got out. They told me I'd be a hero: an Irish patriot jailed by the Brits. Freedom fighter. Me. Bloody funny, isn't it? Me. That's helped fit them all up. Christ, you must despise me.

FRANK *shakes his head*.

FRANK. You have told me in confidence that you are a police informer. I can legitimately keep that out of the case. You have told me you were not part of the conspiracy, and that is

obviously true since you were in fact working against its
purposes. So I can legitimately help you to plead not guilty.
You have also told me you find the bombing of civilian targets
repulsive. This is the basis of a defence. Here's what I suggest.
You go into the witness box. I will ask you about Irish
terrorism. I will ask you about Birmingham for instance. You
will tell the court you think that was the work of animals. You
will say you do not believe in the armed struggle. You will
dissociate yourself completely from the alleged aims of the
conspiracy and from the other men in the dock. You won't
have to incriminate them in any way. But you'll say you are
not one of them. You'll tell the court you do not consider
yourself to be Irish.

EAMONN *drips tears and agrees.*

EAMONN. I see now why they recommended you, Frank.

FRANK. What?

EAMONN. They recommended you. Special Branch. They said
you'd know how to play it in court.

FRANK *stunned.*

32. Exterior. Street outside Brixton Prison. Winter's night.

VINER *and* FRANK *pause after leaving the prison.*
VINER *lights a small cigar and inhales deeply.*

VINER. Thank you. You've given him an outside chance.

FRANK. 'They said you'd know how to play it in court'. 'You'd
know how to play it'. Think of the years of arrogant power
behind a statement like that. There are moments when you
actually feel the monster roll its muscles underneath your feet;
and you've suddenly been moved, you're not standing where
you thought you were. They know they can rely on me to
cobble up a defence for their grass. Presumably we're all
supposed to look surprised when Medway gives him a light
sentence. And they call it blind justice.

33. Interior. Fetter Court. Night.

BINGHAM *working alone. Everybody else has gone home.* FRANK *comes
in from the street. He sits on a desk opposite* BINGHAM. *He chooses some
words.*

FRANK. Eamonn's going to testify.

BINGHAM *thinks about this.*

BINGHAM. Your client knows that my client wasn't in this, Frank.

FRANK *shakes his head.*

FRANK. He knows McFadden wasn't at the Gradys' house.

BINGHAM. He knows McFadden wasn't in the conspiracy. They all know it. Except the women, who don't know anything, God help them. McFadden had his feet under a pub table in Donegal while this was supposed to be going on.

FRANK. Doesn't mean he wasn't in it.

BINGHAM. If Eamonn's going into the box, I'm going to question him.

FRANK. Fair enough.

BINGHAM. Will he admit it? That McFadden wasn't at the Gradys with everybody else?

FRANK. Yes.

BINGHAM (*pleased*). Well, that's something. I now have a one-plank defence instead of a no-plank defence. Thanks.

FRANK *nods. He goes to his desk.* BINGHAM *watches him.*

BINGHAM. Has it occurred to you there's an informer in this?

FRANK. Yes.

BINGHAM. Who do you think it's most likely to be? One of the women? Is that why they seem to know so little?

FRANK. Could be any of them. Conspiracy trials always look like this.

Pause.

BINGHAM. Not Eamonn though?

FRANK. If I knew my client was a police informer, I'd be unlikely to tell you, now wouldn't I?

BINGHAM *leaves it at that.*

34. Exterior. London streets and skyline. Dawn.

Late September 1987.

First light in the streets around the Old Bailey. The quiet is invaded slowly by a helicopter approaching. On the ground around the court, POLICE *are erecting barricades.*

35. Interior. C-Wing. Brixton Prison. Morning.

The MEN *slopping out. As they empty their night-pails into the latrines,* EAMONN *vomits.*

McFADDEN *and the* OTHERS *look sympathetic.*

36. Interior. A bathroom in Surrey. Morning.

PETER STEINSSON *sits in his bathtub sipping tea and listening to Radio 3.*

37. Bingham's bedroom. Morning.

BINGHAM *awake in bed.*
GLORIA *still asleep.*
He's thinking. He looks at his watch and holds his hand over the bedside telephone. At exactly seven thirty it rings.
BINGHAM. Thank you, Operator.
  He puts down the receiver.

38. Interior. C-Wing. Brixton. Morning.

All seven PRISONERS *are lined up and marched off C-Wing.*

39. Interior. Frank's bombsite of a kitchen. Morning.

FRANK, ANNIE *and the three* KIDS *in the usual bedlam. LBC previewing the day's big event at the Old Bailey but almost drowned by domestic noise.* ANNIE *seems more interested in listening to it than* FRANK *who is being his usual slow-starting self.*

40. Exterior. Outside Old Bailey. Morning.

POLICE *everywhere.* JOURNALISTS, CAMERA-CREWS. IRISH SUPPORTERS *with placards.* CROWDS *queueing to get seats in public galleries. Somebody selling sandwiches.*

41. Interior. Judge's chambers. Old Bailey. Morning.

LORD JUSTICE MEDWAY *arrives in his room under armed guard.*

42. Interior. A front room in Surrey. Morning.

PETER STEINSSON *sits dressed and waiting with his briefcase on his knee. Doorbell. The door is opened. His* ARMED POLICE BODYGUARD *comes to tell him his car has arrived.*

43. Exterior. Steinsson's house in Surrey. Morning.

STEINSSON *leaves house and gets into the back of the car with his* BODYGUARD. *He waves to the anxious face of his wife at the window. An* ARMED GUARD *remains on the doorstep.*

44. Exterior. London Underground. Morning.

FRANK *travelling on busy tube, looking at the headlines about today's big story 'Massive Security Alert for Old Bailey Trial'. 'Police fear IRA strike' etc etc.*

45. Exterior. London streets. Morning.

Screaming convoy of vans, cars and bikes bringing the defendants to the Old Bailey.

46. Exterior. London streets. Morning.

In the van, the SEVEN *sit quietly in their thoughts.*

47. Exterior. Outside Old Bailey. Day.

ARMED POLICE *have ringed the immediate area.* BINGHAM *arrives at the security cordon.*

48. Interior. Old Bailey. Day.

BINGHAM *and* OTHERS *being searched as they enter the building. He hears the screaming of the sirens outside that says the Defendants have arrived.*

49. Exterior. Outside Old Bailey. Day.

Helicopters, ARMED POLICE, *barricades, you name it as the convoy arrives.*

50. Interior. Robing Room. Old Bailey. Day.

STEINSSON *and his* JUNIORS; BINGHAM, FRANK *and* OTHER DEFENCE COUNSEL *getting into their cossies.*
FRANK *studies* STEINSSON, *who ignores him.*

51. Interior. Old Bailey. Cell area below Court. Day.

The SEVEN *are herded into the cell area below the courts.* EAMONN *and* McFADDEN *are beside each other.*
McFADDEN. Chin up, Eamonn.
O'BRIEN. Brigid says hello, Eamonn. She says she's proud of you and you're in her prayers.
EAMONN *nods but he's terrified.*
The LAWYERS *start arriving for last minute conferences with their clients.* BINGHAM *and* FRANK *among them.*
EAMONN. God bless us all, eh Ruari?

McFADDEN. Yeh. God bless us all, Eamonn.

52. Interior. Judge's Chambers. Old Bailey. Day.

LORD JUSTICE MEDWAY *puts on his wig with an* ARMED POLICEMAN *watching over him.*

53. Interior. Old Bailey. Cell area below courts. Day.

The lawyers have gone. The SEVEN *are lined up, each handcuffed to* TWO GUARDS. MARGARET *and* DEIRDRA GRADY *are saying quiet Hail Marys. The door opens at the top of the stairs. They are bundled up and we watch them disappear upwards into the light. The door closes behind them.*

54. Interior. Old Bailey court. Day.

The trial is in its sixth week. The jury box is empty.

STEINSSON. My Lord, if in the absence of the jury I might now have the tape recording played so that your Lordship might decide on its admissibility. In the view of the Crown, it reveals Eamonn Hand in conversation with an unknown person in the Republic of Ireland, the two of them discussing the successful acquisition of rocket launchers. As you know, Mr Cartwright is taking objection to it.

JUSTICE MEDWAY *nods. An* USHER *turns on the machine.*

The tape plays. Silence. More silence. Titters. Laughter. McFADDEN *and* O'BRIEN *enjoying it. A sudden cacophony which is obviously somebody talking to somebody else about something.* FRANK *is surprised. People listen intently for a while. Amusement grows.* McFADDEN *smiles encouragingly at* EAMONN. FRANK *studies the imperturbable* STEINSSON.

TESSA *leans into* FRANK.

TESSA (*sotto voce*). You said it was bad. I didn't know it was this bad.

FRANK. It wasn't.

The tape recording ends abruptly. USHER *switches off the machine.* MEDWAY *not happy.* BINGHAM *looks down the row to* FRANK *as if to say 'This is your lucky day.'*

MEDWAY. I think I appreciate Mr Cartwright's objections to this going before the jury. What do you have to say to this, Mr Steinsson?

STEINSSON *confers with his* JUNIOR *and stands.*

STEINSSON. My Lord, I take note of your remarks. On second

consideration and in view of the poor quality of the recording and my learned friend's intention to challenge the Crown's voice print experts with his own, I think it best not to waste the jury's time with this.

Amusement around the court. VINER *pats* FRANK *on the back.* FRANK *studies* STEINSSON *suspiciously.* McFADDEN *and others smile at* EAMONN.

55. Interior. Old Bailey court. Day.

STEINSSON's *junior,* MR KELLY, *is questioning a* SPECIAL BRANCH MAN.

KELLY. And Mr Hand paid for the hire of the lorry by cash? The sum of £218 in cash.

SPECIAL BRANCH MAN. Yes, sir.

FRANK *notices the* DPP's DEPUTY *sliding into a seat behind the Prosecution Benches.*

KELLY. Using the name to the plant hire company of John Flynn and a fictitious address in Chiswick?

SPECIAL BRANCH MAN. Yes, sir.

KELLY *confers with* STEINSSON. FRANK *watches keenly.*

KELLY. Then under constant surveillance by your colleagues, he drove the wagon to Devas Street and parked it outside the home of Mrs Grady and, as it were, delivered it into the hands of the four men who were lodging there and where it was subsequently prepared to receive the four rocket launchers?

SPECIAL BRANCH MAN *is momentarily hesitant. He recovers well.* STEINSSON *glances at* FRANK *who appears to be scribbling away without having noted anything of particular importance.*

SPECIAL BRANCH MAN. Yes, sir.

KELLY. Thank you, Sergeant. You've been most helpful.

KELLY *sits.* MEDWAY *looks to the Defence benches.*

O'BRIEN'S COUNSEL. No questions.

BINGHAM. No questions.

HAGUE'S COUNSEL. No questions.

DUNDAS' COUNSEL. No questions

MARGARET GRADY'S COUNSEL. No questions.

DEIRDRA GRADY'S COUNSEL. No questions.

FRANK *is scribbling but really thinking.* STEINSSON *glances at him.* FRANK *whispers to* TESSA, *giving instructions for a search.*

MEDWAY. Mr Cartwright?

FRANK *stands.*

FRANK. Sergeant. Are you familiar with a phenomenon in the construction industry known as 'lump working'?

SPECIAL BRANCH MAN. Yes, sir.

FRANK. This is – is it not? a form of black economy employment whereby unskilled labour – often Irish – works on sub-contract work on building sites without insurance cards, – thereby avoiding the necessity for the employer to pay insurance stamps and for the employee to pay income tax?

SPECIAL BRANCH MAN. As far as I'm aware, sir, yes.

FRANK. And it's strictly illegal, is it not?

SPECIAL BRANCH MAN. Yes, sir.

FRANK. And therefore if, as my client maintains, he was under the firm impression that he was being asked to hire a lorry for a gang of lump workers, that would be a perfectly reasonable explanation of his use of cash and of a false name and address. Would it not? Would that not seem to you to be a reasonable if not exactly creditable explanation of his behaviour?

SPECIAL BRANCH MAN. Yes, sir.

Reactions in court. McFADDEN *mutters with* O'BRIEN, *who now suspects the game.*

FRANK. In fact his behaviour – would you agree? – need not be interpreted in any way as a culpable contribution to a criminal conspiracy.

SPECIAL BRANCH MAN. Well. Not necessarily, although –

FRANK. Thank you. One more point. You told my learned friend's able junior, Mr Kelly, a moment or two ago that your colleagues kept my client under constant surveillance as he drove the hired lorry back to Devas Street.

SPECIAL BRANCH MAN. Yes, sir.

FRANK. Sergeant, hasn't whoever gave you this story bothered to tell you that my client can't drive?

Reactions. Laughter. McFADDEN *looking grimly at* EAMONN.

FRANK. In fact, if you look at the police depositions, your own written evidence –

SPECIAL BRANCH MAN. I think I got confused.

FRANK. Well let's clear it up, shall we? On page 1068 of . . .

TESSA *hands it to him.*

FRANK. . . . I have it here. (*He flourishes it.*) You will read that you've already stated that my client merely paid for the lorry and delivered the ignition keys to Desmond Hague.

Confusion in the witness box and on the Prosecution benches.

McFADDEN (*leans into* EAMONN). You've got the luck of the Irish, Eamonn.

FRANK. No further questions, My Lord.

He sits. STEINSSON *stands.*

STEINSSON. That concludes the case for the Crown, my Lord.

MEDWAY. Thank you. Mr Steinsson.

STEINSSON *sits.* MEDWAY *looks at the time and thinks about an early*
tea. STEINSSON *at last meets* FRANK's *gaze. A flicker.* FRANK *stands.*
BINGHAM *sees what's coming and is depressed.*

FRANK. My Lord, I have a submission to make in the case of
Eamonn Hand.

MEDWAY. Members of the jury, this is the part of the trial where
we have legal arguments so I'll ask you to leave the court for a
few moments.

USHERS *show out the baffled* JURY. VINER *leans forward.*

VINER. Is this real?

FRANK. Oh yes.

EAMONN *avoids* McFADDEN's *steely gaze.*

MEDWAY. Mr Cartwright. I think you may be pushing at an open
door.

FRANK *stands.*

FRANK. My Lord, I submit that the Prosecution has insufficient
evidence to continue the case against Eamonn Hand since the
forensic evidence has been withdrawn and the police
statements are contradictory and do not in any case override
the clear innocent explanation for every single step of my
client's behaviour. The Prosecution has failed to produce a
shred of evidence which reasonably connects him with the
purpose of this alleged conspiracy. I'm happy to develop this
argument further if your Lordship wishes it.

MEDWAY. No, let me hear what Counsel for the Crown has to
say.

FRANK *sits.* STEINSSON *confers with the* DEPUTY DPP. *He stands.*

STEINSSON. My Lord, given the way the evidence has come out, I
am happy to concede that this is not a case that should trouble
the jury.

Reactions around the court.

MEDWAY. Good. Ask the jury to come back.

The JURY *is brought back in.*

MEDWAY (*to the* JURY). The case against Eamonn Hand – as with
the cases against the other six – once put in motion is in your
charge alone, members of the jury. But on my direction there
is insufficient evidence to continue the case against Mr Hand.
Now my clerk has something to say to you.

CLERK. Have you elected a foreman yet?

JURY *shake their heads.*

CLERK. Then will one of you stand as a temporary foreman now,
please? Will you stand up, please?

He picks the nearest man, who stands, baffled.

CLERK. On the direction of his Lordship do you find the
defendant Eamonn Hand not guilty of conspiracy to cause

explosions under the Explosive Substances Act?

The JURYMAN *looks round at his fellow* JURYMEN *who shrug and nod their heads.*

MEDWAY. Thank you. Release Mr Hand.

EAMONN *has his cuffs taken off. Commotion.* GRADY's *staggered.* EAMONN *is bundled down the stairs to collect his gear.*

CLERK. Quiet. Be quiet in court.

FRANK *stands.*

FRANK. My Lord, may I be released?

MEDWAY. Yes, Mr Cartwright. And can I thank you for conducting this very serious case with such care and good sense?

FRANK. Thank you, my Lord.

FRANK *and* TESSA *and* VINER *leave with all their gear. A lot of backslapping from other briefs. He exchanges a look with* BINGHAM.

56. Interior. Cells below court. Old Bailey. Day.

POLICE *have met* EAMONN. FRANK *arrives with* VINER *and* TESSA. EAMONN *still in shock.*

EAMONN. They're taking me to get my gear.

VINER. Let's go quickly. Now. Come on.

EAMONN (*to* FRANK). How did that happen?

FRANK *shrugs.* EAMONN *goes. He turns.*

EAMONN. Thanks. Thanks. God bless you.

FRANK *nods.* EAMONN *disappears through the doors with* POLICE ESCORT *and* VINER. *The door at the head of the stairs opens and the other* SIX *are brought down from the noisy court which has just adjourned.*

MARGARET GRADY. I don't understand. What's happened? Am I free?

McFADDEN. No, Maggie. Only Eamonn.

MARGARET. How can Eamonn be free and not us? Holy God, what's happening, I don't understand?

57. Interior. Old Bailey Court. Day.

The last stages of the trial. BINGHAM *makes his closing speech to the* JURY.

BINGHAM. The test of a system of justice is how well it can withstand the stresses placed upon it when political considerations enter the legal arena. Can the State, which administers that legal system, deal fairly and justly with people from whom it feels itself to be under direct attack? The answer, in a civilised country, must be 'yes'. Members of the jury, there may be those among you who take the view that the root cause of these difficulties lies in this country's colonial past. There may equally be those among you who take the view that our country bears no responsibility whatever for the appalling events of the last twenty years in Ireland. But whatever your view of Irish history and the causes of the present troubles, I'm quite sure that we must all agree that justice must transcend political allegiance. We perhaps might also agree that it has often been accused of failing to do so because of passion and prejudice. Members of the jury, in the many hours of waiting, you may have had the opportunity to wander in the lower hall of this building. And there you may have noticed a plaque set in the floor. It's a plaque dedicated to you. It's a plaque dedicated to all juries on whom we finally depend for justice. It's a plaque dedicated to a particular jury who, many years ago, withstood the pressures brought by the State to deliver the verdict the State required it to bring. It gives us a reminder. It reminds us all that *you* are the important people here. Not me. Not the Prosecution. Not even his Lordship.

MEDWAY *looking pretty pissed off with all this.*

It's what *you* believe here that matters. The question is whether you really believe that Ruari McFadden will have received real justice if you convict him on the evidence – and only on the evidence – which has actually been brought before you in this trial. Thank you. Thank you, my Lord.

He sits to stony stares from Prosecution and Bench.

58. Interior. Frank's bedroom. Morning.

FRANK *and* ANNIE *are fast asleep.* ALETHEA *comes in with a tray of breakfast cereals and some letters and a small parcel. She turns on the television set at the foot of the bed. She draws back the curtains. She places cereals beside each of them and their mail. She perches on the foot of the bed, watching television news as they drag themselves unwillingly into consciousness.*

TV. The so-called Trial of the Century, the Cenotaph conspiracy case, in which five men and two women faced charges under the Explosive Substances Act, ends today at the Old Bailey after ten weeks. The six Defendants who were found guilty yesterday will be sentenced this morning by Mr Justice Medway. The seventh was acquitted. And they'll be facing very long sentences indeed if one Westminster MP has his way.

Making a surprise intervention into a late-night debate on the new Waterways Bill, Mr Nigel Summerfield, MP for Silkmere, called for salutary sentences to be meted out to terrorists found guilty of attacking what he called the vital organs of state. Mr Summerfield went on to demand how it was, if earlier reports were true that the rocket launchers were supplied by Colonel Gadaffi – that the seven hadn't faced treason charges.

SUMMERFIELD (*who looks like a well-groomed turnip*). Obviously the big attraction of a treason charge is that it carries with it the death penalty and I'm not alone in thinking that the prospect of the hangman's noose might succeed where other –

FRANK. Turn it off.

ALETHEA *turns it off.* ANNIE *and* FRANK *are now sitting up, blearily eating their cornflakes and staring at envelopes.*

ALETHEA (*sings*). Good morning, good morning. You've snored the whole night through.

FRANK *glares at her. He opens the small parcel. A jack in the box nearly gives him a heart attack. A message on it says 'Well done. Bang you're dead'.*

FRANK. Katherine Hughes.

ALETHEA. Do you have to go in to the Bailey?

FRANK. No. Thank God. I hate watching sentencing.

ANNIE. How did you get your man off, Frank? What went right?

FRANK. Prosecution threw it.

ANNIE. Oh.

She reads her letters now and only half listens.

FRANK. I couldn't believe it. I was all-tooled up for a big fight with Steinsson and I didn't have to fire a shot.

ANNIE. This is how men talk, Alethea. Put that down, Alethea.

ALETHEA *has been reading a letter which she now puts down.*

FRANK. I don't think anybody but me and Steinsson had the faintest idea what was happening.

ALETHEA. Has your friend got a better penis than Dad?

FRANK. Well, James could see it.

ANNIE. Oh yeh, I forgot he was in it. How did hot-shot Bingham do?

ALETHEA. Fiona Snodgrass I call him.

FRANK. Bingham's done exactly what a radical lawyer should do in his position. He's focused attention on the burden of proof; he's brought in three good witnesses to say McFadden was elsewhere; he's attempted to put the State's evidence on trial; he's said British justice will be judged by this verdict. The sort of thing that makes you very unpopular in the Chancellor's Office. And he never flinched. He did it exactly right.

Knowing that they would eat him and his witnesses and his fine speeches and spit out the pips. That is that.

59. Interior. Bingham's dream kitchen. Morning.

BINGHAM *and* GLORIA *breakfasting on muesli, fruit juice, coffee, toast, newspapers and silence. Eventually:*

GLORIA. Frank seems to have covered himself with glory.
   Silence.
   Can I just say as an ordinary member of the public who's rather attached to her legs and her arms and her head – that I'm glad they were convicted?
   Silence. He pretends she isn't there.

60. Interior. A pub. Soho. Midday.

EAMONN *drinking beer at the bar and watching the television set. Brisk lunchtime trade building up around him. The one o'clock news starts.*

TV NEWSREADER. The Cenotaph Conspiracy Case has ended in the last few minutes with heavy sentences for the six remaining prisoners. We're going over straightaway to Nick Wilson outside the Old Bailey.
   WILSON, *with* CROWDS OF PEOPLE *behind him.*

WILSON. Within the last few minutes Mr Justice Medway has brought the so-called Trial of The Century to a close. Calling the conspiracy an astonishingly wicked crime, which was no less than an attack on the very heart of British public life, he first sentenced Mrs Margaret Grady and her daughter Deirdra to prison terms of twenty years each.

EAMONN. Oh, Christ. Oh Christ's blood, no.

WILSON. He then sentenced Desmond Hague and Seoras Dundas to thirty years each. And finally, turning to Patrick O'Brien and Ruari McFadden – whom he referred to as the 'mad dogs' of the unit – he sentenced them both to prison terms of thirty-five years.
   EAMONN *is mute in a cheering crowd in front of the television.*

WILSON. When the uproar on the public benches which greeted the sentences had been quieted, and the prisoners had been removed to begin their prison terms – still showing no remorse for their crimes, Mr Justice Medway reserved a final caustic comment for some of the defence barristers whom he accused of trying to turn the trial on its head. 'No reasonable, well-balanced person' he said 'could fail to find in these verdicts that British Justice . . .'

61. Interior. Cells below court, Old Bailey. Day.

Bedlam as the prisoners are being brought down after sentencing.
McFADDEN *is being kicked along the floor by* POLICE. *The others are being restrained. The area is crowded.* BINGHAM *and other counsel enter the area as* McFADDEN *is dragged to his feet.*

62. Interior. Cells below court. Old Bailey. Day.

McFADDEN *and* BINGHAM. McFADDEN *holding his head back to stem flow of blood from his nose. He feels his damaged ribs.* BINGHAM *sighs.*

McFADDEN. You made a very pretty speech, James. I hope you didn't bugger up your chances of silk.
BINGHAM (*laughing*). Well . . .
McFADDEN. Why not accept about yourself that you're a very ambitious feller, eh? Why shouldn't you be a silk?
  McFADDEN *lowers his head gently. Blood has stopped.*
Good.
  McFADDEN *offers his hand.* JAMES *shakes it.*
BINGHAM. Goodbye. Sorry.
McFADDEN. Goodbye, James. Surprise about Eamonn, wasn't it?
  BINGHAM *looks at him carefully.*
McFADDEN. Him turning out to be a grass.
  BINGHAM *says nothing. He goes.*

63. Interior. Robing Room. Old Bailey. Day.

Noisy chat as COUNSEL *get out of cossies and unwind.* STEINSSON *approaches lonely figure of* BINGHAM.
STEINSSON. Bit over the top I thought, Bingham.
BINGHAM. Did you?
STEINSSON. Certainly had Barry Medway worried. Got yourself noticed though – which I imagine was half the point?
  BINGHAM *knows this is true.*
STEINSSON. Well if you're coming up to the Bar Mess I'll have a G and T from you just to show there's no hard feelings.
  BINGHAM *smiles.*

64. Exterior. A London Park. Dusk.

Sitting on a bench, EAMONN *reads a big newspaper spread saying 'How Undercover Men Caught The "Mad Dogs"'.*

65. Exterior. Public telephone in Soho Street. Night.

EAMONN. Hello. I want to talk to Harry Oliver. My name's
Eamonn Hand. Hello? Harry Oliver? What you've written
about the Special Branch is wrong. It's crap. People should be
told the truth.
Pause.
I'm in (*He squints outside.*) Great Newport Street.

66. Exterior. Soho Street. Night.

EAMONN *hanging about waiting, a bedraggled figure, nervous. He
gives up waiting and moves off.*

67. Interior. A Soho pub. Night.

Not very busy. EAMONN *takes a sip from his beer and decides to go for a
pee.*

68. Interior. Pub toilet. Night.

EAMONN *alone, pissing in the toilet.* TWO MEN *come in. One puts a
silenced pistol to* EAMONN's *head and fires three times. They leave
quickly as* EAMONN *dies in his blood on the floor.*
    Fade out.

A Death in the Family

Cast

KATHERINE HUGHES	Jane Lapotaire
FRANK CARTWRIGHT	Jack Shepherd
JAMES BINGHAM	Julian Wadham

Brightpool Park

DAVID CHARNLEY	Bryan Pringle
ANNETTE CHARNLEY	Barbara Pierson
CHIEF CONST. WILKINSON	Richard Kane
DET. INSP. GEE	David Daker
DET. SGT. GRUCOCK	David Fleeshman
WPC REDFORD	Lesley Clare O'Neill
CLIVE CURRAN	Michael Feast
PILBROW	Jonathan Burn
SCHUMACHER	David Baxt
ELLEN THOMPSON	Joanna Foster
SAVILLE	Richard Beale
CROWN COURT JUDGE	Denzil Pugh
CLERK OF THE COURT	C.B. Jones
PROS. COUNSEL	Ray Parkes
JURY FOREMAN	Martin Tomms
TRACEY WILSON	Lisa Hayden
BRYN CHARNLEY	Christopher Green
PAULA CHARNLEY	Alison Green

London

TIM HUDSON	Gerry Sundquist
LORRAINE	Caroline Hutchison
ANNIE CARTWRIGHT	Anna Mottram
TESSA PARKS	Joanne Campbell
HUGH	Eamonn Walker

MICHAEL KHAN	Raad Rawi
KEN GORDON	Tom Marshall
JOANNA DAVIS	Cassie McFarlane
BRENDAN HOLLINGSWORTH	Paul Beringer
DAVID MILNER	John Matshikisa
MOIRA	Sadie Wearing
ROGER ARBISH	Anthony Morton
HIGH COURT JUDGE	Keith Noble
HOSPITAL DOCTOR	Janet Fielding
ALETHEA CARTWRIGHT	Mia Fothergill
PETER CARTWRIGHT	Dan Selby-Plewman
JOHN CARTWRIGHT	Tom Selby-Plewman

Prologue. Exterior. A Northern Cemetery. Day.

A funeral is taking place. Prominent among the mourners is
KATHERINE. *She walks from the graveside with uncles, aunts, cousins
and friends of her father.* ELLEN THOMPSON *catches her up.*

ELLEN. Katherine.
KATHERINE. Oh, Ellen, thank you for coming.
   They embrace. They walk.
ELLEN. When are you going back to London?
KATHERINE. A couple of days. I have to clear his things out of
   the house. I don't really know. I don't know what I'm going to
   do with it all. I suppose I'll give it all to Oxfam. My Dad was a
   hoarder.
ELLEN. How are you?
KATHERINE. Oh. You know. What about you? How's the
   practice?
ELLEN. Same as ever. Maintenance claims, divorce, petty theft.
   Did you talk to him before he died?
KATHERINE. I saw him three months ago. I said 'Why don't you
   come and live with me in London, Dad?'
ELLEN. And?
KATHERINE. He said 'Typical lawyer's question. You wouldn't've
   asked it if you didn't already know the answer.'
   They both smile at this.
   You still live on Brightpool Park?
ELLEN. Yes.
KATHERINE. How is it?
ELLEN. The same, only worse. Come and see. Have a cup of tea.

1. Exterior. Brightpool Park Estate. Day.

Outside the Charnleys' house. A crowd waits.
The CHARNLEYS *with a* WOMAN POLICE CONSTABLE *come out of their
house.*
There is DAVID CHARNLEY *who is fifty-four and* ANNETTE CHARNLEY
who is in her late twenties.
ANNETTE *is leaning very heavily on the* WOMAN POLICE CONSTABLE.
They walk briskly past silent NEIGHBOURS *towards the police car.*
They get into the car with the WOMAN POLICE CONSTABLE *and are
driven quickly away.*

2. Interior. Police Headquarters. Day.

A large room.
Scores of MEDIA REPRESENTATIVES *have assembled for a press*
conference. CAMERA CREWS *are squabbling over positions. There is an*
air of expectation.
DETECTIVE SERGEANT GRUCOCK *looks on unhappily.*
A PRESS OFFICER *is distributing a press release which includes a photo*
of a girl. This is TRACEY.

3. Interior. Police Headquarters. Day.

The office of the CHIEF CONSTABLE, JOHN JESUS WILKINSON. *With*
him is DETECTIVE INSPECTOR KEITH GEE.

JESUS. Might it not have been shrewder to allow this appeal to be
   televised from their house?
GEE. Shrewd?
JESUS. It's a Labour controlled authority responsible for these
   shocking conditions. Frankly I wouldn't let my dogs live in the
   Charnleys' house.
   GEE *finds this pretty grotesque.*
GEE. They wouldn't all fit, sir. The whole of Fleet Street's here.
JESUS. Of course they are. You can't shine the light of publicity
   onto a disaster area like Brightpool Park without questions
   being asked. Very profound questions, one would hope.

4. Exterior. Inside a police car. Day.
The police car is travelling at speed.

WPC REDFORD. Are you religious at all, Annette?
   She doesn't respond. After a while:
CHARNLEY. There's good and bad in us all.
   WPC REDFORD *tries again.*
WPC REDFORD. Are Bryn and Paul coming back tonight?
CHARNLEY. Yeh. Social Services is looking after them just till
   tonight like. We want us kids with us.

5. Interior. Police Headquarters. Day.

Press room. The room is even fuller.
DAN SCHUMACHER *and his crew arrive.*

6. Interior. Jesus's office. Police Headquarters. Day.

JESUS. Is she dead?
GEE. We're just waiting for the body to turn up. They usually do.

JESUS. Not always. A word of caution. I've seen enough in my
time to know what the murder of children can do to people,
even hardened policemen. Remember, Keith, though we may
find ourselves dealing with godless people, don't let it drive
God from your heart.

GEE *nods.*

WILKINSON'S CLERK *comes in.*

They look up. This means the press conference is due to begin.

7. Interior. A corridor. Police Headquarters. Day.

GEE *meets* WPC REDFORD *outside a door. They speak quietly.*

GEE. How are they?

WPC REDFORD *shrugs. He fixes her enquiringly.*

WPC REDFORD. There's something very wrong here, sir.

GEE *nods. He passes on; she goes into the room.*

8. Interior. Police Headquarters. Day.

WPC REDFORD *walks into an ante-room. The* CHARNLEYS *sit there in
silence, smoking. They are a pair of frightened, anxious, distressed
people. There is no eye contact between them.*

9. Interior. Police Headquarters. Day.

The press conference.

GEE *stands on the dais.*

The room quietens.

He is a no-nonsense man who gets respect.

GEE. You are now treading on delicate ground where the utmost
tact and discretion are required.

CLIVE CURRAN *of 'The Scorcher' lights a cigarette.*

The basic facts are as you find them in the press release. It's a
common law marriage, the lady prefers to be known as Mrs
Charnley. The missing girl however still goes under the name
of her natural father. She's Tracey Wilson. She's twelve years
of age. I know there are areas you would like to probe but I
am asking you not to add to the distress of these people.
And please do not invite them to speculate on whether she's
alive or dead. It's only seven days, we're assuming she's alive.

SCHUMACHER. What about Brightpool Park?

GEE *finds him with his eyes.*

GEE. What about it?

SCHUMACHER. Well isn't it true they think she ran away because of the conditions?

GEE. The parents believe this is a possibility.

CURRAN. Are you saying you don't, Chief Superintendent?

GEE. I'm saying I have an open mind.

A buzz of speculation.

GRUCOCK *uneasy.*

CURRAN. You say you're assuming she's alive. Does that mean you think she could be dead?

GRUCOCK cottons on to what's happening. He's not happy.

GRUCOCK. I don't think that's a helpful question, Mr Curran.

PILBROW. It's a fair question. Is there something you're not telling us?

GEE. There are many things I'm not telling you, Mr Pilbrow. There are things I don't even tell my wife. Robin?

Laughter.

GRUCOCK. I'd just like to add: can you all please be particularly careful with Mrs Charnley? Can I hope you understand me?

They are squared.

GEE. OK, will you . . . ?

His CLERK goes to the door. Cameras, microphones poised.

The door opens.

Camera motors whirr, flashes explode as ANNETTE, supported by WPC REDFORD, and CHARNLEY enter.

10. Interior. Police Headquarters. Day.

The press room as Scene 9.
CHARNLEY *is speaking to the world through the news media.*
WPC REDFORD *sits close to* ANNETTE.

CHARNLEY. Tracey. If you're watching. We know you're out there somewhere. Come home, love. Or get in touch. Your Mam and me knows things has been bad. Things has been bad for all of us. We've hit rock bottom. But we want you back.

He pauses.

Flashes pop.

He lights a cigarette with shaking hands.

GEE *is studying him hard.*

WPC REDFORD. Do you want to say anything, Annette?

ANNETTE. Just. If somebody's got Tracey. Please don't harm her. (*She weeps.*)

Flashes pop all around.

PILBROW. Mr Charnley, do you think you step-daughter might've been abducted?

CHARNLEY (*after some thought*). There are people capable of it. I've asked the police that they should be rounded up, all the known ones, and looked at. But I don't know where she is. All I know is, animals shouldn't have to live like we've had to.

CHARNLEY *begins to falter. He looks at the pathetic state* ANNETTE *is in.*

GEE *looks at* CURRAN.

CHARNLEY. Nobody could blame Tracey. Nobody who came and saw how we're fixed could blame anybody for anything.

He's gone far enough. He stops.

The cameras whirr. More questions are shouted.

CHARNLEY *looks to* GRUCOCK. GRUCOCK *stands.*

GRUCOCK. Right. Well, I think . . .

GEE *glances again at* CURRAN, *who is ready and willing.*

CURRAN. Mr Charnley, why did you wait four days to report her absence?

CHARNLEY *loses his temper.*

CHARNLEY. The show's over. Out the bloody road, go on. The show's over – you've had your pound of flesh.

He pushes ANNETTE *towards the door.*

Flashes pop.

11. Interior. Gee's office. Police Headquarters. Day.

GEE *and* GRUCOCK *sit.*

GEE. 'Nobody could blame anybody for anything'. Now what else could that mean? He's got a potential motive.

GRUCOCK. Could mean all sorts of things. Why didn't you tell me you were using Curran to smoke him out?

GEE. Two separate accounts from neighbours of the child being unwilling to go home at night. She was seen a number of times to prefer to sleep on a balcony.

GRUCOCK. So would I.

GEE. And she's hinted to a local shopkeeper about abuse. Sexual abuse. I doubt if the wife really knows what's what. She's practically ESN, Robin. Listen, how many times have you seen it? It's an epidemic. Charnley stinks, he's lying.

GRUCOCK. Lying isn't murder. Sexual abuse isn't murder. What *is* his motive?

GEE. Say she was threatening to blow the whistle on him.

GRUCOCK. There's no actual evidence of it. I spoke to Mrs Houghton yesterday.

GEE *interrupts.*

GEE. Mrs Houghton couldn't find her own backside with both hands. Social Services have let kids down time and again on this issue.

There is a pause.

GRUCOCK. Well, I've trawled the canals. I've looked down all the manholes and opened up all the lock-up garages. I've looked in every disused flat and house on the estate. I've hauled in every child molester in a fifty mile radius. I've covered every inch of that estate. And Charnley has no transport, Keith.

GEE. She'll turn up. I don't know where he's put her but she'll turn up.

GRUCOCK. What did Jesus want?

GEE. To remind me to keep God in my heart.

12. Interior. The Charnleys' house. Evening.

Bare light bulbs light the rooms as SCHUMACHER *and his* CAMERAMAN *are given a silent guided tour by* CHARNLEY.

Dirt and decay. SCHUMACHER *indicates to his man to get footage of the kitchen.*

CHARNLEY. People should be told. We shouldn't be brought down to this. It wasn't my fault.

SCHUMACHER *nods.*

13. Exterior. Near the Charnleys' house. Light fading.

SCHUMACHER *is about to begin talking to camera.*

A crowd, mainly CHILDREN, *watches silently.*

His camera pans across the waste-ground, the graffiti saying 'Eat the Rich', the CHARNLEY *house, the* P.C. *on guard outside the house and on to* SCHUMACHER.

SCHUMACHER. The man who in other times and in other places we would call the head of the household, David Charnley, last worked in a local slaughterhouse five years ago. This is not unusual on an estate on which male unemployment is running at eighty-nine per cent and which is widely regarded by the residents themselves as a dumping ground. One called it a bantustan, a tribal homeland for the dispossessed.

Here's another statistic: on this estate one child in three is on the Social Services' 'At Risk Register'. Another observer put it like this: Brightpool Park is the unacceptable face of the Thatcher revolution. It's nearly night now on this grotesquely misnamed estate, and the media circus is packing up for the day. In the eerie half light of a northern English evening the grim blocks once more cast their shadows. And in the shadow of one family's agonizing wait, a hundred smaller agonies of poverty, waste and despair are being played out nightly.

14. Interior. Ellen's flat. Night.

ELLEN *and* KATHERINE *are watching* SCHUMACHER *on television.*

SCHUMACHER (*on television*). Tracey Wilson may well have run
away from a life too bleak to contemplate. Whatever the truth
of this particular tragedy, the harshness of life on Brightpool
Park is posing a challenge to this country, which may at last be
re-discovering its slumbering social conscience. This is Dan
Schumacher for CBS News, Brightpool Park, England.

ELLEN. Slumbering social conscience. More like terminal coma.
You've forgotten what it's like, I bet.

KATHERINE. It's not a bed of roses down in London.

15. Interior. Fetter Court. Day.

LORRAINE *and* HUGH *are busy, but* LORRAINE *is also being distracted
by* JOANNA DAVIS.

FRANK *and* BINGHAM *pass through.*

LORRAINE *calls out.*

LORRAINE. I can't do more than keep asking, Joanna.

JOANNA. Yes, I know, but –

LORRAINE. Frank, big business. Tim Hudson megastar.

FRANK. Thanks, Lorraine. I have my dark glasses ready.

*He goes to his desk, picks up the brief and thence into a conference
room.* BRENDAN HOLLINGSWORTH *arrives with a mug of tea and
takes up a seat to watch the action.*

LORRAINE. I know it doesn't help but you aren't the only one.
Frank's got unpaid fees going back twelve months.

JOANNA (*quietly*). Yes, but Frank's a big earner. I can't afford not
to get paid.

LORRAINE. Who can afford not to get paid?

JOANNA (*becoming distressed*). I don't think you actually
understand. Will you ring them now?

LORRAINE. No, actually I won't because I have actually got a lot
on my plate (LORRAINE *and* JOANNA *overlap with each other.*) –
and I wrote to them again yesterday.

JOANNA (*speaking alongside* LORRAINE). – because there's nothing
in it for you. I haven't worked for four weeks.

LORRAINE. Yes I know that.

The telephone rings.

Hugh, take that, will you?

JOANNA. Because I find it hard to believe, Lorraine, that there's
nothing for me. I mean there's got to be a reason for that.

MICHAEL KHAN *has come over, so has* KEN GORDON *and* BINGHAM
is monitoring it from his desk. LORRAINE *grits her teeth and starts to
work on books.*

JOANNA. Ignoring me won't solve the problem.

HUGH. It's for you really.

LORRAINE *takes the telephone.*

MICHAEL KHAN. Come on, come on, Joanna.

LORRAINE. Hello, oh hello. (*She drags the court diary across the desk.*)

JOANNA. It's time we had this out because it's not just me.

LORRAINE (*underneath this*). OK, go ahead with it, Colin. Yes, I'll
do that. OK thanks, bye.

She puts the telephone down.

MICHAEL KHAN. Did Frank go out again? He should be here.

HUGH. Conference.

MICHAEL KHAN *goes off looking for* FRANK.

LORRAINE. So what you're actually accusing me of is pushing
work towards the whites in the set. Let's start speaking plainly
shall we Joanna or we'll be here all week?

16. Interior. Fetter Court. Conference Room. Day.

FRANK, TIM HUDSON *and his solicitor* NIGEL CONWAY.

HUDSON. I can honestly say (*He pauses for effect.*) – I have never
dealt in drugs, ever. OK. I've been a bad boy and I've been
found out. The two grammes found on my person was mine,
but the thirty grammes, no.

FRANK. Police planted it.

HUDSON. They brought it through the door with them. Took it
out of his pocket, put it on my table. Hello, hello, hello, what's
this we see here? I'm arresting you, can I have your autograph
for my daughter? Simple as that.

FRANK *nods and sniffs.*

FRANK. Ah.

HUDSON. You don't really believe me.

FRANK. I don't have to believe you. I have to construct an
account based strictly on this – (*Touches the brief.*) – which a
jury will believe in the face of some rather persuasive police
evidence.

HUDSON. Oh come on. Juries are getting pretty wise to the way
the filth get their arrests.

FRANK. You think so? OK, this is my story then. Ladies and
gentlemen of the jury. I'm sitting at home one night in
Hampstead minding my own business when a group of
detectives from the Drugs Squad arrest me for dealing in a

quantity of cocaine which they've brought along specially for
the occasion. I see you asking yourselves why. Why would they
do this to me? Well, what other motive could it be than that
time-honoured obsession which repeatedly drives detectives to
nick actors with uncles in the Tory government? I should
think you'd get five years.

There is a pause. HUDSON *looks at* CONWAY.

HUDSON. Well I have to say your reputation and your fees had
led me to expect you might come up with something rather
more irresistible than that.

FRANK. Really? Please don't feel obliged to me. There are many,
many barristers in the Temple who would be delighted to
charge you even higher fees to run this engaging story past
twelve intelligent people.

FRANK *is coldly angry.*

CONWAY *lets his client stew, unaided.*

HUDSON *stands.*

CONWAY *and* FRANK *stand.*

HUDSON. I think Nigel and I should have another talk before we
go any further.

FRANK. Yes, so do I.

HUDSON *makes for the door.*

17. Interior. Fetter Court. Day.

A full-scale row is going on around the clerks' desks.
LORRAINE *is getting into a rage.*
JOANNA DAVIS, BINGHAM, BRENDAN HOLLINGSWORTH, KEN
GORDON *and* HUGH *are all there.*

LORRAINE. Nor frankly do I see why I should be responsible for
having to chivvy you lot into paying your rent. If you want the
bills left unpaid for months on end that's fine by me.

KEN GORDON. This is it. This is what really annoys you. Money.

LORRAINE. Nothing annoys me, I'm not annoyed.

KEN GORDON. You're complaining about being a hired hand,
aren't you?

FRANK *and* MICHAEL KHAN *join them at this point.*

If you want a rise why not come out and say so?

LORRAINE. I'm not asking for a rise and I didn't start with the
complaints. Only don't blame me if the phones get cut off.

KEN GORDON. We're not talking about phone bills and this is not
a personal attack on anybody.

MICHAEL KHAN. I have to go to court. This whole area has to be
aired by the entire set, Lorraine.

LORRAINE. Well air it then. But I'm not prepared to be the whipping boy for everything that goes wrong. I can't help it if solicitors won't pay fees promptly.

JOANNA *leaves at this point.*

And I'm not the person to complain to if you don't happen to like the teabags.

KEN GORDON. We're not talking about teabags, darling.

LORRAINE. Don't call me 'darling', you great sexist slob.

KEN GORDON. Oh that's great. A post-feminist critique.

MICHAEL KHAN. Frank, we have to get this sorted out.

FRANK. Yes I know, Michael. Lorraine –

LORRAINE. The trouble is, Frank, you are running around like headless chickens because you never sorted yourselves out about who you are and what you are.

KEN GORDON. Oh bollocks to this.

KEN GORDON *leaves for his desk in disgust.*

LORRAINE. I'm going to the Clerks' Office now to try and help some of you lot get your cases into court because I'm not a lawyer. I'm not paid to stand around arguing. Frankly that's a luxury I can't afford on these wages.

She goes.

KEN *comes back.*

KEN GORDON. God, she'll not be happy till she's on a percentage and pulling in fifty grand a year like all the other clerks. And that's not on in this Chambers. I've got a con arriving.

He goes away again.

FRANK *sighs.*

FRANK. Is Katherine in?

HUGH. In court as usual.

BRENDAN *pipes up from his perch.*

BRENDAN HOLLINGSWORTH. It seems to me: what Lorraine's saying is: what really is the difference between Fetter Court and, you know, Pump Court or Grimshaws or anywhere else? I can't say it's immediately visible to the untrained eye, apart from in Fetter Court we all sit around in one big draughty room.

18.   Interior. Frank's house. Night.

FRANK *and* ANNIE *are eating supper.*
ALETHEA *sits apart, staring into a mirror.*

FRANK. To have a twenty-two year old pupil telling me I might as well not have bothered setting up Fetter Court! What is it they expect? Do they think it wasn't a struggle for *me*?

ANNIE *gets up to clear things off the table and he realises he's droned on and vented his anger all through supper.*

ALETHEA (*to herself*). I'm *so* ugly.

FRANK. Thanks, Annie, that was delicious. I'm sorry I forgot to say I was going out again.

ANNIE. That's all right.

FRANK. Are you OK?

ANNIE. Headache.

FRANK. Oh I'm sorry, I'm sorry, I've droned on. Here sit down and have some wine.

ANNIE. I've got a headache. Bed, Alethea.

She goes to the sink.

ALETHEA gets up, still transfixed by her ugliness, and goes.

FRANK slugs some wine, and dials a number. No reply.

FRANK. Come on, Katherine. Be in for a change.

She shakes her head at him.

ANNIE. Frank, you'll give yourself ulcers.

She's clearing worktops.

He's trying to think of something positive to say to change the subject somehow but:

FRANK. Bingham wants me to apply for silk.

ANNIE. He's just a careerist.

FRANK. Advise me.

ANNIE. You've always said you wouldn't allow them to absorb you or buy you off. Unless you've changed your mind you're not going to apply for silk.

FRANK gets up and stands nearer to her. He leans against the wall where she washes up.

FRANK. I was thinking about us today. We're not the greatest marriage in the world but we've survived. Nineteen years. I feel rather proud of us.

His clumsiness just irritates her.

ANNIE. You're never going to let me live it down are you? I have one brief affair which God knows wasn't worth the effort and . . .

FRANK. I'm talking about us, not you.

There is a pause.

Oh look I've got to go. I'll try not to be too late . . .

ANNIE. What does it matter? I've got a book to read, you've got a key.

FRANK goes.

19. Exterior. Brightpool Park. Day.

The area round the CHARNLEYS' *house.*
The graffiti is being amended to read 'Eat the rich, not their shit.'
A Post Office van is parked on the road and two postmen are delivering
sacks of letters and presents to the CHARNLEYS.
The PC *takes delivery at the door.*
All of the windows in the house are curtained.
Lots of cars are now dotted around, belonging to the JOURNALISTS —
most of whom are in or outside the nearby pub.
A hot-dog stand is doing a brisk trade.

20. Interior. Charnleys' house. Day.

ANNETTE, BRYN *and* PAUL *stand amazed at the piles of parcels and*
letters.
The BOYS *and* ANNETTE *start opening them: cards from well-wishers,*
some containing money. Parcels contain toys, food and clothes.

21. Exterior. Brightpool Park. Day.

PILBROW *and* CURRAN *among the boozers finishing hot dogs. They*
saunter across the waste ground. CURRAN *finishes his lager and chucks*
the can over his shoulder.

CURRAN. Jesus, what a shitheap! I'm going back to the hotel.
   Unless they dig a body up quick I can't see my editor letting
   me fart about up here much longer. Heard anything about
   this woman in Gateshead's apparently got three tits?
PILBROW. Yeh, it's a con, Clive. When you take a close look
   there's nothing really there.
CURRAN. Same as here.
   He sees something.
   Hello, Hello. I bet he's done a runner.

22. Exterior. Brightpool Park. Day.

A crowd of JOURNALISTS *including* PILBROW *and* CURRAN *follows*
ANNETTE, BRYN *and* PAUL *through the shopping arcade to* ELLEN's
office.

23. Interior. Police Headquarters. Day.
Press Conference.
GEE, GRUCOCK *and the assembled* PRESS *including* CURRAN *and*
SCHUMACHER.

GEE. I consider it a matter of extreme urgency that we find

David Charnley. We have requested the assistance of every
police force in the country.

CURRAN. Is he going to be arrested?

GEE. We wish to put a few questions to him.

PILBROW. Will you be asking him to explain the four-day delay?

CURRAN. What about Tracey?

GEE. I urge you not to let your imaginations run riot. We now
have two missing persons we're desperate to find.

He looks like a man whose suspicions are being borne out.

24. Exterior. A seaside resort. Pier. Day.

DAVID CHARNLEY *sits in a shelter on the pier.*
Beside him is 'The Scorcher' with a front page picture of him and the
headline: 'Desperately Seeking Tracey – And Her Dad'.

25. Exterior. A forest. Day.

A steep track in the forest. The trees are so dense it's almost permanent
semi-darkness. It's raining heavily.
SAVILLE, *a healthy sixty-five-year old man with rosy cheeks and a clear*
eye is climbing the track. He decides to take cover in the abandoned croft
up ahead. He goes in. He stands in the doorway looking out. After a few
seconds his eye is caught by something down among the trees twenty yards
away.
It's something flapping around. It seems to be beckoning to SAVILLE.
He walks down through the trees and reaches the thing that caught his
eyes.
After a while we see real horror on his face.
He looks around for help. His half-choked scream echoes down through
the trees.

26. Interior. The Charnleys' house on Brightpool Park. Day.

ANNETTE *watches mesmerised as* MRS HOUGHTON *of the social services*
takes BRYN *and* PAUL *away out of the room and out of the house.*
WPC REDFORD *sits and takes* ANNETTE's *hand.*
ANNETTE *knows what's to come.*

ANNETTE. Oh no, no. No no.

27. Interior. Police Headquarters. Evening.
A massive press presence in the press conference room.
JESUS, GEE *and* GRUCOCK *enter and sit.*
GEE, *white-juced grips a piece of paper from which he reads a prepared*
statement.

GEE. At approximately 13.30 hours today the remains of a young girl were discovered in Gorton Forest. The remains have not yet been positively identified. The gentleman who found the remains is presently under sedation. That is all.

There are howls of protest and a cacophony of questions.
Is it Tracey? How did she die? etc.

28. Exterior. A forest road. Day.

JESUS *gives impromptu press conference.*

JESUS. I can't comment for obvious reasons on this particular set of circumstances but one thing must be getting abundantly clear and that is that we in our society face an epidemic of sickening violence directed at the weak and defenceless, the very young and the very old, and that this is part and parcel of the relentless moral decline facing our nation.

29. Interior. A Chinese takeaway.

CHARNLEY *watches television. He sees film of police activity in a forest, a stretcher, a spot on a map. A photograph of Tracey.*
JESUS *talking sadly.*
CHARNLEY *realises what has happened.*

30. Exterior. Beach. Dawn.

CHARNLEY *is huddled in the doorway of a gents toilet asleep. Beside him a copy of 'The Scorcher', also empty beer cans. He's waking up.*
A police car pulls up silently on the road.
He's lighting a cigarette. He sees two COPS walking towards him. He gets up, his legs are stiff. He hobbles, he trots, he runs. He's pursued across the road and down on to the beach and for a hundred yards out towards the sea. He gets in the sea up to his waist before he is dragged out.

31. Interior. New Road Station. Night.

DAVE CHARNLEY, ROBIN GRUCOCK *and* KEITH GEE *sit in an interview room.*
Silence.

CHARNLEY. When did she die?
GEE. Why do you ask?
CHARNLEY. How long was she kept alive?
GEE. You tell me.

GEE. How can I tell you?

There is a pause.

GEE. I can understand how one thing leads to another. I've got
two daughters. I always enjoyed a cuddle with them. There's
nothing more natural. And I can understand it getting out of
hand. You wouldn't be the first or the last. (*Pause.*) Maybe you
can tell me when she died if I remind you how she died.

CHARNLEY. Why should I kill her?

GEE. Because she was threatening to expose you.

*CHARNLEY dismisses this idea with something between a groan and a
laugh. He shakes his head.*

GEE controls his anger and revulsion.

Because of the damage you did her in the last sexual attack.

CHARNLEY. Damage?

GEE. Where did it happen? Not at home? Somewhere on
Brightpool Park or elsewhere? You lost control of yourself.
There must have been a lot of blood. You were drunk maybe?
You couldn't stop the blood. The child was hysterical. You
couldn't take her to hospital, could you? But you had to stop
her crying somehow.

CHARNLEY. How bad was the damage?

GEE. If she'd survived she'd have needed a colostomy bag.

CHARNLEY gasps and gags on rising vomit.

You couldn't stop the blood but you could stop her crying,
couldn't you?

GEE takes a roll of Sellotape from his pocket.

With Sellotape wound round and round her face. (*He puts the
Sellotape round and round his clenched fist.*) Is that when it began to
get out of control? It wasn't really Tracey, just a rag doll. Was
that it? It wasn't real pain. And she was going to bleed to death
anyway so why not find out how it feels when you really let go of
everything inside you?

CHARNLEY groans.

Do you want to see what you did?

He produces a large photograph. CHARNLEY refuses to look.

CHARNLEY. You're making a mistake.

GEE. You made a mistake. Why did you wait four days before
you reported her missing? Did you think you could wipe this
little chicken off the face of the earth and nobody would
notice?

CHARNLEY. I thought she'd run away. She'd done it before.

GEE. Because of your filthy abuse, but why this, why this?

CHARNLEY refuses to look at the photograph.

*GEE grabs him by the hair and holds the photograph in front of his
face.*

Why this?
CHARNLEY *opens his eyes and screams.*

32. Interior. Magistrates Court. Day.

Silence.
A door opens below the dock.
CHARNLEY *steps up into the dock in handcuffs.*
For the packed court room this is their first glimpse of him.
ELLEN THOMPSON, *his solicitor, is there.*
The eyes of virtually every person in the room are on CHARNLEY *as if scrutinising some extraordinary exotic creature from another world. While the* STIPENDIARY MAGISTRATE *fiddles with his papers and* JOURNALISTS *scribble their impressions onto paper and* ARTISTS *do quick sketches,* CHARNLEY *looks around slowly through dead eyes. The effect is eerie, specially when seen from* CHARNLEY'*s point of view. He hisses at them.*

CHARNLEY. Satan.

33. Exterior. Brightpool Park. Night falling.

An angry crowd is gathering outside CHARNLEY'*s house.*
PC *on door looking worried.*
CURRAN *arrives with four* MINDERS. *They push through the crowd to the door.*

34. Interior. Charnleys' House. Night.

ELLEN *with* WPC REDFORD *and* ANNETTE.
CURRAN *comes in.*
ANNETTE *is terrified.*

ELLEN. Are you sure this is what you want, Annette?
CURRAN. She's sure.
  He puts a contract and a pen on the table in front of her.
  ANNETTE *signs her name painfully slowly.*
  A half brick comes through the window.
  Right. Let's go.
  The MINDERS *grab her.*

35. Interior. Fetter Court. Night.

All the BARRISTERS *are present. There is a noisy debate going on.*

FRANK. If people will stop shouting for a minute, I might be able to hear you.

Quiet.

DAVID MILNER *(repeating)*. Why are you defending Tim Hudson?

FRANK. I'm not sure that I *am* any more but why not?

JOANNA. Because he's a rich man who wants a left wing brief to do his dirty work for him.

MICHAEL KHAN. This is the point, deep down what are we? Who are we serving?

KATHERINE. Maybe he briefed Frank because he needed a good barrister, you know?

DAVID MILNER. Nobody's having a go at Frank.

KATHERINE. I know when somebody's having a go at somebody.

DAVID MILNER. The point is: we can't afford to be seen to be operating as just another set of mercenaries.

MICHAEL KHAN. We need a very clear policy. We can't have a kind of de facto First Eleven that gets big political, criminal, and trades union work, while the Second Eleven slogs away at the bread and butter, immigration, gay rights, petty crime – and because we're the B team nobody has to take us seriously.

FRANK. You want a co-operative.

The younger ones like this idea.

KEN GORDON. Why don't we just go for total anarchy?

MICHAEL KHAN. Nobody's talking about anarchy, just a commitment to an agreed policy.

TESSA. Which should include all members taking on a share of the less sexy work.

OTHERS. Hear, hear.

FRANK. Where would the 'sexy' work I would thereby be passing up go to? Would a solicitor who I've turned down therefore offer his murder case to you, Alison, or you, Joanna?

MICHAEL KHAN. Eventually, yes.

KATHERINE. Oh, that's garbage, Michael. 'Eventually' they will be offered those cases anyway or not, but it won't have anything to do with anybody else moving aside. It'll be to do with gaining experience and getting your communities to instruct its solicitors to brief black barristers.

FRANK. OK, say we've got our co-operative. Do we pool our fees and each draw a salary? Purse-sharing?

MICHAEL KHAN. Based on years of service. Graded. Solicitors all do it. It's a perfectly easy thing to organise.

People think.

KATHERINE *is shaking her head.*

JOANNA. Nobody's saying it's a perfect solution. There's a price to pay for progress.

KEN GORDON. Who's being asked to pay it, that's what I want to know.

DAVID MILNER. *We* are at the moment.

There is an impasse.

People ponder.

BINGHAM *picks his moment.*

BINGHAM. Going back to something Michael said. I think the entire chambers lacks a bit of credibility.

FRANK *can see what's coming.*

I think we'd all benefit if Frank took silk.

There is a stony silence.

It isn't being absorbed or bought off, it's saying the left should have its share of senior counsel.

KATHERINE. James, I understand what you're saying. But I've listened to this for fifteen years. Taking silk is joining the establishment. Full stop.

FRANK. I'm not in principle against any of us applying for silk but for me it's a personal decision I made years ago which I see no reason to change.

OTHERS. Hear, hear.

TESSA. I think you should. If I thought I'd get it I'd apply.

JOANNA, DAVID, *and* ALISON *are taken aback.*

BRENDAN. Ridiculous.

TESSA. No it's not ridiculous. You don't know the difference it would mean to me and what I could do with my practice.

BRENDAN. No, Frank's ridiculous.

FRANK *is amazed.*

You're going on as if this was 1968. Frank, it isn't radical politics anymore. It's more important than that. The politics of gesture are buried. The class war is now being waged increasingly in the courts. That's what we've been talking about all night, I thought. If that's where the war is, let's get serious about it. There's nothing sell-out about strapping on the best armour if you're in a fight. That presupposes it's some kind of self-indulgent personal crusade. It isn't. The basic rights of a whole class are being stripped off us by the most reactionary government for fifty years and there's no time for pussy-footing about. If Frank Cartwright QC can speak louder in the fight than Frank Cartwright can, then get your form and fill it in. It isn't 1968. The world's moved on.

There is a silence.

Well that's what I think.

Silence.

There is a knock at the door, LORRAINE *puts her head round the door.*

LORRAINE. Are you ready for me?

FRANK. Yes. Sorry about this, Lorraine.

She comes in and sits.

Silence.

LORRAINE. That's all right. I asked to be allowed to talk to you, I won't mince words. I joined Fetter Court for the same reasons as everybody else. Because I believed in it and I was led to believe I would be treated as somebody who had a share in what we were trying to do. But I find that there are basically two workers here – me and Hugh – and eleven bosses. And there have been times when – I have to say it – you have simply exploited us. So I'm going to make your choice very simple for you. You must either devise a means of paying me which reflects the relationship I thought you wanted, or find someone else to employ. I'll leave you to it.

She goes.

Silence.

KEN. Why don't we break a habit of a lifetime. And actually make a decision.

FRANK. OK. A vote. Do we offer her more money? In favour. Against.

A muted cheer.

Meeting quickly breaks up.

KATHERINE. Well that's a crying shame.

36. Interior. The same. Later.

FRANK *and* KATHERINE *alone. Both tired and a bit sad.*

KATHERINE. They're trying to wish away a basic fact of life: barristers are hired guns, and no amount of policy making or purse sharing can change that.

FRANK. Would you leave if we became a co-operative?

KATHERINE. Yes. Because it wouldn't be a co-operative. It would be me, you, Bingham and Ken Gordon subsidising the others. That's a recipe for disaster.

FRANK *is caught in a double bind and knows it.*

FRANK. Aaaargh. I'm going home.

They start to switch off and lock up.

Actually, I have to go and tell Lorraine. Shit. Shit, shit, shit.

37. Exterior. Brightpool Park. Day.

The CHARNLEY *house boarded up. The door has been unboarded.*

ELLEN *is leaning on the wall waiting.*

A council WORKMAN *stands nearby.*

Out of the house steps KATHERINE HUGHES.
ELLEN *thanks the* WORKMAN.

ELLEN. Thanks.
   The WORKMAN *immediately starts nailing up the boards again.*
   ELLEN *and* KATHERINE *walk.*
KATHERINE. Where's the wife?
ELLEN. In a safe house with a journalist called Curran.
KATHERINE. Oh Christ.
ELLEN. Know him?
KATHERINE. Yeh. Do we have access to her?
ELLEN. If we must, but he's not keen on the process of justice
   screwing up his exclusive. The two boys are in care. She'll have
   a hard job getting them back.
KATHERINE. Does she know that?
ELLEN. God, Katherine, it's hard to figure out what she knows.
   She's a mess really.
   They walk. ELLEN *lets* KATHERINE *think a bit.*
KATHERINE. I don't know. I don't think I can help you.
ELLEN. I don't think he killed her.
KATHERINE. Why?
ELLEN. How did he get the girl to the place where she finally
   died? He has no transport. They say he must have taken her
   there by public transport and carried out the final sexual
   attack there in anger because she was threatening to expose
   him, but, I mean, not a hint of a witness to the journey.
KATHERINE. You think briefing a woman will help Charnley's
   case?
ELLEN. I think it'll help *me*.
KATHERINE. Ever done a case like this before?
ELLEN. No.
KATHERINE. You'll be OK. Don't worry. Just don't spend too
   much time looking at the post-mortem stuff. OK?
   ELLEN *nods.*
   They are walking past 'Eat the Rich, Not their Shit'.
   How is he mentally?
ELLEN. Falling apart at the seams. He's already tried to kill
   himself. I think he'll try again. He's also been attacked by
   other prisoners twice. One lot beat his head in and another lot
   tried to sit him on a hotplate.
   KATHERINE *thinks a bit more. She stops walking and looks* ELLEN *in
   the eye.*
KATHERINE. What made him confess?
ELLEN. I don't know.
KATHERINE. Has he ever tried to claim the cops beat it out of
   him?

ELLEN. No.

KATHERINE. Is the other stuff true, Ellen? Was he raping her?

ELLEN. I don't know.

KATHERINE. Let's go and ask him, shall we?

38. Exterior. Risley Remand Centre. Day.

ELLEN *and* KATHERINE *arrive in* ELLEN'*s battered old car.*

39. Interior. Risley Remand Centre. Day.

A corridor.

ELLEN *and* KATHERINE *are walking along the corridor with a* SCREW.

ELLEN. Since when?

SCREW. Since supper last night, Madam.

40. Interior. Risley Remand Centre. Day.

An interview room.

CHARNLEY *sits waiting.*

ELLEN *brings* KATHERINE *in.*

CHARNLEY *doesn't acknowledge them.*

KATHERINE *has her first look at the Beast of Brightpool Park.*

ELLEN. David, this is Katherine Hughes. She's going to defend
  you.

KATHERINE. Hello.

  CHARNLEY *nods without looking at them.*

  They sit.

  We're told you've taken no food today, David.

  Silence.

CHARNLEY (*to* ELLEN). Ask them for a match, please.

  CHARNLEY *puts a cigarette to his lips with unsteady hands.*

  ELLEN *goes out to the* SCREWS.

  A SCREW *comes in and lights his cigarette for him. The* SCREW *leaves
  again.*

  CHARNLEY *smokes.*

KATHERINE. Have there been any more attacks on you?

  CHARNLEY *shakes his head.*

  What about the screws? Are they OK with you?

  He nods.

  David, whatever else you may have done to Tracey – and we
  are going to have to talk about all of it – you didn't kill her.
  Despite what you confessed to.

  He shakes his head.

Hang on to that then. You're not guilty of what you're charged with. That's all that really matters.
CHARNLEY *doesn't respond. He stubs out his cigarette and puts the remainder back in the packet.*
KATHERINE. David, what they say was your motive, that you'd been sexually abusing her, what about that?
Silence.
He seems to be unaware of the question.
I have to ask you. How is it that there's clear forensic evidence of long term sexual activity?
There is a long pause.
CHARNLEY *starts to crumple.*
CHARNLEY. Oh Christ, oh Christ.
He gets down on the floor and curls up, hiding his face in his hands.

41. Exterior. Car Park. Risley Remand Centre. Day.

KATHERINE *and* ELLEN *sit crying miserably in* ELLEN's car.

KATHERINE. Ellen, this fellow's never gonna get to court. I've seen this before. He wants to die. Jesus Christ he should die. She was only a little girl. He deserves to die, the shit. I'd like to kill him myself. Listen, if he won't eat he'll very quickly go beyond the point at which we can help him. Get the shrinks back into him. I think he should have something drastic. Come on get us out of here, I want to go home.
ELLEN *starts the car.*

42. Interior. Frank's House. Evening.

FRANK's *getting ready to leave.*
He's dashing downstairs from his study to the bedroom.
The noise of children's television very loud in another room.
ALETHEA *is pestering him.*

ALETHEA. Oh please I'll sit quietly.
FRANK. He's horrible anyway. He's a fat bore.
ALETHEA. Actually, he's fantastic. He's a true star. I could meet Lorraine as well and actually he isn't fat.
FRANK. Lorraine's left.
ALETHEA. Because you're so horrible to her I expect. I can come then, can I?
FRANK *can't argue any more.*

43. Interior. Frank's house. Bedroom. Evening.

ANNIE *is lying on the bed, eyes closed.*

FRANK *and* ALETHEA *come in.*

FRANK. Alethea's coming with me to ogle Tim Hudson. Is that all right?

ANNIE. I need her to look after the boys.

ALETHEA. No, why should I?

ANNIE. Oh God!

ALETHEA *bangs the furniture.*
The telephone rings.

FRANK. Alethea, listen. Behave. I'll make it up to you. I'll get a signed photo.

ALETHEA. I'm sick of her.

ANNIE. Oh for God's sake go.

FRANK. No listen. Let me handle this.

ALETHEA *rushes out of the room.*
FRANK *gets the telephone.*

FRANK. Yes? Yes, Hugh, I'm on my way. We said 5.30. You *told* me 5.30. Oh, shit.

He slams down the telephone and goes.

ANNIE (*shouting*). Tell them to turn down the TV!

44. Interior. Fetter Court. Late in the day.

HUGH *is working hard at his desk with a new junior called* MOIRA.
BINGHAM *is at his desk working.*
Others are dotted about including MICHAEL KHAN.
FRANK *hurries in and parks* ALETHEA *in the clerks' area.*
He fixes HUGH *with a look that could kill.*

HUGH. Sorry, Frank.

FRANK. Alethea, this is Moira. Moira, Alethea. Where are they?

HUGH *points at a conference room.*

Have they had some coffee?

MOIRA *realises she's forgotten to do it.*
She looks guilty.
FRANK *looks angry and exasperated.*

FRANK. Christ!

He goes to the conference room.
KEN GORDON *comes in and goes to his desk, pissed off. What a day he's had.*
MICHAEL KHAN *can see it.*

MICHAEL KHAN (*smilingly*). One of those days, Ken?

KEN GORDON. One of those days, Michael. Michael, tell me, have you ever tried finishing a case in Snaresbrook at 12.30, and starting another one in Aylesbury Crown Court at 2?

He says this loudly for HUGH's *benefit.*

Does our clerk know something I don't about British Rail, or
does he think we all possess bloody helicopters?

HUGH (*under his breath*). Oh, piss off. Bloody prima donnas.

The telephone rings, he answers it.

KEN GORDON. Is anybody coming for a drink?

*KEN GORDON goes out as a RUNNER arrives from a solicitor's office
with a brief. He puts it on HUGH's desk, waves and goes.*

*HUGH looks at it, reads it, scrambles for the court diary, consults it,
dies inside. Looks across at BINGHAM's desk.*

*ALETHEA and MOIRA watch the pantomime and sneak a glance at
each other.*

45. Interior. Fetter Court. Late in the day.

*HUGH has sent MOIRA across with the brief which she plops on to
BINGHAM's desk with a smile and sets off back to the clerks' area.
BINGHAM glances at the brief.*

BINGHAM. Moira, what's this?

MOIRA. It's your brief for tomorrow. It's just arrived.

BINGHAM assumes she's made a mistake.

BINGHAM. I'm not in court tomorrow.

He looks at the brief. His name is on it. She scuttles off.

*BINGHAM takes the brief to HUGH who is already on his feet ready to
defend to himself.*

Hugh.

HUGH. OK. It's a cock up, James. I'm ready to admit it.

MOIRA. It's my fault.

HUGH. No, it's my fault. Well it's *her* fault in a sense. It came
over the phone and I scribbled it on a piece of paper and . . .

The telephone goes. Since no one bothers with it, ALETHEA answers.

I didn't realise Moira hadn't put it in the diary and it just got
forgotten about.

ALETHEA. Who? Sorry he's tied up.

BINGHAM. I see. And what is it?

HUGH. Well it's incompetence. I know that.

ALETHEA. Who? Yes she's here. I'm Alethea.

BINGHAM (*losing his temper*). The case. I'm talking about the case
I'm apparently doing tomorrow. What is it?

MOIRA bursts into tears.

ALETHEA (*shouting*). Dad, Dad!

46. Interior. Fetter Court in the Conference Room. End of the day.

*FRANK, HUDSON and CONWAY, but ALETHEA is shouting outside the
door.*

FRANK. You're now telling me the entire cast used illegal substances?

ALETHEA (*shouting*). Dad, Dad.

FRANK *can't believe this interruption.*

HUGH (*shouting outside*). Frank.

BINGHAM (*shouting outside*). Frank.

FRANK. Excuse me.

FRANK *goes out quickly.*

HUDSON *and* CONWAY *are left feeling foolish.* HUDSON *lights a cigarette.*

HUDSON. Well, is it a wrap?

CONWAY *looks out and sees* HUGH *trying to get somebody on the telephone.*

There's no sign of FRANK *or* ALETHEA *or* BINGHAM.

HUGH (*into telephone*). Hello. Lorraine. It's Hugh.

47. Interior. A hospital. Summer evening.

A corridor.

FRANK *arrives in intensive care unit with* ALETHEA *and* BINGHAM.
A FEMALE NEIGHBOUR *is there with the two boys* JOHN *and* PETER.
A SISTER *arrives.*

FRANK. Alethea, look after Peter and John.

48. Interior. Hospital. Evening.

We watch through glass as FRANK *sits in a* SISTER'*s room being told grave news by a* WOMAN *in a white coat.*

49. Interior. Hospital. Evening.

LORRAINE *arrives to take over the* KIDS *and the* FEMALE NEIGHBOUR *goes home.*
KATHERINE *arrives.*

50. Interior. Hospital. Evening.

In the intensive care unit itself FRANK *is allowed to sit a while watching* ANNIE *on a ventilator.*

51. Interior. Hospital. Night.

Day room.
PETER *and* JOHN *are asleep on* LORRAINE.

ALETHEA *curled up on* KATHERINE.
BINGHAM stares into space.
A NURSE *comes in.*
LORRAINE (*softly*). Should we take them home?
  The NURSE *nods.*
ALETHEA (*sobbing*). No, no.
KATHERINE. Come on, sweetheart.

52. Interior. Hospital. Night.

Much later, in the day room.
FRANK *is sitting with* BINGHAM *in silence.*
The WOMAN DOCTOR *arrives and sits with him.*

WOMAN DOCTOR. With this kind of massive brain haemorrhage
  there's really not much doubt. Only the ventilator is keeping
  her going. I'm really terribly sorry. Perhaps you should go and
  attempt some sleep. Come back later.
  She looks to BINGHAM *to get him to go home.*
FRANK. I see. Thank you.
  BINGHAM *gets him up to go.*
  Would it have made any difference if I'd been there when she
  collapsed?
WOMAN DOCTOR. None whatever.
FRANK. I see. Thank you.

53. Exterior. Outside Frank's house. Dawn.

BINGHAM *and* FRANK *arrive in* BINGHAM's *car and pull up.*
BINGHAM. Want me to come in?
  FRANK *shakes his head.*
  Got a key?
  FRANK *nods.*
  He gets out of the car.
  FRANK *collects his wits a bit.*
FRANK. Thank you James.
BINGHAM. Are you in court today?
FRANK. Umm . . .
  FRANK *has no idea. He's gone inside.*
BINGHAM. Don't worry. I'll sort everything out. Just get some
  sleep.
  FRANK *nods and goes off to the house.*

54. Interior. Frank's house. Early morning.

FRANK *arrives home to his empty house. He looks into various rooms and wonders 'What am I going to do?'*

55. Interior. Hospital. Day.

Intensive care. A DOCTOR *switches off the ventilator and leaves* FRANK *alone with* ANNIE's *body.*

56. Interior. Hospital Psychiatric Unit. Day.

CHARNLEY *sedated on a trolley, is wheeled along a corridor and into a room where quickly and matter-of-factly he's given a single charge of electricity into his head.*
Music ends.

57. Interior. Remand Centre. Day.

ELLEN, KATHERINE, CHARNLEY.
CHARNLEY *sits in silence. He puts a cigarette between his lips.*
KATHERINE *whips out a lighter and lights it for him.*
CHARNLEY *starts to speak.*
CHARNLEY. I worked my arse off on farms, in factories, wherever there was labour wanted. Roads. I worked on the M62. I worked on the M63. M56. When they didn't want any more roads, they give me the bullet. I moved on. Pickin' spuds. Smashin' up batteries for the lead in them.
Three years carrying carcasses in an abattoir, then finish, knackered. Forty-nine years old, finished.
KATHERINE. What's this got to do with Tracey?
CHARNLEY *focuses on her.*
He speaks matter-of-factly.
CHARNLEY. You have to sell what people want to buy. This is a law of life Katherine, a law of life.
ELLEN *and* KATHERINE *are aghast, hardly believing this.*
We had to survive.

58. Interior. A country house. Day.

Main hall.
JESUS *on a dais, speaking to the wealthy of the county.*
JESUS. And in a sense what I have to say to you today as we sit in these splendid surroundings is about survival. Spiritual survival in a world which is disintegrating before our astonished eyes.
During the remainder of the speech we have a good look at the wealthy of the county.

For I would like to take as my theme what St Paul called the
furniture of the mind. Those large, familiar, everyday articles
of faith on which so much depends if we are to make our
journey to God. Furniture that has grown less fashionable, less
comfortable, less convenient in these times. Such a thing as
personal responsibility.

This draws applause from the audience.

We've heard a lot – and mark my words we are about to hear
a lot more in connection with a certain case I needn't name to
you – about poverty and deprivation being the causes of this
epidemic of violence . . .

There is more applause.

And no doubt it is in some minor way, in some cases, a
contributory factor, but the time draws near when even the
blind who lead the blind must begin to see that crime is not a
disease but a sin.

There is great applause.

If it is a disease it's a moral sickness. A tide of cheap, trashy,
pseudo-scientific, pseudo-philosophical, off-the-shelf morality,
which is all but engulfing St Paul's sturdy furniture. The 'Me'
generation – with its throw-away marriages and its disposable
children – is now giving way to its offspring: the 'not me'
generation. Criminal behaviour? Not me. Subversive civil
disorder? Not me. Theft, violence and mayhem on a scale
unparalleled in modern times? Oh no, it's not me. It's the
government to blame for not giving me a job. It's the housing
officer to blame for not giving me a house; but you can't
blame *me*, it's not *me*.

There is rising applause throughout the latter part of the speech.

59. Exterior. A suburban house. Day.

KATHERINE *and* ELLEN *arrive by car outside.*

60. Interior. The house. Day.

Two minders, CURRAN *and* ELLEN *downstairs.*

ELLEN. Where is she?

CURRAN. Upstairs. Wasting our time. All she's capable of is
   sitting all day in front of the telly like Nelly the Elephant.
   What is it anyway? (*A sudden horrible thought strikes him.*) He
   hasn't topped himself, has he?

ELLEN. Ruin your investment, would it? What's it going to be?
   'Life with the Butcher of Brightpool Park?' No, he hasn't
   topped himself. (*She goes to the stairs.*)

CURRAN. Where's La Passionara then?

ELLEN. Barristers aren't allowed to talk to potential witnesses.

CURRAN. Witness? Listen: I've got a right to be in on this if it affects the case.

ELLEN. Do you want me to get a court order?

He relents.

ELLEN *goes up.*

61. Interior. The house. Day.

ELLEN *goes upstairs. She pushes open the door into the bedroom. The curtains are drawn.*

ANNETTE *is sitting watching a soap on television.* ELLEN *looks at her for a second pityingly.*

ELLEN. Annette?

ELLEN *switches off the set.*

ANNETTE *gawps at her, mouth open. She starts to remember things she's been trying to forget.*

A couple of things I have to ask you, love.

ANNETTE *looks very worried and upset.*

62. Interior. The house. Day.

ELLEN *comes back downstairs.*

CURRAN. If there was any chance of a copy of the post-mortem photos you'd be astonished at how grateful I would be.

ELLEN. Like what?

CURRAN. Half a year's salary. I don't know. What do solicitors pull down? I bet you're not making what *she's* making. Or a new car delivered to your door. No one would ever know. Tell me what you'd like.

ELLEN. Well . . .

CURRAN. Go on. What would you really like?

ELLEN. What I'd really like is to hang your balls round your neck.

CURRAN. Are you a dyke?

ELLEN. That woman needs help.

CURRAN. I've got certificates saying there's nothing wrong with her mentally.

ELLEN *heading for the front door.*

She needs a roof over her head and food in her mouth. She needs thirty grand, darling. Are you going to give it to her, or am I?

ELLEN. Provided her husband is found guilty of murdering her daughter. If not she gets nothing, right?

CURRAN. You mean she should get paid either way – like you?

ELLEN *tries to appeal to* CURRAN'*s humanity.*

ELLEN. Why don't you arrange for her to visit the kids?

CURRAN. I've offered, but they won't allow a photographer.

ELLEN *goes.*

63. Exterior. In the car. Day.

ELLEN. If she knew what was going on, she's not admitting it. Even to herself. I dunno. I really don't want to put her in the box, Katherine.

KATHERINE. OK. Charnley has to do it all alone.

64. Exterior. A London common. Winter. Day.

FRANK *is walking alone in the rain. He's unshaven and this is probably the first time we've seen him dressed in anything but a suit.*

65. Interior. Fetter Court. End of the day.

HUGH *and* BINGHAM *are sweating over the chambers' accounts. Both are innumerate: they're like a pair of celibates on their wedding night.*

HUGH. If you just put that there. Or move that bit over there . . . ?

BINGHAM. But it doesn't add up. Why won't these stupid numbers add up?

HUGH. Well it's not supposed to, is it?

BINGHAM. Of course it's supposed to. If this won't add up to the same as this then this bit is missing in the middle.

HUGH. Yeh. Well when that happened Frank used to write a cheque to cover the bills.

BINGHAM. What? I'm going home before I go mad.

He thinks.

He looks at HUGH *who is defeated by the task.*

BINGHAM *takes out his cheque book, he checks the figure.*

He writes a cheque.

Tomorrow we get these audited and work out a proper accounting system.

HUGH. When is Frank coming back, James?

BINGHAM (*aggressively*). He was exhausted for God's sake.

HUGH. Well what am I gonna do with this Hudson brief? Frank doesn't return my calls.

BINGHAM *rubs his eyes. He's knackered as well.*

HUGH *looks at him.*

BINGHAM. Give me that bloody thing.

He picks up the brief and pulls on his raincoat.

66. Interior. Frank's house. Night.

ALETHEA *answers the front door to* BINGHAM. *She brightens up at the sight of him.*

ALETHEA. Hello, James.
BINGHAM. Hello, sweetheart.
  They walk along to the stairs hand in hand.
  Where's Frank?
  ALETHEA. In his room. As usual.
  ALETHEA *returns to her thoughts and her book and he pities her loneliness and sadness.*

67. Interior. Frank's study. Night.

BINGHAM *waves the brief and chucks it on to* FRANK's *desk.*
FRANK *looks at it.*

FRANK. Oh yes.
BINGHAM. Hudson's solicitor's getting rather desperate. Word
  around the Bailey is that Cartwright's retired. Burnt-out case.
  FRANK *chucks it across the desk.*
  BINGHAM *unwraps a bottle of Beaune.*
FRANK. Ah!

68. Interior. Frank's study. Night.

The bottle of Beaune is three-quarters drunk.

BINGHAM. I know we can never be close friends, personally,
  politically, in the way for instance that you and Katherine are.
FRANK. You and Gloria have my undying gratitude and
  friendship. The things you've done for the kids, and –
BINGHAM. Yes, I know. I know all that, I realise I'm about to be
  presumptuous but I simply wanted to talk to you as a
  colleague and admirer. When you come back to Fetter Court
  and I hope it will be soon, don't allow yourself to be
  sidetracked by esoteric disputes about 'what is democracy'. You
  should go for the big issues and fix your mind on the
  important questions of the time. And take silk.
  There is a pause.
FRANK. Thank you, James.
  BINGHAM *waits for more.*
  Nothing.
  He accepts this and gets on his feet.

FRANK *hands him the brief.*

FRANK. You know Hudson, don't you?

BINGHAM (*in despair*). Yes, vaguely, but —

FRANK. Could you possibly manage it?

BINGHAM. Yes, of course, Frank. (*He goes to the door.*)

FRANK. I won't forget this, James.

BINGHAM *goes.*

69. Exterior. Old Bailey. Day.

Cameras click as TIM HUDSON *arrives and goes into the building with* CONWAY, *his* CHARACTER WITNESSES, *his* PARENTS, *etc. They're all tight-lipped.*

70. Interior. Old Bailey concourse. Day.

HUDSON *and* CONWAY, PARENTS, CHARACTER WITNESSES, *and* FRIENDS *meet* BINGHAM.

HUDSON. James.

BINGHAM. Hello, Tim. Good heavens, what a glittering array. Look, have a cup of tea. I'm going upstairs to have a word with prosecuting counsel and I'll see you again before we go in.

HUDSON. I'm sure justice will be done.

BINGHAM. Well if so we can always appeal. Only a joke, Tim.

71. Interior. Old Bailey. Day.

The Men's Robing Room.

BINGHAM *seeks and finds* ARBISH, *a large, amiable man.*

BINGHAM. Roger, I'm glad I've bumped into you.

ARBISH *continues getting into his gear.*

ARBISH. James! What can I do for you?

BINGHAM. We're against each other this morning.

ARBISH. Ah yes. Mister Tim Hudson. He's a naughty man.

BINGHAM. Not at all. It's all a ghastly mistake.

ARBISH. You astound me.

BINGHAM. Let me tell you the facts. I was given the coke by a dressing room visitor. An American film star.

ARBISH. Good heavens!

BINGHAM. It was a gift for the cast of the play to share at a party. No question of me dealing in the stuff at all. A very common practice in the business. In fact I have a theatrical knight to tell the jury all about this side of backstage life.

ARBISH. Will the jury have to wear costume? (*He adjusts his wig in a mirror.*)

BINGHAM. I don't need to make money this way. I'm a very successful actor. I'm of good character. So good that I've got as a character witness a member of the Privy Council.

ARBISH. Well I know at least four members of the Privy Council who should be in prison themselves. What are you suggesting, James?

BINGHAM. I'll plead possession with very heavy mitigation. Public gallery looking like Who's Who of the theatre and politics.

ARBISH. Ah. The full Monty, eh?

BINGHAM. Frankly, I don't think the jury's going to believe I'm a dealer. I think you should think again about that charge. The police – God bless them – have made an honest mistake.

Two BARRISTERS *come in.*

ARBISH *stands up.*

ARBISH. I'm afraid not, James. Let's stand it up in front of a jury, shall we? (*He goes out.*)

BINGHAM *is crestfallen.*

72. Interior. Court Number Two. Old Bailey. Day.

HUDSON *is in the witness box sweating and stammering.*
The gallery is dismayed.

HUDSON. He put it on the table, yes. No, no. Actually a tobacco tin.

BINGHAM. Yes, we've understood that. What I'm trying to –

HUDSON. Get me to say. Right. OK.

BINGHAM. No, not get you to say. I'm not trying to get you to say anything.

ARBISH *is loving it.*

I'm trying to get you to convey to the court what exactly became of the tobacco tin.

HUDSON. The tobacco tin had nothing to do with me. (*This is said passionately and unconvincingly to the* JURY.)

JUDGE. Your counsel is doing his best to assist you, Mr Hudson. If you could listen to his questions a little more carefully.

HUDSON. I'm frightfully sorry.

BINGHAM. That's all right. I'm grateful to Your Honour. It's my fault, I'm not making myself clear. Was the cocaine in the tobacco tin when you first saw it produced?

There is a long pause.

HUDSON. I'm sorry. I've completely gone. No, sorry it's gone.

There is terrible embarrassment and silence.

73. Interior. Old Bailey canteen. Day.

Very busy.
BINGHAM, HUDSON, CONWAY *are at a table in despair.*

HUDSON (*quietly and resignedly*). The bloody ironic thing is I really
was telling the truth.
For the first time BINGHAM *actually believes the story.*
BINGHAM (*unconvincingly*). Well, let's wait and see. Jury's are
strange creatures.
HUDSON. If you've kept me out of prison, James, I'll do anything
for you.
BINGHAM. Well actually there might be something –
A VOICE *on the tannoy.*
VOICE. Defendant and counsel in the case of Timothy Hudson,
please.
HUDSON. Oh God: I'm on.

74. Interior. Frank's house. Day.

ALETHEA *sits dressed for a lunch date.*
FRANK *is waiting with her.*

FRANK. You look great.
ALETHEA looks miserable.
Alethea.
The door bell rings. She gets up.
Alethea.
ALETHEA *pauses and looks at him for the first time.*
It will all work out.
ALETHEA. James is waiting to take me to lunch and I have to go.
She is unconvinced by him. She goes to the door. She opens the door to
TIM HUDSON *who's carrying flowers for her. She's gobsmacked.*
HUDSON. Alethea Cartwright?
ALETHEA. Yes.
HUDSON. I hope you don't mind. James said I could join you for
lunch. Is that all right?
ALETHEA. Yes. That'll be all right.
HUDSON escorts her away down the path observed by FRANK.
BINGHAM steps in.
BINGHAM. Well cheer up, Frank.
FRANK. Cheer up? You're taking my daughter to lunch with a
drug abuser.
BINGHAM. He got off, didn't he?
FRANK. The jury must have been fully paid-up members of his
fan club is all I can say.

BINGHAM. No they just thought anybody who would go to the trouble of inventing a story as bad as that would have learned his lines better.

FRANK. I don't want him touching her. You sit in the middle, right?

BINGHAM. OK.

FRANK. Thanks.

BINGHAM *nods and goes.*

Empty house again. FRANK *doesn't fancy it. He picks up the telephone and dials.*

75. Interior. Katherine's flat. Day.

KATHERINE *is half packed and continuing with the job.*
A large suitcase. FRANK *watches.*

FRANK. How's your man?

KATHERINE. Half crackers.

FRANK. And how are you?

KATHERINE. Panicking.

FRANK. You can never tell with juries.

KATHERINE. No, not about the result. It's just that there's only so much of it you can do. Only so much of yourself you can use up, when there's nothing good in your life to renew you. As if I needed to tell you that. How are you? I can't imagine it.

FRANK. Grief is like chronic pain. It's very isolating. Still about ten per cent of the time I'm hallucinating. But what's really knocked me sideways is the guilt.

KATHERINE. About what?

FRANK. About everything, everything. Being alive. My marriage. My job. It's a revelation I can tell you. You go through life thinking you're rational. You're not. You think you're emotionally placid. You're not. In fact I don't know what I am. I'm not convinced I know who this I is who takes over every sentence, every thought, every feeling. Here I am, this must be me. I've got my clothes on. Sorry, it's very embarrassing. The other thing about grief is that it keeps delivering you into situations where you find your friends standing there looking sympathetic because you're talking incomprehensible crap. Actually I don't really want lunch. I want to say something to you. Katherine, the grief that has me by the throat, *now still*, is rooted not in a love that was cut down but in that guilt I've nursed for ten years about sacrificing my marriage and my family to my job, to my *career*.

KATHERINE *shakes her head in disagreement.*

So I'm saying to you: don't do it. Don't let your self be

crucified by Brightpool Park or anything else. It isn't worth it.

KATHERINE. You're ready for work again.

FRANK. Yes. Soon.

KATHERINE. And ready for silk too.

FRANK. What would you say?

KATHERINE. I'd say: if that's what you want you should do it.

FRANK. That's what I think.

KATHERINE. Then you should do it.

> *There is a pause.*

> I have to go. I've got a train to catch. The circus is moving town.

76. Exterior. In a completely sealed prison van. Day.

CHARNLEY *in a completely blacked-out prison van with four* PRISON OFFICERS. *The van slows. He and we can hear muffled sounds of traffic. It slows down. He hears the sounds of large numbers of people. Individual women's* VOICES *shouting 'Hang the bastard'. Missiles hitting the sides of the van. The van is moving slowly. It speeds up leaving the noise of the crowd behind.*

It goes down a ramp. It stops. Most of this is done from CHARNLEY's *point of view. And so it continues.*

The back door opens. He jumps down out of the van with the POLICE. *You hear the noise again. He goes through the heavy doors. They close behind him.*

He's marched along the corridor down into cells where ELLEN THOMPSON *is waiting with a brave smile.*

And now we see him as she sees him for the first time. He's hollow-faced, he's old, he's gaunt.

77. Interior. The cells below court. Day.

ELLEN, KATHERINE *in her gear and* CHARNLEY.

KATHERINE. Say it.

> *There's a pause.*

CHARNLEY. Not guilty.

KATHERINE. I want you to say it as if you meant it. Say sorry to spoil the party, cop this: not guilty!

78. Interior. The courtroom. Day.

The court is jammed. It's also hushed.

CHARNLEY (*much too loudly*). Not guilty. (*He looks and sounds half crackers.*)

79. The same. Later.

SAVILLE *is in the box. Sturdy, nut brown, but with a shadow across him forever. The court is hushed.* CHARNLEY's *eyes are closed.*

PROSECUTING COUNSEL. Could you describe to us what met your eyes as you looked into that darkness?

SAVILLE. Yes, sir.
But he has to steady himself and make a physical effort to speak.
I went down out because I saw something waving at me. There was something on the ground or half-way out of the ground. At first I thought it was a doll. And then I saw it was a girl. Her eyes were closed and her head was on one side. And I was on the point of speaking, saying could I help her up. But in that instant I saw the rope around her neck.
He daren't speak another word yet. He shakes his head to the JUDGE.

JUDGE. Would you like some water?
SAVILLE *nods and the* USHER *brings him some water.*
KATHERINE *leans back to* ELLEN.

KATHERINE (*whispers*). I'm going to cross-examine him.

ELLEN. Why?

KATHERINE. I just want the jury to see me being nice to somebody.

80. Interior. The courtroom. Day.

SAVILLE *is still in the box.*

JUDGE. Miss Hughes.
KATHERINE *stands.*

KATHERINE. Mr Saville, we've all been distressed by your description. It's easy for those of us who are here in a professional capacity to forget what being a witness can really mean. I want to clarify one small detail. Did you stumble across this croft or did you know its location already, in what is, by your own evidence, a very dense part of the forest?

SAVILLE. No, I knew it well. I'd used it many times for shelter.

KATHERINE. It can't be seen, by chance, from any road or footpath, can it?

SAVILLE. Oh no.

KATHERINE. Thank you again, Mr Saville. No further questions, Your Honour.
She sits.

81. Exterior. Police Headquarters car park. Night.

Lots of JOURNALISTS, *restless, angry, milling about, fed up.*
Some of them sing 'Why are we waiting? Why are we waiting?'

82. Interior. Police Headquarters. Night.

GRUCOCK *and* GEE.
JESUS *comes in.*

JESUS. What in God's name is happening?
GRUCOCK. A girl's body's been found, sir. Raped. Beaten.
  Strangled with rope.
JESUS. Oh, hell.
GEE. She was an eighteen-year-old woman. She went out to work
  two nights ago and never came back.
JESUS. Work?
GEE. She's on our books. She was a prostitute.
JESUS. Keep me informed.
  JESUS *goes.* GEE *closes his eyes.*
  GRUCOCK *looks at the* JOURNALISTS *out of the window.*

83. Interior. Hotel dining room. Chester. Night.

A small but rowdy table of JOURNALISTS.
At another table, alone, KATHERINE *eating.*
At another, SCHUMACHER *alone, reading. The noise annoys him. He*
leaves. As he passes them.

PILBROW. You'll have to excuse us, Daniel. It's the conditions
  we're forced to live in!
  They scream with laughter.
  He walks towards the door past KATHERINE's *table. He sits. She pours*
  him wine.
SCHUMACHER. You hear the news?
KATHERINE. No.
SCHUMACHER. A girl went missing. She's been killed.
KATHERINE. More lurid headlines for you lot.
SCHUMACHER. No, she ruined the story by being a prostitute.
  Who cares about whores? Still we'll make something out of it.
  She dressed young for guys who are into school girls. There's
  our story.
  She stares at him.
  Hey I'm joking.
KATHERINE. Yes. Are the police making any connection between
  them?

SCHUMACHER. No. Should they?

KATHERINE. Cheers.

84. Same. Later.

They are now alone in the dining room. He's picking at her left-overs.

KATHERINE. What was the feeling around the time of Tracey's disappearance?

SCHUMACHER. Sick.

KATHERINE. Why?

SCHUMACHER. We were waiting for a body to be found.

KATHERINE. No, I mean right at the beginning. When she was just a runaway.

SCHUMACHER. Sure. Gee made it clear right away he didn't expect the girl to turn up alive.

This confirms what she thought.

KATHERINE. I see.

He's smiling, trying to figure this out.

SCHUMACHER. Am I helping you in some way?

KATHERINE. What's Gee like? Is he a villain?

SCHUMACHER. He drinks a lot.

KATHERINE. That's not unheard of in a cop.

SCHUMACHER. Or a lawyer.

She bristles. She starts to think about turning in.

Why you want to know about Gee?

KATHERINE. What's your problem? You like this man?

SCHUMACHER. He gets respect. He's honest. That's what I feel.

KATHERINE. Well, he'll be all right then, won't he? Bedtime.

For a second he wonders if that's an offer, but:

Goodnight, Mr Schumacher.

SCHUMACHER. Goodnight, Miss Hughes.

85. Interior. The courtroom. Day.

GEE *is in the box.*

KATHERINE. Inspector Gee, you've had the responsibility for this case from the outset?

GEE. Yes.

KATHERINE. Its conduct has been your personal responsibility?

GEE. My professional responsibility, but mine solely.

KATHERINE. My client was taken in for questioning on May 7th, on the day after the discovery of the body and eleven days after Tracey went missing. Is that correct?

GEE. That's correct.

KATHERINE. You must have been very relieved that my client had been apprehended. Is that correct?

GEE. I don't think that's what I felt.

KATHERINE. But hadn't you by then already formed a very strong conviction that my client was the murderer?

GEE. No, not at all.

KATHERINE. Are you saying you still had an open mind?

GEE. Of course.

KATHERINE. Because in fact there was no evidence to link him with the crime, was there?

GEE. Forensic evidence showed matching traces of fibres of his pullover under the girl's fingernails.

KATHERINE. Yes, forensic tests made after his arrest linked him with the girl, but not with the crime. And this is hardly surprising, is it, that he should be linked with his daughter, since they lived in the same house? So it can't have been that that persuaded you that a nationwide manhunt was necessary.

GEE. It was clear from a preliminary examination that the girl had suffered sexual abuse over a long period of time. A number of years, not days.

KATHERINE. So you suspected him of having sexually abused his daughter, once you received this preliminary report?

GEE. Yes.

KATHERINE. But not before then? You didn't suspect that before? *There is a pause.*

GEE. Yes, I did.

KATHERINE. You did? That's interesting. Why was that?

GEE. Because I asked myself 'If you believe your daughter's run away, why wait four days before telling anybody?'

KATHERINE. And what answer did you come up with?

GEE. I had an open mind.

PROSECUTION *smirks.*

KATHERINE. Did it seem to you that my client was behaving like a guilty man?

GEE. He struck me as a man who had something he needed to hide.

KATHERINE. I see. Did my client offer any other explanation for his stepdaughter's disappearance?

GEE. Yes.

KATHERINE. He did insist that Tracey might've been abducted, didn't he?

GEE. He came up with this once or twice.

KATHERINE. Did you question all the known sex offenders on your books?

GEE. Yes.

KATHERINE. And drew a blank in each case?

GEE. Yes.

KATHERINE. When was this?

GEE. My colleague. Sergeant Grucock, handled this within forty-eight hours of us knowing she was missing.

KATHERINE. So you were in fact waiting for a body to be discovered.

GEE. Absolutely not.

KATHERINE. But you weren't looking for her with anything like the same commitment of time and resources.

GEE. No.

KATHERINE. Why not? Was it because you were convinced she was already dead?

GEE. She *was* already dead. Charnley's confession makes it clear she died on the 26th and he waited four days –

KATHERINE. But you didn't know that at the time.

GEE. No.

KATHERINE. So why weren't you looking for her? I put it to you again: you had already decided my client was guilty of a murder you couldn't even be sure had taken place.

GEE. Absolutely not.

KATHERINE. But you've just said he looked like a man who was hiding something. What was it he was hiding?

GEE. Well his confession makes that clear.

KATHERINE. Chief Superintendent, I'm talking about *then* not *now*. At the time before my client made the confession which he retracted as soon as he had access to legal advice; at a time at which – and the forensic report makes this perfectly clear – Tracey may well still have been alive; at a time when you were nevertheless winding down the enquiry which was your sole responsibility: what was it you thought my client David Charnley was hiding?

Pause.

GEE. Well what else could it have been?

KATHERINE. No further questions, Your Honour. (*She sits.*)

GEE, *and the bulk of the Court, are baffled.*

86. Interior. The cells below the courts. Day.

CHARNLEY *is in bad shape.*

ELLEN *and* KATHERINE *sit near him.* KATHERINE *begins to pity him.*

CHARNLEY. I don't deserve to live. I'm just shit. I'm an animal. I should be put on telly and given rat poison.

KATHERINE *moves close to him. Nobody has given* CHARNLEY *a shred of human warmth for months.*

KATHERINE. David, where would any of us be if we got what we deserved?

CHARNLEY. I want to plead guilty. I'm guilty. I don't want to show my face.

ELLEN's face shows near panic.

KATHERINE keeps her head.

CHARNLEY weeps.

KATHERINE puts one hand round CHARNLEY's shoulders and the other on his clenched fists. He shakes his head.

CHARNLEY. Oh, Jesus Christ. Christ's blood.

She understands. She nods.

KATHERINE. You have to say it all, shall I help you?

CHARNLEY shakes his head.

Shall I say it for you? You told Gee the truth about how you felt about Tracey, didn't you?

CHARNLEY weeps.

KATHERINE. You can say it now. Go on, you couldn't resist her, could you, this little girl? But you didn't kill her.

CHARNLEY weeps and shakes his head.

KATHERINE strokes him.

ELLEN recoils from this scene.

No, of course not, she was your little girl. You can say it. You can say it out loud, all you did to her.

CHARNLEY wails.

KATHERINE. You're not guilty, David. When we get up there today, I want you to forget about everybody else in the court but me. Just talk to me, OK?

87. Interior. Crown court building. Ladies toilets. Day.

KATHERINE is washing her hands thoroughly. She dries them. She sprays cologne on her wrists. She smells it. She sprays some on her sleeve where it touched his shoulders. She gets her composure.

She looks herself in the eye in the mirror. She inhales a big breath and cut.

88. Interior. The courtroom. Day.

CHARNLEY is in the box. He looks only at KATHERINE.

KATHERINE. Mr Charnley, you know, don't you, that nothing that's been said here so far in this trial and nothing that will be said will do anything to bring Tracey back? You know that?

CHARNLEY. Yes.

KATHERINE. And nothing that we say can cause her any more

suffering. You know that?

CHARNLEY. Yes.

KATHERINE. And you know that what this court is concerned with is whether or not you murdered her, nothing else? You know that?

CHARNLEY. Yes.

KATHERINE. Mr Charnley, did you murder Tracey?

CHARNLEY. No.

KATHERINE. On the night of the 8th May and during the following day, you made statements to Chief Superintendent Gee which culminated in you signing the confession which was read earlier in the trial. Is that correct?

CHARNLEY. Yes.

KATHERINE. Was it in any part accurate?

CHARNLEY. Yes.

KATHERINE. Which part do you say was accurate?

CHARNLEY. The bit about having sex with Tracey.

KATHERINE. Mr Charnley, are you prepared to be completely frank with the court?

CHARNLEY. Yes.

KATHERINE. When did you start having sex with Tracey?

CHARNLEY. After the boys were born.

KATHERINE. What were your sexual relations with Annette like at this time?

CHARNLEY. She didn't want any.

KATHERINE. How old was Tracey?

CHARNLEY. Eight.

KATHERINE. What did you get Tracey to do with you?
Pause.

CHARNLEY. At first . . . at first it was just touching. I asked her to touch my private parts. And I touched her private parts. Then I got her to masturbate me. Then in the end I was going all the way with her.

KATHERINE. Can you tell the court exactly what that means?

CHARNLEY. Intercourse.

KATHERINE. You had full sexual intercourse with her?

CHARNLEY. Yes.
Pause.

KATHERINE. As well as normal sexual intercourse, was there abnormal sexual intercourse?

CHARNLEY. Yes. Erm . . . anal intercourse.

KATHERINE. How old was Tracey when you first had actual sexual intercourse with her?

CHARNLEY. Eight.

KATHERINE. For how long did these sexual acts continue?

CHARNLEY. Till she went missing. Five years.

KATHERINE. Mr Charnley, was Tracey in any sense a willing partner in this?

He shakes his head.

I'm afraid you'll have to tell the court. Was she a willing partner?

CHARNLEY. Oh, help me, God. No, she wasn't.

GEE is disgusted with him, never takes his eyes off him.

KATHERINE. In your statement you said that in the spring of this year it became clear to you that Tracey was becoming so desperately unhappy that she might expose you to the authorities in order to escape your sexual advances. Is that part of your statement accurate?

CHARNLEY. No.

KATHERINE. What is inaccurate about it? Was she not miserably unhappy?

There is a pause.

KATHERINE *repeats the question.*

Was she?

CHARNLEY. Yes, she was.

KATHERINE. Was she threatening to expose you?

CHARNLEY. No. She knew we needed her.

KATHERINE. You needed her? You're not now talking about your sexual needs, are you?

CHARNLEY. No.

There is a pause.

GEE is watching very closely.

KATHERINE. In what way did you need her?

CHARNLEY. We needed the money?

KATHERINE. What money?

He's on the brink of collapse.

Mr Charnley, it's very important that you now tell the court the whole truth.

CHARNLEY. We needed the money she started earning.

GEE can suddenly see it coming. Hell is truth learned too late.

KATHERINE. How did she earn this money?

There is a pause.

CHARNLEY. At first pornographic videos. After that: Prostitution.

GEE's world falls apart.

89. Exterior. Court building. Night.

GEE is leaving the court building after the day's hearing.
He's completely silent and grim as he pushes his way through a crowd of
JOURNALISTS *into a car in which he is driven away.*

90. Interior. Fetter Court. Daytime but dark. 5 p.m.

Busy. Most people there at desks. Talking, etc, signs of Christmas. Cards on desks and on room dividers and walls. Christmas shopping dotted about the place.
FRANK *arrives from the street unexpectedly.*
MICHAEL KHAN *notices him first.*

MICHAEL KHAN. Frank.
FRANK. Merry Christmas.
OTHERS. Frank.
  They seem pleased to see him. They gather round to welcome him back.
  BINGHAM *beams. Most of them haven't actually clapped eyes on*
  FRANK *for months.*

91. Interior. Same. Later.

Everybody present bar HUGH *and* KATHERINE.

FRANK. I've just come from a meeting with Hugh. At which I
  made it plain that he cannot continue as our senior clerk. I
  also made it plain that it was our mistake not his to have asked
  him to do it in the first place. I asked him to consider staying
  as junior clerk.
JOANNA DAVIS. I think that's appalling.
FRANK. Just a second, Joanna, please. I've also had a meeting
  with Lorraine today at which I asked her on behalf of Fetter
  Court to come back. She has accepted and I have offered her
  the customary terms to clerks in the Temple.
  They all knew this was in the offing but KEN *wants it clear.*
KEN GORDON. A percentage?
FRANK. Correct. I have also made an application for silk. I
  apologise for my prolonged absence. I am coming back in the
  New Year to lead this Chambers into what I believe will be a
  crucial period. This is a time for those of us who value truth,
  justice and *democracy* to discipline ourselves and be ready to
  fight. That is what Fetter Court was set up to do. I hope I
  have your support.
  Pause.
JOANNA DAVIS. Is the implication of that that anybody who
  doesn't share your approach is *not* committed to truth, justice
  and democracy?
FRANK. Not at all, Joanna.
  He says no more.
JOANNA DAVIS. Well I'd like a democratic vote about Fetter Court
  becoming a co-operative.

FRANK. By all means. Will those in favour please show?

JOANNA, ALISON, DAVID, MARTIN *and* MICHAEL *raise hands.*

Those against.

FRANK, JAMES, KEN, TESSA, BRENDAN.

Katherine cannot be here tonight but she wished to record her vote against this motion. Should it come up.

They realise he has come well-prepared.

I would hope that you would all accept that.

DAVID. Yes. I do.

MICHAEL *and* ALISON *nod.* JOANNA *and* DAVID MILNER *shake their heads. They leave.*

Silence.

TESSA *damp-eyed.*

FRANK *sad but determined.*

92. Interior. Police Headquarters. Night.

JESUS's *room.*

JESUS *is with* GEE.

Hundreds of Christmas cards everywhere.

JESUS. Whatever the outcome of the trial, Keith, it's perhaps time you began to think in terms of a well-deserved retirement after this is all over. If that's a problem pensionwise, then let's by all means have a look at a long term leave of absence on medical grounds.

GEE. Yes, sir.

93. Interior. The court. Day.

KATHERINE *stands in the packed court to make her closing speech.*

KATHERINE. Members of the Jury, this is the part of the trial when I'm allowed to speak directly to you.

The JURY *looks pretty hostile. One or two are looking at her in the eye defiantly. Others are studying the floors and the ceiling.*

You've had the harrowing task of listening to and examining the evidence of a quite repugnant crime committed against a child.

One or two of the JURY *look at* CHARNLEY.

You have also heard a terrible account from the mouth of the defendant, filled with self-disgust and shame, about the way in which he exploited his young stepdaughter. How he slowly began the process of taking advantage of her sexually, subjecting her to indignity and misery for his own satisfaction and eventually pressing her to provide similar sexual service for other men.

His account was monstrous and it would be impossible for us to deny our sense of outrage against anyone who could visit such inhumanity on someone in his care, our hearts wrenched at the thought of this little girl robbed of her childhood, our whole beings sickened by the way she was forced to sell her body and soul. But members of the Jury, to allow these deep and powerful emotions to cloud your judgement in this case would be adding another monstrous act to the ones we have heard about. It would be a terrible miscarriage of justice. You've heard that on somewhere between the 26th April and the 4th May she was taken to a remote woodland where she was savagely attacked, raped, strangled and her remains buried. You've also heard that David Charnley possesses no means of transport. That travelling from Brightpool Park to the scene of the murder would be long indeed by public transport. And you've seen that no witnesses to any such journey have been produced in court. You've heard Chief Superintendent Gee agree that no forensic evidence exists to link David Charnley with the crime or its location. Then why, you may begin to ask, was my client ever charged with this crime? It was because he confessed. Why did he confess? Imagine. Your stepdaughter has been missing for eleven days and you have reason to fear the worst for her, you and your family have become the focus of national concern and speculation, and you have two appalling secrets to live with, both of which cause you deep feelings of guilt. So much so that you can't stand it any more. You run away. Your stepdaughter's body is found in a shallow grave. You are apprehended and then interrogated by the force's most experienced detective. You are shown a photograph of her remains. What might that do to a mind struggling for eleven days to block out its own imaginings of the torments and indignities the child may have suffered in her last days and hours, at the hands perhaps of one of the men who for five years have picked her up on street corners in order that she might serve them sexually.

You admit abuse. Finally you confess to murder too. Naturally, the gentlemen of the press then have a field day. Taking the high moral ground, they have called my client a beast, a monster, a butcher – a man who has sunk to depths which no human should. Yes, there's no doubt no human should reach those depths . . . but what makes it possible?

Ladies and gentlemen, the fact is we don't know exactly how Tracey died. But we do know exactly how and where she lived. She lived in a corner of late twentieth century England called Brightpool Park. She lived in the kind of grinding poverty that few of us in this room can imagine having to endure. In a house so damp that the floorboards were rotting away, with half of the windows shattered and boarded up, without a constant supply of electricity. Where a bed in winter was a blanket on the floor, huddled with her brothers for warmth. Where a meal was a packet of crisps with tomato ketchup.

If we pity her death we should pity too her life, and ask ourselves, is this acceptable that a child at her age should go into prostitution in order to help feed her parents and her younger brothers? And if she hadn't gone into prostitution would she have died?

But who is responsible for putting her onto the streets? Well, surely this man here, David Charnley. Yes, he's responsible. He let it happen. Yes, he put his daughter on the streets. The head of the family clinging to the ledge of existence, he took the only option that seemed open to him. He had no skill to sell and no one wanted to hire his strength any longer. But there was a market for his daughter. What would you do? How much are your children worth? It's a ridiculous question, isn't it? It's an insult for a human being to be asked such a vile question. David Charnley was asked it. If it's an insult to be asked 'How much for your daughter?' when you have all you need, then what is it when your other children are desperate for the bare necessities of life?

What is it to be reduced to the ultimate service industry, where your own flesh and blood is for sale? By his own words David Charnley denies killing Tracey but confesses to you that he did the unspeakable. But you may feel that the unspeakable was being done to him and his – in our name. This case is an indictment – but not just of David Charnley. Members of the Jury, David Charnley confessed to murder precisely because he had *not* lost all moral sense. Precisely because he was overcome with guilt. He took personal responsibility for her death, and you now know why. But you are not trying him for sexual abuse. You are not trying him for pimping for a child. You are trying him for the most serious crime in the calendar. Your task has been harrowing but your duty is clear. If you convict David Charnley, then let it be understood what his real crime has been: not murder, but poverty and powerlessness.

She sits.

94. Interior. The courtroom. Day.

It's packed.
CURRAN's *in the press box,* SCHUMACHER *too.*
The JURY *files in.*
The JUDGE *comes in.*
They all stand.
He sits.
They all sit.

CLERK. Will the defendant stand, please?
  CHARNLEY *stands.*
  Members of the Jury, have you reached a decision?
  The FOREMAN *stands.*
FOREMAN. We have.
CLERK. Do you find the accused guilty or not guilty to the charge of murder?
FOREMAN. Not guilty.
  There is amazement and noise all round the court.
  CURRAN *can't believe it.*
  SCHUMACHER *pats him on the back.*
  CHARNLEY *grips the stand and sways.*
  ELLEN *hugs* KATHERINE.

95. Exterior. A cemetery in London. Day.

A headstone has been put on ANNIE's *grave.*
FRANK, JOHN, PETER *and* ALETHEA *are reading it.*

ALETHEA. It looks nice. We'll have to keep it very tidy, won't we?
FRANK. Oh yes.
  The boys nod solemnly.
ALETHEA. Can I be in charge of that?
FRANK. Yes.
  She is very pleased about this and so is FRANK.
  OK, from the right then, turn, quick march.
  As the children walk towards the gates FRANK *turns and looks at the headstone.*

96. Exterior. A cemetery in the north. Day.

A small posse of PHOTOGRAPHERS *snaps away as* CHARNLEY *and* ANNETTE *hand in hand approach* TRACEY's *grave.*
He kneels.
There is no headstone yet, just a mountain of flowers.
Cut.
Silence.

EPISODE FIVE

Permanent Blue

Cast

KATHERINE HUGHES	Jane Lapotaire
FRANK CARTWRIGHT	Jack Shepherd
JAMES BINGHAM	Julian Wadham
DAVID VALENTINE	Ronald Lacey
BILL TURNER	Nick Stringer
TYLER	James Faulkner
SENIOR ATTORNEY	Douglas Wilmer
DEPUTY TO THE DPP	Charles Lewson
REV. BILL TURNER	David King
SIR CHARLES BINGHAM	Wensley Pithey
GEORGE VINER	Bill Wallis
LORRAINE	Caroline Hutchison
TESSA PARKS	Joanne Campbell
HUGH	Eamonn Walker
MICHAEL KHAN	Raad Rawi
KEN GORDON	Tom Marshall
ALETHEA CARTWRIGHT	Mia Fothergill
FRANK'S MOTHER	Irene Richmond
JOHN WOODHAM	John McGlynn
WPC ORTON	Chloe Rackow
GEOFFREY KATZ	Joel Cutrara
VAN DRIVER	Paul Heasman
VAN PASSENGER	Harry (Aitch) Fielder
ASIF KHADRI	Azeem Sheikh
MICHAEL CROWE	Philip Manikum
TV INTERVIEWER	Andrew Hilton
JOHN SHANDLEY	Dennis Ramsden
TELECOM ENGINEER	Robin Summers
POLICE INSPECTOR	Robert Hickson
POLICE PATROLMAN	Gareth Milne
TAXI DRIVER	David McEwan

THUG 1	Colin Skeaping
THUG 2	Terry Forrestal
THUG 3	Chris Webb
JAZZ BAND	Groove Juice Special

1. Interior. Westminster Hall. Day.

Forty new barristers are being appointed, including FRANK
CARTWRIGHT. *They are wearing knee breeches and full bottomed wigs.
Behind them sit their* CLERKS, *in morning dress – except for* LORRAINE,
who is nevertheless dressed very smartly. FAMILIES *are present –
including* FRANK's *parents,* MR *and* MRS CARTWRIGHT, *and his
children,* ALETHEA, JOHN *and* PETER. FRANK *makes his declaration to
the* LORD CHANCELLOR.

FRANK. 'I Francis Thomas Hugh Cartwright do sincerely promise
and declare that I will well and truly serve her Majesty Queen
Elizabeth the Second and all whom I may be lawfully called
upon to serve in the office of one of her Majesty's Counsel,
learned in the law according to the best of my skill and
understanding'.
FRANK is handed his letters patent.

2. Exterior. London Street. Day.

An unmarked van is travelling. There are two MEN *in the front.*

3. Interior. Back of van. Day.

In the back of a windowless van, KATZ, *a forty-year-old American is
swigging a bottle of Jack Daniels. By his side is a plastic bag containing
more duty-free booze and cigarettes and a flight bag. All around him are
wooden crates. He's singing as he undoes his trousers.*

KATZ. (*singing*). 'Oh say can you see my ass, if you can then you
must be a Brit'.
He bangs on the dividing wall.

4. Interior. Front of van. Day.

A MAN *in the passenger seat opens the sliding window and is confronted
with* KATZ's *backside. This is soon replaced by his grinning face.*

KATZ. Hi, I have to take a crap.
The MAN *closes the window. Both men in the front are exasperated but
immediately start looking for a toilet.*
KATZ *bangs on the wall again.*

MAN (*in the passenger seat*). There's a pub over there. Watch it!

A five-year-old boy has stepped out in front of them.
The DRIVER *sees him too late.*

5. Interior. Fetter Court. Day.

A big party to celebrate FRANK's *appointment as a silk. Those present are the whole of the chambers (except* HUGH, *and* KATHERINE), *his* KIDS, *his* MUM *and* DAD, *many* COLLEAGUES, FRIENDS *and a* JAZZ BAND. *There is a lot of food and drink; champagne corks are flying, the band is playing.*
FRANK *is introducing his* MUM *and* DAD, MR *and* MRS CARTWRIGHT *to people.*
FRANK *is still wearing the full monty. People occasionally borrow his wig to use for posing in photographs.* ALETHEA *is reading out the Letters Patent to* MICHAEL KHAN, KEN, TESSA *and* LORRAINE, *who is wearing top hat and tails.*

FRANK. You remember James Bingham.
MRS CARTWRIGHT. Hello again, James, nice to meet you again in happier circumstances.
BINGHAM. Hello, Mrs Cartwright, Mr Cartwright, congratulations Frank.
ALETHEA (*reading*). Elizabeth the Second by grace of God of the United Kingdom of Great Britain and Northern Ireland. Then all the other places she's chief of. Greetings, know ye that we have appointed our loyal subject Francis Thomas Hugh Cartwright . . .
  MICHAEL, KEN, TESSA *and* LORRAINE *scream with laughter.*
FRANK. I think that's everybody. Oh. Hugh.
MRS CARTWRIGHT. What about Katherine? I've been looking forward to meeting her again.
  FRANK *looks around, realising* KATHERINE *isn't there.*

6. Exterior. London Street. Day.

A traffic jam. KATHERINE *and* HUGH *are in her car. They are in a side street thirty yards from a main road. They are dressed for a party. There's no visible reason for the delay.*

KATHERINE. Oh for God's sake. Let's have a shufti.
  They get out and walk towards the main road.

7. Exterior. London Street. Day.

They walk past jammed traffic and discover a small crowd surrounding the scene of an accident. An ambulance is arriving. Two police cars are already there.

The van we saw earlier is now on the side of the road, its back doors are open and a crate has spilled out on to the street.
The TWO MEN *from the van are loading the contents of the crate quickly back into the van. The lid of the crate is damaged and what looks like a machine gun is momentarily visible to them both.*
KATZ *is being sick.*
The police are re-starting the traffic.
KATZ *looks at* HUGH *looking at him as he wipes his mouth and spits.*
KATHERINE *approaches* KATZ.

KATHERINE. What happened?
KATZ. Take a walk lady.
The ambulance arrives.
A stretcher with a covered body is put into the ambulance.
An ASIAN WOMAN *in shock goes with the stretcher.*
They watch. KATHERINE *sees the van driving away.*
KATHERINE. Hey, Hugh – remember this. D500 FYE.

8. Exterior. London Street. Day.

The van has gone completely. The ambulance leaves.
Three of the COPS *from the two patrol cars are talking together. One of them is female. She is* WPC OSMAN.
The fourth is supervising the flow of traffic which is now fine.
He rejoins his colleagues. They all confer.
A young man turns to HUGH.

YOUNG MAN. All over, hit and run, little boy dead.
HUGH. Was it the van?
YOUNG MAN. What van?
KATHERINE. There was a blue van, there was a crate in the road.
The YOUNG MAN *leaves, not interested.*
YOUNG MAN. I dunno love, I got here too late.
HUGH goes to people nearby.
HUGH. Did you see what happened? Excuse me did you see what happened?
They shake their heads.
KATHERINE. C'mon, Hugh.

9. Interior. Fetter Court. Day.

The party continues but is more muted.
The jazz band is playing mood music, people are dancing.
KATHERINE *and* HUGH *are sitting at her desk by a telephone.* MICHAEL KHAN *is talking to* HUGH.

FRANK *approaches them.*

FRANK. As someone once said, shall we dance? After all, this is a party.
FRANK and KATHERINE *dance, close.*

KATHERINE. Congratulations.

FRANK. Thank you, and thank you for your support, I'll always wear it. I've only been a silk for an hour. I haven't been asked to do their bidding.

KATHERINE. Just think of me when you're sitting with the Attorney General in the Garrick.

FRANK. Who were you phoning? Don't you ever stop working?

KATHERINE. I'm sorry, I didn't want to spoil your day. Hugh and I were held up by an accident. A little boy was run over, killed.
They stop dancing.
The band goes into upbeat music again.
The telephone rings on KATHERINE's *desk.* HUGH *answers it.*
KEN *drags* LORRAINE *up to dance.*
TESSA *drags* ALETHEA *up to dance.*
As KATHERINE *answers her telephone, making notes as she does,*
MICHAEL KHAN *joins* FRANK.

MICHAEL KHAN (*to* FRANK). Katherine's convinced she saw a crate full of kalashnikovs.

FRANK. What? (*He looks over at* KATHERINE, *who has taken the phone.*)

KHAN. Makes a change from little green men.

10. Interior. Fetter Court. Day.

The party is ending, people are leaving.
HUGH, FRANK *and* KATHERINE *sit quietly apart from the others.*

KATHERINE. The phone call was a journalist friend. He's got a mate in the police to ring vehicle licensing at Swansea. The van number belongs to the Metropolitan Police.
A COUPLE *of people come over to say goodbye to* FRANK.

FRANK. Thanks for coming, sweet of you.
The COUPLE *go.*
BINGHAM *joins them.*
So does KEN GORDON.

HUGH. I know what I saw, I know what kalashnikovs look like.

KATHERINE. What were they doing in a van in the middle of a London street? Hit and run, a little boy died. But what happened? I mean you know me, I think our policemen are wonderful.

HUGH. And there was this American guy being sick.

BINGHAM. How do you know he was American?

KEN GORDON. He was being sick with an American accent. An American, eh? CIA. You know what CIA stands for, don't you?

BINGHAM. Just about anything these days.

KEN and BINGHAM laugh.

KEN GORDON. I was going to say Caught in The Act but yours is funnier, James.

KEN and BINGHAM laugh again.

HUGH and KATHERINE can't bear this.

There is silence.

FRANK. Well, look, OK, why not do the obvious thing? Call the press office at Scotland Yard and ask them. See what they say.

HUGH takes this as an insult.

KATHERINE collects her bag.

KATHERINE. Hugh, I'll drop you off, eh? Frank, congratulations. I'm chuffed for you.

HUGH and KATHERINE leave.

KEN GORDON shakes his head.

KEN. Listen I know I'm a bit pissed but . . . I mean: Hugh's one thing, but how can she get to her age and do what she's done, and achieve what she's achieved and still believe all this conspiracy stuff? It's juvenile. She'll get the loony left a bad name.

FRANK looks angry.

11. Interior. Newspaper office. Day.

JOHN WOODHAM *is reading their affidavit.*
KATHERINE *is searching through a bulging folder.*
He finishes reading.

KATHERINE. Can you do something with it? Run a little story?

WOODHAM looks doubtful.

WOODHAM. Kalashnikovs on the streets of England aren't exactly unheard of these days.

KATHERINE. Not a crateful.

WOODHAM nods.

WOODHAM. If I get a quiet day next week I'll do half a column, seeing as it's you.

KATHERINE. Say we're asking for other eye witnesses, will you?

WOODHAM nods.

Listen, if you get a quiet day next week come to my Peace Camp case. Five women and three Japanese Buddhist monks, no?

WOODHAM *would like to really, but –*

WOODHAM. Peace Camp stories really are last week's news.

KATHERINE. Can I borrow this?

WOODHAM. (*surprised*). Sure, ehm, twenty-four hours.

KATHERINE *closes the folder; it's six inches thick and marked* CIA.

KATHERINE. Thanks. See you.

WOODHAM. Yeh, take care, Katherine. How's your sex life?

KATHERINE. Celibacy, John. Get into it.

WOODHAM. I was into it for twelve years. We called it marriage in those days.

KATHERINE *laughs as she goes.*

I don't believe you.

12. Interior. Katherine's flat. Night.

KATHERINE *is in bed with the folder.*

She finds a photograph of KATZ. *She reads the caption.* KATHERINE *finds an asterisk and a note. She reads.*

KATHERINE (*reading*). Believed to be a member of the so-called Secret Team.

She pulls over the telephone and lifts off the receiver. There's no dialling tone but she doesn't notice. She's looking up JOHN WOODHAM's *number in her book. She starts to dial. She notices. She tries to get a dialling tone. Nothing. She replaces the receiver. She lifts it again. Nothing.*

KATHERINE *is just beginning to suspect mischief when she notices her telephone isn't plugged in. She plugs it in, smiling. The dialling tone arrives. She dials.*

JOHN WOODHAM *answers.*

KATHERINE. John, Katherine, hi listen: I think you're going to want to run that story – the guy we saw was Geoffrey Katz. CIA, formerly ex Deputy Station Tehran, now believed to be a member of the Secret Team. What's the Secret Team?

13. Exterior. Curzon Street. Early morning.

BILL TURNER *arrives outside an anonymous office block. There is no name on the door.*

Video cameras scan the street.

He stares up at the curtained windows.

Cameras watch him as he moves about the street.

He takes a stone from his pocket and hurls it at a camera, missing. He throws his A to Z at the camera. He waits.

A police car enters the street quickly and pulls up beside him.

BILL *starts taking his clothes off.*

Two uniformed POLICE CONSTABLES *get out of the car and approach him.*

FIRST PC. Can I ask you what you think you're doing?

BILL TURNER. Piss off.

FIRST PC. Come on, I want you to move on.

BILL TURNER. Piss off. Don't touch me.

FIRST PC *puts his hand on* BILL *to restrain him.*

You touched me, that's assault. (*To the* SECOND PC) You're my witness, he's assaulting me. Right: I'm arresting you.

FIRST PC. Come on.

They both try to grab him. He struggles.

BILL TURNER. Right, you're both under arrest.

FIRST PC. Bloody fruitcake.

BILL *elbows the* FIRST PC *on the nose. Blood pours out.*

The THE SECOND PC *draws his truncheon.*

14. Interior. Fetter Court. Day.

It's quiet.

JAMES BINGHAM *is at his desk talking to* FRANK CARTWRIGHT. KEN GORDON *listens in from his desk, drinking tea.*

BINGHAM. I'm a forty-four year old man. For twenty years I had my own little business, an electrical sub-contractor. I'm one of the sparrows who get the crumbs when they divide up big contracts, mainly defence contracts. Very small beer but it's a good living. I vote Tory. I'm perfectly clear that I live in the best country in the world. I'm a blood donor.

FRANK *is chuckling.*

I'm involved in the Boy Scout movement and apparently I not only do not think that's remotely funny but I don't even know anybody who would think it was funny.

FRANK. I don't like you very much.

BINGHAM. One day I'm on some trivial defence job and I'm suddenly ordered off-site. My contract is torn up because my work isn't up to scratch.

FRANK. Serves you right, you're a toad eater.

BINGHAM. My business goes bust. The building society repossesses the house. Finance company tows away the Volvo. I finally discover the explanation for all my troubles. I'm the victim of a conspiracy.

FRANK. Ah, that one, lot of it about. Why?

BINGHAM. Because there's no other explanation. I write to my MP; she's no use. I write long letters to anybody I can think of; nobody's interested. Except the people watching me from

their cars, tapping my telephone when I had one and
interfering with my mail.

KEN GORDON. Oh, oh.

BINGHAM. Finally after a bit of striptease in Mayfair I apparently
go berserk in a Chelmsford police station in front of a small
but attentive crowd of police . . .

FRANK and KEN are laughing.

. . . witnesses and am now up on charges of wasting police
time, actual bodily harm on two police officers, causing fifteen
hundred quids worth of damage to police vehicles and
property, what do you think?

Even BINGHAM has to chuckle.

Why *me*?

15. Interior. Fetter Court. Day.

*On the stairs BILL TURNER and his solicitor JOHN SHANDLY ascend in
step. BILL TURNER looks determined with jaw jutting and eyes staring.*

16. Interior. Fetter Court. Day.

In a conference room BINGHAM, TURNER, SHANDLY.
SHANDLY *is a fifty-year-old man who has represented TURNER for years.*
BILL TURNER *is looking at the posters on the wall.*

BINGHAM. Mr Turner, do you mind if I ask you this? When you
went to Curzon Street and stood outside that building –

BILL TURNER. MI5 Headquarters.

BINGHAM. Yes, why did you take all your clothes off?

BILL TURNER. That was my low point, Mr Bingham. I felt like I
was at rock bottom you know; I felt here I am, I'm nothing,
you've reduced me to nothing, what next. What else can you
take away? And of course I got my answer within the hour,
didn't I? All I've got left is my liberty.

JOHN SHANDLY. I don't really think there's much point in
dwelling on that part of the story. The police are not charging
Bill with indecent exposure or with anything else he says
happened in that particular street. In fact they say they know
nothing about you being in that street, they're solely interested
in events after you arrived –

BILL TURNER *bristles.*

JOHN SHANDLY. – were *brought* to Lansdowne Road Police Station.

BILL TURNER. Well obviously they would deny it; they're part of
the conspiracy against me.

JOHN SHANDLY. Yes, but, Bill, all I'm saying is let's not complicate things. You're charged with actual bodily harm, with attacking policemen. The reason I thought Mr Bingham would be a suitable barrister is that this chambers specialises in that sort of difficulty. But I don't honestly see the helpfulness of the other business.

BINGHAM. The reason I asked, Mr Shandly, is that I feel that until I understand this conspiracy business I can't get hold of Mr Turner as a whole.

BILL TURNER. Quite right.

JOHN SHANDLY. Well can we at least begin with the strictly relevant information?

BINGHAM. Alright. Let's go back to Curzon Street.

JOHN SHANDLY *sighs*.

You'd been drinking.

BILL TURNER. Yes, I was drunk as a monkey in fact.

BINGHAM. But you have a clear memory of what happened after you were arrested?

BILL TURNER. I was driven out of London back to Essex to a police station and I was assaulted by police officers.

BINGHAM. Well there must be more to it than – ?

BILL TURNER. Let me ask you a question, Mr Bingham. Do you vote Conservative, I mean habitually?

BINGHAM. No. Not at all in fact.

TURNER. No I didn't think you did. Do you believe in the profit motive? Is it what makes the world go round as far as you can see?

BINGHAM. No.

BILL TURNER. No. Were you glad when we beat the Argies?

BINGHAM. No, I can't say I was 'glad' about that episode.

SHANDLY *rubs his eyes*.

BILL TURNER. No, fair enough, would you say you believed in this country?

BINGHAM. Believed in it?

BILL TURNER. Love it? Do you love this country?

SHANDLY *is in despair*.

JOHN SHANDLY. Bill, I've explained about the Radical Bar.

BINGHAM. Yes. I do love this country.

BILL TURNER. What do you love? Answer me straight.

BINGHAM. I love my friends, I love the countryside, English literature, cream teas, White Christmases.

BILL TURNER. No, balls to that, excuse my French. Do you love this country, not the promised land, but do you believe we've got it basically right here? That we do a lot of things better than a lot of other people?

BINGHAM. Such as?

BILL TURNER. For example, fair play. Do you believe in good old British fair play?

BINGHAM. I believe a lot of people believe in it.

BILL TURNER. You're a slippery customer. John said you would be.
SHANDLY *goes red.*

JOHN SHANDLY. Well . . .

BILL TURNER. Let me tell you what I think. (*He leans forward.*) It's all a load of shit. Answer me one more question. Do you believe the British legal system can be relied on to give me justice?

There is a pause.

BINGHAM. No.

At first TURNER *is a little disappointed. Then he nods to himself and seems quite surprisedly content with this reply. He sits back and accepts his fate.*

BILL TURNER. I place myself entirely in your hands, Mr Bingham. Tell me what to do and I'll do it, with one proviso. I want the whole story told in court.

BINGHAM. The court can only hear evidence which bears directly on the charges. I think you'll have to accept that it would be wise to plead guilty to the charges and then let me bring out the rest of the story in mitigation.

BILL TURNER. As long as you believe me, Mr Bingham.

BINGHAM. Well, as it happens yes, I do. It occurs to me, Mr Turner, that there must be a possibility that what we are dealing with here is not a conspiracy.

BILL TURNER *looks hostile.*

But that somebody somewhere might have made a ghastly mistake.

BILL TURNER. Who?

17. Interior. Curzon House. Day.

A darkened room. A microfilm viewer.

DAVID VALENTINE, *fifty, sits winding a microfilm of a newspaper. He finds the article he wants, he zooms in on it; it is headled* 'The Strange Case of the Hit and Run'. *It runs to half a page and features a sub-heading:*

'Katz Eyed'.

And the now-familiar photograph of GEOFFREY KATZ.

VALENTINE *reads, he switches off the machine.*

18. Interior. Fetter Court. Day.

A TELECOM ENGINEER *is reassembling the telephone on* HUGH's *desk.*

KATHERINE *is pinning a blow-up of* JOHN WOODHAM's *article on to the wall in a prominent place.*

KEN GORDON *is pretending not to notice.*

BINGHAM *is working at his desk.*

TELECOM ENGINEER. Not much wrong there either.

LORRAINE. Well I'm telling you there's a fault.

TELECOM ENGINEER. I'm not doubting it, but intermittent faults are tricky. Can I . . .?

He's picking up the telephone on KATHERINE's *desk.*

FRANK *arrives from the street. He pauses to admire* KATHERINE's *handiwork.*

KATHERINE. Help yourself.

The ENGINEER *has the back off* KATHERINE's *telephone.*

FRANK. Great stuff.

KATHERINE. Ta.

FRANK *speaks confidentially to* KATHERINE.

FRANK. Making any progress?

KATHERINE. Not yet.

ENGINEER *re-assembles* KATHERINE's *telephone.*

LORRAINE. Well?

TELECOM ENGINEER. Not yet.

He works on another telephone.

LORRAINE. I dunno. How come it takes three days to get you round here? Honestly: you make two billion quid a year out of us.

TELECOM ENGINEER. I know.

MICHAEL KHAN. Lorraine, he doesn't own Telecom, he's a worker.

LORRAINE. Michael, will you leave this to me? I know what he is. It's bloody inconvenient.

LORRAINE *heads back to her desk.*

TELECOM ENGINEER. Well I have actually got a few shares.

KATHERINE. Lorraine, I'm off in a minute. I'm in Ipswich tomorrow. Peace Camp case. I'll be back as quick as I can – John Woodham's got another witness.

LORRAINE. Good luck.

TELECOM ENGINEER. Can I try this one, please?

ENGINEER *picks up* BINGHAM's *telephone.* BINGHAM *looks up and nods absent-mindedly. He double-takes, he looks up again, he sees and hears a small commotion and looks over to the clerks' desks.*

He blinks, BILL TURNER *is there.* BILL TURNER *has just seen* BINGHAM *and is coming over.*

LORRAINE *is following him.*

LORRAINE. Look, I'm sorry, but . . .

BILL TURNER. It's alright, dear, I see him.

He comes over to BINGHAM's *desk followed by* LORRAINE.

BINGHAM's *aghast.*

Mr Bingham, I've been doing some research about what you said: mistakes. Mistakes *have* been made.

LORRAINE. James, I'm sorry –

BINGHAM. It's alright, Lorraine, I'll explain.

LORRAINE (*as she goes back to her desk*). OK.

BINGHAM. Katherine, could you . . .?

KATHERINE. Sorry, James. Bye. (*She leaves.*)

FRANK *sees* BINGHAM's *problem and sits in as a witness to the conversation.*

BINGHAM. The fact is, Mr Turner –

BILL TURNER. Bill.

BINGHAM. Bill. The fact is, Bill, I'm not allowed to talk to you except in the presence of your solicitor. You have to talk to him first and he'll arrange a –

BILL TURNER. I've sacked him, he was useless. I'll get another one, but you'll continue with the case. I'm hanging on to you, you've got the right attitude. Read this. (*He hands over a file of press cuttings.*) All cases of mistakes being made, mistaken identity. There was one woman sacked from her job and it turned out she had the same name and similar national insurance number to one of these, you know, one of these bitches in CND, bloody terrorist. It's all in here. Excuse my French, won't you?

FRANK *hates him.*

BINGHAM. Well look I'll read it, I promise.

BILL TURNER. And I've finally had a reply from the Prime Minister.

BINGHAM. Prime Minister?

BILL TURNER. Well shall I say the Prime Minister's office? (*He reads the letter.*) 'Dear Mr Turner, thank you for your letter. I regret to inform you that this is not a matter with which the Prime Minister can become personally involved. She suggests you take it up with your Member of Parliament'. As if I haven't. 'Yours sincerely'. Thirty-six words. In my opinion the Prime Minister hadn't even read my letter. It doesn't end here, I refuse to lay down and die. I will make my presence felt directly in Downing Street. What I need is publicity.

BINGHAM. Please don't, Bill, you're on bail.

BILL TURNER *starts to look very emotional. He's in turmoil.*

BILL TURNER. I've always behaved myself, Mr Bingham; it's against my beliefs to act like a hooligan.

The whole room is now watching, including the ENGINEER.

TURNER *pulls himself together.*

OK, I'll do it the proper way, due process of law. Recommend another solicitor.

BINGHAM. That's not really the correct thing . . .

BILL TURNER *looks desperate.*

BINGHAM *is desperate.*

FRANK *helps. He rummages on his desk, picks up a compliments slip.*

FRANK. Here. She's good.

BILL TURNER, *reading with lips still quivering.*

BILL TURNER. Helen Robinson. Is she . . . ?

FRANK. She's a Communist.

BILL TURNER. Good. I need hardliners if I'm taking on the secret state. I'll go now. (*He goes.*)

There's a pause.

FRANK. You're going to put this maniac into the witness box?

BINGHAM *sighs. He flicks through the file.*

BINGHAM. It *is* amazing how many people believe they're being watched by . . . you know, the powers that be, MI5 tapping their phones, CIA interfering with their milk deliveries. I mean I know it doesn't happen, but . . .

He looks at the news cutting above KATHERINE's *desk.*

19. Interior. Crown Court. Day.

Court room. INSPECTOR MADDEN *is in the box. Five* WOMEN *and three Buddhist* MONKS *are in the dock.* MR JUSTICE CLOUGH *is on the bench.* KATHERINE HUGHES *is cross-examining.*

KATHERINE. So on March 6th last at 4 a.m., yourself and forty-three officers of the Thames Valley constabulary went to this nuclear air base and apprehended my clients as they were, you allege, preparing to attack and breach the perimeter security fence?

INSPECTOR. Yes.

KATHERINE. Why?

INSPECTOR. I'm sorry, Madam, are you asking me why we apprehended them?

KATHERINE. Why did you go? Why weren't you at home tucked up in bed, instead of roaming the countryside?

INSPECTOR. I'm sure we'd all prefer to be tucked up in bed at 4 a.m. on a frosty morning.

KATHERINE. Why weren't you then? Why were forty-four of you careering around the countryside in a big bus?

INSPECTOR. I'm tempted to answer 'because you can't fit forty-four men in a little bus'.

There is laughter. Someone translates for the Japanese MONKS: *they laugh.*

KATHERINE. Your Honour, I'd like you to instruct the witness to answer my question.

MR JUSTICE CLOUGH. I'm not sure any of us knows what your question is, Miss Hughes.

KATHERINE. Inspector Madden, how did you come to pick on that spot at that time? If, as you say my clients were conspiring together to damage the fence, how did you know they were conspiring?

INSPECTOR. We knew because we saw them doing it.

KATHERINE. How did you know they were going to be there? Are the forty-four of you some sort of flying anti-pickets? Are you condemned to patrol the back roads at night forever and ever for some sins you've committed in another life? Or did you consult your horoscope perhaps? 'Be careful with money today, oh and by the way if you are at West Markham Airbase at 4 a.m. tomorrow morning you'll get a nice surprise'?
There is laughter in the court.

INSPECTOR. Information was received.

KATHERINE. From?
There is silence. There are jeers from the public gallery. There are a lot of women supporting the defendants.

INSPECTOR. Your honour, this is obviously not relevant.

MR JUSTICE CLOUGH. Allow me to decide that.
There are cheers from the public gallery.

MR JUSTICE CLOUGH. Be quiet. The witness will answer.

INSPECTOR. I don't think I can give the court an accurate answer.

KATHERINE. Why not? You commanded this police operation. You uncovered this dreadful conspiracy. How? Who told you about it?

INSPECTOR. The conspiracy . . . the evidence for the conspiracy has already been given. The monks for instance have admitted discussing the break-in in advance.

KATHERINE. That's already been dealt with, Inspector; the Japanese monks don't speak very good English, if you ask them a question they tend to nod.

INSPECTOR. Nevertheless they gave statements.

KATHERINE. Nevertheless nothing. We're not talking about evidence gathered *afterwards*, we're talking about how you knew how to be there at 4 a.m. with your dogs, and your sticks, and all the other paraphernalia of the paranoid state. Did your information come from inside your force?

INSPECTOR. I'm not in a position to say.
There is more noise on the public benches.

KATHERINE. Inspector, I know I'm asking you to do something
you may find goes against the grain.

PROSECUTING COUNSEL *gets to his feet.*

PROSECUTING COUNSEL. I object, your Honour. Counsel for
defence is insulting the witness by suggesting he might not tell
the truth.

There is a pause. There is laughter in the court.

KATHERINE. Your Honour, it hadn't occurred to me to suggest
that, but I thank my learned friend for putting me on my
guard.

There is more laughter in court.

MR JUSTICE CLOUGH. Don't go too far please, Miss Hughes.

KATHERINE. Inspector Madden, was your information the result
of surveillance by the security services?

There is a pause.

A phone tap? If so, then you presumably believed you were
being given evidence of a conspiracy. Why didn't you arrest
my clients at that point?

There is another pause.

Instead of waiting.

There is another pause.

There can really only be two explanations. Either you knew
there was no conspiracy or else you believed there was but
couldn't say so because your only evidence had been gathered
by means which you were worried might actually be illegal. Is
that not so?

INSPECTOR. Absolutely not.

KATHERINE. And if you believe the phone tapping was an illegal
or quasi-legal abuse of my clients' civil rights then no doubt
you've already been down to MI5 and told them to watch it or
you'll be round to feel a few collars, yes, have you? Have you
been round to Curzon Street and asked them what they think
they're playing at, bugging the telephones of ordinary British
women with whose politics they happen to disagree?

20. Interior. Crown Court building. Day.

In the canteen. KATHERINE, *a* SOLICITOR, *and the* DEFENDANTS *sit
together drinking tea. At the other end of the canteen sit police constables*
COOPER *and* McMILLAN *and* INSPECTOR MADDEN.

INSPECTOR. Have you noticed how they grin all the time?

COOPER. What are Buddhists anyway? I mean when they're not
over here laying down in front of missile launchers. Is it
Allah?

INSPECTOR. You wasn't paying attention to Miss Hughes
yesterday, which is a pity 'cos she was paying a lot of attention
to you. It's not all peace and love and butter wouldn't melt in
their mouths.

COOPER *looking at his bandaged thumb.*

COOPER. Oh yeh, that's obvious. But I mean, is it all part of
Indian Buddhism, vegetable curry and all that?

INSPECTOR. It's all reincarnation, isn't it?

McMILLAN. Oh my wife's one then; she believes all that.

INSPECTOR. What?

McMILLAN. Yeh, she reckons we've all been here before and we'll
all be back again. I told her: you do what you like but don't
expect to find me here. I said if I was you I'd try and get a
decent pair of tits next time an all.

He says this very loudly, the WOMEN *all look across. Several* WOMEN
mutter, quietly, 'pig'.

An USHER *hurries in.*

USHER. Ladies, could you please come back into court
immediately, the jury's on its way back?

They all get up and leave including the INSPECTOR. McMILLAN *and*
COOPER *follow on at leisure.*

21. Interior. Crown Court building. Day.

In the court room the JURY *has just sat down, the room is crowded and
hushed.* MR JUSTICE CLOUGH *comes back in, he sits.*

CLERK. Would the defendants please go into the dock?

All eight DEFENDANTS *walk into the dock.*

MR JUSTICE CLOUGH. Will you please tell the Japanese gentlemen
that the jury is now going to deliver its verdict?

The INTERPRETER *does so. The* MONKS *smile and nod. One of them
speaks.*

INTERPRETER. He says 'thank you', Your Honour.

MR JUSTICE CLOUGH. Yes, thank you. Now.

22. Interior. Crown Court building. Day.

Corridor outside the court room. COOPER *and* McMILLAN *sit.*

COOPER. What do you think?

MCMILLAN. What? The lies that's been told in there this week,
they'll get off, won't they? Just 'ordinary people', aren't they?
What right have *we* to stop them conspiring to cause criminal
damage on crown property? If their consciences tell them
that's what they should do, I mean: who the fuck are *we*?

A cheer goes up in the court, COOPER *and* McMILLAN *pull on their hats.*

MCMILLAN. Would you bloody credit it, eh?

The doors open from the court. Two or three of the PUBLIC *rush out into the street excited.* INSPECTOR MADDEN *comes out, dischuffed.*

MCMILLAN. Juries; I'd do away with them.

INSPECTOR. Unbelievable. The jury *convicted* them. The judge goes and gives them twenty-one days suspended sentences. Enough to make a glass eye cry.

23. Exterior. English countryside. Dusk.

KATHERINE *is driving her car home and listening to loud music.*
KATHERINE *grins. She's happy.*

KATHERINE. Wallop. Take that. Five acquittals!

She sees something ahead, above. She stops the car.

24. Exterior. English countryside. Dusk.

KATHERINE *stands watching a large flock of starlings, grouping and regrouping as they sweep back and forwards across the sky, like images of violence on a screen.*
She suddenly feels cold. Her elation has gone.
Clouds are building up in the darkening sky.
She has a road map in her hand, she consults it, not quite sure of her bearings. She looks up to identify landmarks. She notices a van slowly approaching half a mile away.

25. Exterior. English countryside. Dusk.

KATHERINE *is driving.*
The van overtakes at speed on the narrow road and disappears round a bend.

26. Exterior. English countryside. Dusk.

KATHERINE *reaches a farmyard. She parks on the road and gets out.*
One or two chickens are about but no people, no lights, no vehicles. She's about to approach the house.
The van reappears and rams her car head on. She watches in stunned fear and silence as it rams it twice more, moving it ten yards along the road.
Three men in combat gear and balaclavas appear.
She starts to run. They pick her up and duck her in a horse trough.
Drenched and screaming she's thrown into manure. They beat her across

the back and legs with rubber truncheons. They urinate on her.
They go back to their van and drive away.

27. Interior. Street door. Katherine's house. Day.

TESSA *opens the street door to* FRANK *and they go upstairs.*

TESSA. The doctor's just gone. Nothing's broken, but a lot of
   bruising.

28. Interior. Katherine's flat. Day.

The curtains are closed.
FRANK *and* TESSA *go into her bedroom, passing* JOHN WOODHAM *who
is sitting in the lounge.*
KATHERINE *is in bed,* LORRAINE *is sitting with her, her eyes red from
crying.*
FRANK *sits on the bed in silence.*

KATHERINE. Please don't tell anybody else. I don't want anyone
   else to know yet.
FRANK. Katherine, you should tell the police.
   KATHERINE *shakes her head, it's obvious from their reactions that*
   LORRAINE *and* TESSA *have been through this with her already.*
KATHERINE. No. Not them. Why me?
   Everybody laughs.
   Give me a kiss, Frank.

29. Exterior. A London pub. Day.

WOODHAM *sits at a garden table.*
WPC OSMAN *joins him. She wears a car coat over her uniform.*
WOODHAM'*s surprised to realise she's a cop.*
OSMAN. Now you know why I have to be careful.
   Look, they were right, there was a van, and it was a police van.
   It killed that little boy, I'm certain. I was on the scene within
   minutes, there was no sign of any other vehicle, no other skid
   marks, no other debris, nothing. This is all wrong.
   OSMAN'*s not going to say any more unless she is asked.*
   WOODHAM *is making notes.*
WOODHAM. Were the drivers policemen?
OSMAN. Yes, I know they were, they showed us their warrant
   cards. Anyway I knew one of them by sight.
WOODHAM. What about the guy who was being sick, the
   American?
OSMAN. No idea; he'd crapped himself that's all I know.

There is a pause.

WOODHAM. The weapons.

OSMAN. Kalashnikovs, nightsights.

WOODHAM. Who's keeping it quiet?

OSMAN. I don't know. Somebody very senior, because the pressure we're under to shut up is nobody's business. Official Secrets Act, old pals act, you name it, us four are getting it chucked at us. It's sickened me and I'm not the only one. But it's wrong.

She starts to become emotional.

I for one would like to know why that little boy was run over, and I'm not a hero, and I'm not looking for trouble, but I'm not going to help protect the people responsible. I've got a five-year-old myself.

WOODHAM. It would really help if I knew who those cops were.

There is a pause.

OSMAN. Anti-terrorist squad.

WOODHAM. You said someone very senior. Bob Fine?

OSMAN *shakes her head.*

OSMAN. I find it hard to believe. If he'd had officers under him who'd done something like this he'd be the first to do something about it. Commander Fine . . . I mean he's a legend.

30. Interior. Curzon House. Day.

VALENTINE'*s office.*
His SECRETARY *speaks to him by intercom.*

SECRETARY'S VOICE. David, it's Commander Fine again.

VALENTINE. Tell him I've gone on holiday.

VALENTINE *types the name* KATHERINE HUGHES *into his computer terminal and waits.*
KATHERINE'*s file comes up on the screen.*

31. Interior. Katherine's flat. Night.

KATHERINE *is in a dressing gown on the settee, very withdrawn.*
WOODHAM *is talking to her.*
The local television news is on, soundlessly.

WOODHAM. The Secret Team is a state within a state. Past or present members of the CIA, depending on your point of view, operating huge drugs and arm smuggling businesses in order to finance, well who knows what, arms to the Contras, but what else?

KATHERINE. Is there an English branch of this Secret Team?
WOODHAM *shrugs*.

KATHERINE. Did they offer any explanation for the sudden
resignation of Bob Fine?

WOODHAM. A spokesman in the Metropolitan Police expressed
his regret. Resignation of one of the forces most experienced
officers. Offers of posts on the board of several companies.
Latest in a string of top men being lost to the private
sector . . . Blah, Blah . . .
KATHERINE *nods*.

WOODHAM. How are you?

KATHERINE. I'm OK.
But KATHERINE *is lifeless*.

WOODHAM. Katherine, I don't honestly feel that having got this
far I can let this drop. But there's no longer any compelling
reason why you shouldn't take a very remote back seat.

KATHERINE. No. No back seat.

32. Exterior. English countryside. Dusk.

KATHERINE *is at the wheel of her car. She sees a van overtake her at
speed on the narrow road and disappear round the bend.*

33. Interior. Katherine's flat. Night.

KATHERINE *is with* WOODHAM.

KATHERINE. I want to get as much of this public as soon as
possible.

34. Interior. Katherine's flat. Night.

Five or six JOURNALISTS.

KATHERINE. We now have information from a witness within the
Metropolitan Police that the vehicle which killed five-year-old
Asif Khadri was a Metropolitan Police van being driven by
out-of-uniform officers of the anti-terrorist squad.

35. Exterior. In Tyler's car. Night.

TYLER *is driving.* KATZ *is reading* WOODHAM'*s article.*

KATZ. 'It is now positively established that the third man at the
scene of the accident that killed five-year-old Asif Khadri, the
former or serving CIA officer Geoffrey Katz, was indicted by a

Federal Grand Jury in New York in August 1982 on charges
of running arms shipments to Middle East terrorist
organisations.' Aw shucks. I didn't do it all alone. My buddies
helped me.

They arrive at the gates of a US Airforce base.

36. Interior. Room on US Airforce base. Night.

TYLER *reads* WOODHAM's *article as* KATZ *changes his clothes.*

TYLER. Were you really in Chile in '73?

KATZ. He say that?

TYLER *(reading)*. 'Acted in the events leading to the overthrow
and murder of the democratically elected President Salvador
Allende'.

KATZ. You sound surprised.

TYLER *(smiling)*. You don't look old enough, Geoffrey.

KATZ *now dressed in the uniform of a US Airforce colonel.*

KATZ. Be seeing you. Sorry to leave you to clean up the mess.

TYLER. No problem. I'm taking care of it.

37. Exterior. Tyler's car. Night.

Outside the base. TYLER *watches a military plane taking off. He drives
away reaching for his cellular phone. He dials a number.*

TYLER. Michael Crowe, please.

38. Interior. Valentine's flat. Night.

VALENTINE *watches a late night news and current affairs programme,
while consuming tumblers full of scotch.*
*The television shows a drawing of irate Members of Parliament in the
Chamber. We hear rowdy noise on the backbenches.*

MINISTER. I can assure the house that if it were shown . . . that
there was any substance to these allegations. *(He is drowned out
by the jeers from the backbenches.)* Then the journalists in question
have a duty to place any evidence they have in the hands of
the police.
There is derisive laughter from Labour benches.
The picture cuts to MICHAEL CROWE *live in the studio. This sobers*
VALENTINE *up a bit.*

INTERVIEWER. That was the Home Secretary answering questions
about suspected MI5 involvement in the Khadri case following
reports in today's newspapers. With me now is an

acknowledged expert and author on security matters, Harry
Ollerton. Harry Ollerton, do you give *any* credence to this
theory, that the CIA and the Metropolitan Police could be
involved in arms smuggling?

OLLERTON. I think it's possible. Until a year or two ago I'd have
said 'no, utterly non-feasible'. But recent developments inside
the security community have changed my thinking. Frankly,
almost anything is now believable.

INTERVIEWER. What sort of development?

OLLERTON. What I understand is this: there is a group inside
MI5 – a small but influential group, extremely patriotic, let it
be said, *extremely* patriotic – led by a charismatic senior officer
whom I obviously cannot name, who has allowed his ideology
to lead them into some very murky operational areas.

INTERVIEWER. Can you tell us more about this officer?

OLLERTON. I really can't. Except to say –. You see, what people
don't understand at all well are the stresses and strains these
men live with day in, day out – is it any wonder if occasionally
an element of instability creeps in?

VALENTINE. Bastards.

39. Interior. Curzon House. Night.

VALENTINE's *office.*
He types into his computer terminal. On his screen appear the words
'Sorry. The registry is closed'.

40. Interior. Curzon House. Night.

Four BIG MEN, *led by* TYLER, *walk purposefully along a corridor.*

41. Interior. Curzon House. Night.

VALENTINE's *office.*
He sits waiting.
A knock. He ignores it.
A key is put into the lock and turned. TYLER *comes in with his* MEN.
They take hold of VALENTINE.

42. Interior. Curzon House. Night.

TYLER *and his* MEN *march* VALENTINE *down a corridor and into a*
waiting lift.

43. Interior. Curzon House. Night.

In the lift, silence as they descend.

VALENTINE. I want to talk to the Director.
  The lift bottoms, they march him out.

44. Exterior. Curzon Street. Night.

VALENTINE *is politely escorted out of the front door, and left without a word on the street.*
He looks up to see the starlings flocking and chattering overhead.

45. Interior. A gentleman's club. Day.

A large indoor swimming pool, empty except for SIR CHARLES BINGHAM *who is thrashing his way through his daily five lengths.*
JAMES *arrives, clothed.*
He waits.

BINGHAM. Dad.
  SIR CHARLES *sees him and paddles over.*
SIR CHARLES. James, not coming in?
BINGHAM. I'm due back in court in half an hour.
SIR CHARLES. Not staying for lunch then?
BINGHAM. Thanks all the same, Dad. Well?
SIR CHARLES. Ah yes. They weren't terribly keen to be helpful, even for an old friend. You certainly picked your moment to ask a favour, what with your friend the harpy banging on to all and sundry about Scotland Yard selling Chieftan tanks to the ayatollahs. Are you still telling me that woman's got all her marbles?
BINGHAM. There's no connection. It's a simple question. Are they sure they haven't made a mistake and got the wrong Bill Turner?
SIR CHARLES. But say the answer was 'yes'. You see, from their point of view, yet another opportunity for somebody to get up a story in the papers poking MI5 in the eye with a burnt stick. More opposition MPs sinking their yellow teeth into the poor old Home Secretary's legs.
BINGHAM. The answer was 'no' then?
SIR CHARLES. I'm promised this is definitely kosher, James. There's no mistake. Your client failed a routine security vetting.
  BINGHAM *can't see this being true.*
BINGHAM. Did they say why, for God's sake?

SIR CHARLES. Now, James, you asked me to ask a simple question, the answer was 'no'. You didn't ask me to ask, and I wouldn't have agreed to ask, any supplementaries. It's supposed to be a bloody secret service you know, though you wouldn't know it these days.

He submerges in the pool.

46. Exterior. English countryside. Dusk.

KATHERINE *turns and sees her car being rammed and shunted along the road by the van.*

Overlay sound of a telephone ringing.

47. Interior. Katherine's flat. Night.

The telephone is ringing.

KATHERINE *alone, all the lights are on. She's sitting on the sofa, thinking.*

Eventually she picks up the receiver.

KATHERINE. Katherine Hughes.

48. Exterior. Riverboat on Thames. Day.

KATHERINE *looking for someone.*

VALENTINE *is in the cabin drinking tea. He waves. She joins him.*

KATHERINE. How did you know me?

VALENTINE. From photographs. What can I get you?

KATHERINE. Who are you?

VALENTINE. I thought it would be easier if we sat in here.

He looks around.

She looks around.

We clock a man and a woman at a table.

KATHERINE. Your friends, are they?

VALENTINE. Former colleagues. That's why I suggested your flat, I thought it would save them the trouble.

KATHERINE *understands.*

KATHERINE. My flat is bugged.

VALENTINE *blinks at her.*

What gives you people the right to do that?

VALENTINE. National security, of course.

KATHERINE. Am I on file too?

VALENTINE *finds this is a ridiculous question.*

VALENTINE. Of course you are. Surely you all know you are? You spend enough time muttering your jeremiads about the secret state. I mean to say if you're not a legitimate target I really don't know who is.

KATHERINE. You wanted to say something to me, and presumably to your former friends.

VALENTINE. First of all a few facts about myself, to counter-balance the disinformation.

KATHERINE. You're him. (*She laughs.*) So you're what Harry Ollerton thinks of as charismatic. (*She laughs some more.*)

VALENTINE. Yes. I've been an MI5 officer since coming down from Oxford in 1957. I spent eight years as head of F Branch, domestic subversion. For the past three years I've led, charismatically or otherwise, a special unit whose existence will never be admitted in any circumstances by my superiors, or their political masters. One of my duties was to assist an operation called Desert Song. You stumbled across a dusty corner of Operation Desert Song. Desert Song is the supply of arms to terrorist bases in Gadaffi's Libya. It's primarily a covert CIA operation. Our American cousins bring the weaponry into Heathrow and we supervise the police moving it across London to Stansted where it's flown on to Libya.

KATHERINE. What was in it for Commander Fine?

VALENTINE. Purely money. Buckets full of it; greedy, greedy man.

KATHERINE. Why guns to Libya?

VALENTINE. Theoretically the rationale is that by getting someone like Katz into terrorist bases in Libya, Western intelligence can monitor who's being trained to do what. The thought that those weapons might reappear in European cities to murder young police-women apparently doesn't matter.

KATHERINE. Harry Ollerton says you're crackers.

VALENTINE. I have received psychiatric counsel for a number of years for normal stresses and strains. I'm not unstable.

KATHERINE. Why are you telling me any of this?

VALENTINE. I expect to be charged within a day or two.

KATHERINE. With what?

VALENTINE. I don't know. If Mrs T's feeling brave, Section 2. Like you, I'm becoming devoted to the idea of openness, freedom of information. As a token of my goodwill, I've sent some information on Desert Song to your journalist friend. I've also sent something to Mr Bingham which he may find helpful.

KATHERINE. Why do you need our goodwill?

VALENTINE. I'm going to need good lawyers. I know you and Cartwright are good. All your mail intercepts came across my desk for eight years.

There is a pause.
He drinks up his tea.

KATHERINE. Aren't you going to offer me some kind of explanation?

VALENTINE. Oh that? What explanation do you need?

KATHERINE. It wasn't Santiago, this was England. It was the middle of the English countryside.

VALENTINE. Yes. It was England, wasn't it? TTFN.

The boat docks.
He leaves.

49. Interior. Katherine's flat. Day.

KATHERINE *is alone.*

50. Exterior. Thames river boat. Day.

VALENTINE. Yes. It was England, wasn't it?

51. Interior. Katherine's flat. Night.

KATHERINE *throws things into two suitcases and a briefcase. She looks around her flat.*

KATHERINE. You won't get away with driving me out. I'll be back. (*She leaves.*)

52. Interior. Dingy bedsit. Night.

A bed, a table, a chair, a wardrobe, a cooker, a sink.
BILL TURNER *sits in silence eating a pie with a knife and fork.*
On the wall he's pinned a photograph of the house he used to live in and the car he used to drive.

53. Interior. Frank's. Night.

KATHERINE *sets down a bottle of wine and three glasses on the table.*
BINGHAM *is watching* FRANK *reading documents.*

KATHERINE. He said it was a token of goodwill for the Radical Bar.

BINGHAM *nods and takes the glass of wine she's offering him. He's containing his anger.*

He was really talking to his ex-colleagues – saying 'If you make me the scapegoat I will not go quietly'.

FRANK *finishes reading.*

FRANK. So there is another Bill Turner?

BINGHAM. What sort of country is it where they can just throw away a man's life like this? And they lied to my father.

KATHERINE *chokes on wine as she bursts out laughing.*

BINGHAM. Something funny Katherine?

KATHERINE. I'm sorry James.

BINGHAM. No please share the joke.

KATHERINE. Well it's just that these people piss all over Bill Turner and me – in his case metaphorically – and you get aerated about the fact that they lied to your father. I think he got off lightly. I wish I'd been wearing the right school tie, maybe I'd have got off with being slipped a couple of white lies instead of being beaten up and thrown in the shit.

BINGHAM. I'm afraid I find class prejudice hard to stomach even in these circumstances.

KATHERINE. Class prejudice?

BINGHAM. Just because he's my father and doesn't happen to live in a tenement house in Salford doesn't mean his feelings don't matter.

KATHERINE. I just think it's ridiculous – but ridiculously, wonderfully eloquent about you, James – that the first time I've ever clapped eyes on you being angry it's caused by some petty piece of public school 'bad form'. 'They lied to my father'. I mean what does that make your father? I mean for God's sake it's exactly that knowledge that the country is being run by a secret club of overgrown schoolboys that drives me round the bend.

BINGHAM. Oh that's what drives you round the bend? I thought it might be the strain of being such a rude, opinionated, bigoted hypocrite.

KATHERINE. Oh I'm a hypocrite as well, am I?

BINGHAM. Yes, you are. I'm a life member of this secret club, I suppose?

KATHERINE. Yes, you are, because you were born in to your class, James and there's nothing you can do to get out of it.

BINGHAM. You seem to have managed, Katherine.

They are both rather stunned by what they have said.

FRANK *clears his throat. A truce.* FRANK *tries not to smirk. He breathes a deep sigh of relief. At last that's over. He drinks.*

54. Exterior. Bingham's BMW. Day.

BINGHAM, HELEN ROBINSON, BILL TURNER.

They drive slowly down a street in Essex looking for a number on a door.

BILL TURNER. The same name, virtually the same national insurance number, but a real subversive, it's like coming face to face with your doppelganger. Doctor Jekyll is about to meet Mr Hyde. (*They pull up.*)

55. Exterior. A street in Essex. Day.

BINGHAM, HELEN ROBINSON *and* BILL TURNER *go to a door and press a bell.*
There is a chime.
BILL TURNER *is very keen to meet his namesake.*
A vicar comes to the door. He is as open and jovial a man as you could wish to meet.

REVEREND BILL TURNER (*for it is he*). Hello, come in.

56. Interior. Reverend Bill Turner's workroom. Day.

The walls are full of Peace Movement posters. BILL TURNER *looks it over with distaste.*

REVEREND BILL TURNER. Welcome to the hub of my network of subversion. Bill Turner, I presume?
He offers his hand to BINGHAM.
BINGHAM *points to* BILL TURNER, *who is staring at the* REAGAN/THATCHER *'Gone with the Wind' poster.*
The BILL TURNERS *shake hands.*
REVEREND BILL TURNER. As you can see I'm active in the Peace Movement. Funnily enough I've always been a bit annoyed, you know, that nobody ever tampered with my mail. I mean a lot of my friends have had their phones tapped, and I never have, you know. I was beginning to feel 'I wonder if it's a plot to make me look like an informer', or make me look even more insignificant than I already am. Thank goodness there's an explanation at last. The security services are completely incompetent.
He laughs. They all like him and his joke, except BILL TURNER.
BILL TURNER. I don't think your activities are funny I'm afraid, Reverend; I've paid the price for all this.
REVEREND BILL TURNER. Actually I do little more than lick stamps.
BILL TURNER. Someone obviously thinks there's more to it than that.
BINGHAM *can't believe his ears.*
He hands REVEREND BILL TURNER *the file.*
BINGHAM. This belongs to you rightfully. We haven't made a

copy. But we would like you to consider giving evidence.

REVEREND BILL TURNER. Of course, of course. Oh wonderful, my very own MI5 file, it's like Eamonn Andrews.

BILL TURNER. Just a minute, that's my evidence. That's my liberty you're handing over.

He grabs the file. There is a struggle.

57. Interior. Fetter Court. Evening.

BINGHAM *and* FRANK.

BINGHAM. I hate Bill Turner.

FRANK. Which one?

BINGHAM. I hope he gets ten years. You were right; he's a toad eater. He's learnt nothing. He gets a ton and a half of liquid manure poured over his life and what does he say to the man it was intended for? 'There's no smoke without fire'.

58. Interior. Police Station. Day.

A uniformed INSPECTOR *is formally charging* VALENTINE. VALENTINE *is a bit drunk.*
The INSPECTOR *is a bit embarrassed.*
A SERGEANT *makes notes.*

INSPECTOR. David Valentine, you are charged under Section 2 of the Official Secrets Act –

VALENTINE. They must be out of their minds.

INSPECTOR. – in that you have retained notes and documents in your possession, having no right to retain them and in that you communicated them contrary to your duty to a person not authorised under the act –

VALENTINE. Don't talk to me about duty, sonny boy. I was doing my duty when you were doing your O-levels.

INSPECTOR. – to receive them. Do you wish to say anything?

VALENTINE. Oh yes.

INSPECTOR. You're not obliged to say anything unless you wish to do so –

VALENTINE. I do, I do.

INSPECTOR. – but whatever you say will be taken down in writing and maybe given in evidence.

VALENTINE. Write this down. The law is a monkey on a stick.

A knock on the door. A MAN *enters.*

Who's this?

INSPECTOR. It's your solicitor.

VALENTINE (*to the* SOLICITOR). Well you can bugger off for a start. I'm not talking to this idiot. I've told you, sonny Jim, the first thing they've got to get straight is this: I'll be choosing my own lawyers.

59. Interior. Fetter Court. Day.

FRANK, KATHERINE *and other* MEMBERS OF THE CHAMBERS *and* VINER *watching as a heavy safe is manhandled into the chambers by a* TEAM OF MEN. *Another two* MEN, *led by* TYLER *are electronically sweeping the whole area.*

TYLER. Which area will be used for case conferences?

FRANK. We have three conference rooms.

TYLER. You'll have to undertake to use one only, it's a lot simpler that way.

KATHERINE. For whom?

TYLER. Now you must understand, all documents relating to the case have to be kept under lock and key at all times when not actually being worked from. You cannot take any papers away from the chambers and no other members of the chambers can be allowed to see any of the documents.

This causes amusement among the LAWYERS *watching.*

I'd like to speak to you now, privately.

He goes to one of the conference rooms, KATHERINE, FRANK *and* VINER *follows. They walk past* HUGH *who is ostentatiously reading a copy of 'Spycatcher'.*

60. Interior. Conference room. Day.

TYLER *produces three documents.*

TYLER. I'd like you all to read and sign this.

FRANK. What is it?

TYLER. It's a copy of the relevant part of the Official Secrets Act.

VINER. We're already bound by the Official Secrets Act, in the same way as we're bound by the Road Traffic Act or the Historic Monuments Act. Why not ask us to sign those?

TYLER. Are you refusing to sign?

FRANK. This is straightforward intimidation. Can I drink after time because I haven't signed a copy of the Licensing Act?

TYLER (*to* KATHERINE). You are required to sign this by law.

KATHERINE. I know what the law is.

TYLER. Alright, not my problem. We'll go back out now and I'll tap in the combination number.

FRANK. Why?

TYLER. So you can use the safe.

FRANK. Why do you need to know the combination? Whose safe is it anyway?

TYLER. Ours.

KATHERINE. Well take it back with you; we didn't ask for it.

TYLER gives in. He hands over a sheaf of paper.

TYLER. Here are the instructions.

61. Interior. Fetter Court. Day.

They come back out of the conference room into the main room.
The safe team and the sweepers are waiting to go. TYLER signals them to leave. As he goes he taps HUGH's book.

TYLER. Fantasy.

He leaves.
There is silence, and there is nervous laughter and chatter from HUGH, MICHAEL, KEN GORDON and others.

62. Interior. Fetter Court. Evening.

On the stairs VINER and VALENTINE ascending.

63. Interior. Fetter Court. Evening.

It's empty but for FRANK and KATHERINE at FRANK's desk, waiting.
They hear footsteps on the stairs.
VINER and VALENTINE arrive.

64. Interior. Fetter Court. Evening.

VINER, VALENTINE, KATHERINE and FRANK shake hands in the middle of the room.

VALENTINE. Have they been?

FRANK. They claimed to be sweeping the entire place for bugs.

VALENTINE. And did they pronounce any room in particular to be more free of eavesdropping devices than the rest?

FRANK. The conference room up there seems safest, they thought.

VALENTINE. Good let's use it. I want them to be in no doubt about what I intend to make known.

65. Interior. Fetter Court. Evening.

In the conference room.
VALENTINE, VINER, KATHERINE and FRANK.

VALENTINE. I'm afraid I can't oblige you with a nice 'right to
know' defence à la Ponting, for the simple reason that I don't
believe people do have a right to know. My defence is as
follows. I'm charged with retaining and/or communicating
information contained in three batches of documents. I have
copies here for you.

He takes one batch of documents out from his briefcase.

The first batch was the file on the second Mr Turner. If they
wish to run an Official Secrets case against me on that they'll
make themselves look even bigger fools than they really are.
The second batch refers to Desert Song. Frank, have you been
indoctrinated into Desert Song?

FRANK *nods.*

VALENTINE *is holding up the batch of papers he's just taken out of his
case.*

Desert Song is a straightforward money-making scam being
run by people who are little better than animals in my humble
opinion. I'm referring here to our senior partners in the
intelligence community, the Americans, whose bidding we are
obliged to do every time they come up with some idiotic
scheme.

FRANK. But I thought the purpose of Desert Song is to infiltrate
CIA agents into terrorist training camps in Libya?

VALENTINE. The purpose of Desert Song is to make a lot of
money; this is my point. They cannot accuse me of prejudicing
the national interest by disclosing the operation when the
operation is straightforward private enterprise. Don't you
think it's beautifully ironic that we're now colonised by
barbarians?

VINER. I don't understand. If Desert Song is private enterprise,
where does all the money go, and why did you go on helping
it?

VALENTINE. Because I was ordered to do so. Where the money
went is the biggest question of all. At first: weapons for the
contras, weapons for the Mujihadeen, for their own terrorist
training camps in America. But after that: homes, swimming
pools, hotel bills, and all the paraphernalia of bribery and
corruption.

KATHERINE. There's a third batch of documents you said.

There is a pause.

VALENTINE *closes his briefcase.*

VALENTINE. I think that's enough for today. It doesn't do to
over-egg the pudding, does it?

They are surprised to end so quickly.

He stands.

They all stand.
They go out through the main room. As he passes KATHERINE'*s desk*
VALENTINE *spins the monkey on a stick.*

66. Interior. Fetter Court. Night.

VALENTINE *and* KATHERINE *are descending the stairs.*
FRANK *is putting* 'Desert Song' *into the safe.* VINER *looks on.*

VALENTINE. The men who were here, did anyone give a name?
KATHERINE. Tyler.
   VALENTINE *nods.*
VALENTINE. It's a racing certainty that Tyler was behind the
   attack on you. Of course, he'll have put it out to tender. Ta ta
   for now.
   KATHERINE *finds this hard to bear.*
   FRANK *arrives with the keys and unlocks the street door.*

67. Interior. Fetter Court. Night.

KATHERINE *sees* FRANK *and* VINER *talking.*

FRANK. George is worried about you being in the defence team.
VINER. We should face the fact that the Bar Council might take
   issue with you doing it, given that you have made some public
   utterances on all this.
KATHERINE. No I haven't. I've spoken about something I saw in
   the street. What's that got to do with Valentine blowing the
   whistle?
VINER. If the Prosecution wanted to be nasty, they might say
   there's a risk you have evidence which might – just might –
   have to be used in the case.
KATHERINE. They can call Hugh. They can call WPC Osman.
   How many witnesses do they need? I'm doing this case and
   I'm not going to let some manoeuvre dressed up as etiquette
   stop me.
FRANK. OK. We're all in it.

68. Interior. Offices of the DPP. Day.

VINER, KATHERINE *and* FRANK *sit waiting.*
They are reading newspapers. The case is front page headlines.
A man comes for them. They stand.

69. Interior. Offices of the DPP. Day.

VINER, KATHERINE *and* FRANK *come into the* DPP's *office.*
A DEPUTY *to the* DPP *sits behind his desk. He stands, smiles and shakes their hands. They sit.*

DDPP. Thank you for coming. Now clearly we all have an enormous problem.

70. Exterior. English countryside. Dusk.

A van rams KATHERINE's *car twice head on.*

71. Interior. DPP's office. Day.

DDPP. And that is how to ensure that your client has the fairest possible trial without national security being at all prejudiced. I understand that you've refused, as yet, to sign a copy of the Act. I have to say that that refusal is certain to be detrimental to your client's case. You see, the prosecution will prove its case by establishing that Valentine has a wealth of potentially damaging information which he must be prevented from disclosing.

FRANK. Politically damaging, to the security services and to the Government, not to national security, that's not an issue.

DDPP. You simply aren't in a position to know that. We can't give you the documentary evidence which proves that unless you give solemn and binding undertakings never to disclose it afterwards. The case itself of course will be heard in camera.

KATHERINE. That's for the Judge to decide.

DDPP. I think we can all assume it.

VINER. Are you telling me we can't see the evidence against our client if we don't sign?

FRANK. Are you going to blindfold us when it's produced in court? Or do you intend to hold the trial not only in the absence of the press and the public, but in the absence of the defence lawyers? Very democratic.

DDPP. The jury is made up of members of the public.

VINER. Will the jury be allowed to see and hear everything?

DDPP. Well that again will be for the Judge to decide.

They don't like the sound of this.

KATHERINE. Will the jury be allowed to see and hear anything?

FRANK. Sir, I will undertake here and now not to disclose anything likely to be prejudicial to the security of the nation and if I ever do so the Attorney General can have me charged under the Act. But I will not undertake to help keep secret the facts about so-called intelligence operations which are clearly politically or commercially motivated. And in case you have any doubt, let me tell you exactly: our client's defence is exactly that.

The DDPP is squirming in his seat.

72. Interior. Fetter Court. Day.

HUGH *answers the telephone.*

HUGH. Fetter Court. Hang on a minute.
  He finishes writing something.
  Yeh? What Attorney?
  He goes silent. He puts his hand over the telephone.
  (*To* LORRAINE.) Is Frank in?
LORRAINE. Who is it? The papers?
HUGH. Attorney General.

73. Interior. Garrick Club. Day.

FRANK *is shown into a lounge. The* ATTORNEY GENERAL *rises from a club chair to greet him.*

ATTORNEY. Cartwright.
  FRANK *joins him. They sit.*
  Get you a drink?
FRANK. No. Thank you.
ATTORNEY. Congratulations on your silk. Long overdue. Absurd that an advocate of your distinction spent so long as junior counsel.
FRANK. Well, being junior counsel has its advantages.
ATTORNEY. Well, yes . . . Now then. This business. We really have to get it sorted out. We can't go into court on this basis. As you know, it wasn't my idea to prosecute the fellow but prosecuted he will be. Make no mistake about it. The government won't run away from this.
FRANK. Fine.
ATTORNEY. What I need from you – I mean to hell with all this rubbish about solemn undertakings. There *are* people in Westminster who regard the radical bar as Agents of the Kremlin, but you know me and I know you. I know you're a professional barrister. So all we need is a gentlemen's agreement.
FRANK. About what?
  ATTORNEY GENERAL *shuffling in his seat.*
ATTORNEY. Cartwright. Even I won't be allowed to see absolutely

everything that's relevant to the case.

FRANK. You're going to prosecute Valentine without seeing all of the evidence?

ATTORNEY GENERAL *shuffling again.*

ATTORNEY. The fact is: it's not really *you* who poses the problem. But Katherine Hughes is a different matter. She's a splendid advocate. But politically . . . emotionally volatile. We would need to know that you were able to guarantee her discretion too.

FRANK. Ah. I see. I see. Yes.

ATTORNEY. Good. Can I then rely on you to be decent about this?

FRANK. No. You can't.

ATTORNEY. Well you're a bloody fool, Cartwright. Bad show.

74. Interior. Fetter Court. Night.

The Conference Room. VINER, VALENTINE, KATHERINE, FRANK. VALENTINE *produces third batch of documents.*

VALENTINE. The year 1974 was a turning point for the country. With the Heath government being humiliated by the mineworkers for the second time in two years and Wilson winning two successive elections on a policy of naked appeasement towards militant workers, many of us became convinced that the rot had to be stopped. The measures that were taken are now more or less common knowledge thanks to Massiter and Wright. Three years ago, the service was reorganised so that there would be no more whistle blowing. The third batch of documents is called wheatsheaf.

FRANK. Wheatsheaf?

VALENTINE. It is about the workings of a secret team. In fact we're known as the Safe Team.

75. Interior. Curzon House. Night.

In a room with a tape recorder TYLER *listens.*
On the tape recorder the voice of VALENTINE.

VALENTINE. The only objectives of the Safe Team, were to continue to ensure that no left leaning party would ever again be returned to power in this nation. To prepare the ground for action against it if it ever happened. To encourage and forge strong links with those on the political scene who would wish to move the Conservative party permanently to the right.

76. Interior. Fetter Court. Night.

KATHERINE. What about parliamentary democracy?

VALENTINE. We care as much about parliamentary democracy as you do, Miss Hughes. Like you, we regard it as necessary window dressing. We've done the Unions for good, we've done the Labour Party. We've done CND and other such riff-raff. We've done what we know the country wanted.

FRANK. So what went wrong?

VALENTINE. When the Americans came along with Desert Song, I was opposed to Safe Team participation. I was however, overruled. When I was subsequently able to establish to my superiors what Desert Song really was, I was again overruled. I was instructed that this was the opportunity we'd been looking for to achieve venture capital. I was to receive a cut of the money the American team was making. Our operations could now be funded by participatory profits in arms and drug smuggling.

77. Interior. Curzon House. Night.

TYLER (*smiling*). I thought it was a neat idea.

78. Interior. Fetter Court. Night.

Silence.

VALENTINE. The publicity surrounding the death of the child meant that a scapegoat was required.

KATHERINE. Why you?

VALENTINE. Just because I'm an anachronism. It became apparent that the Safe Team – or should I say Tyler – and I no longer shared the same values. I think his loyalty is not primarily to this country, though he disputes that, but to absolutes of power and secrecy.

79. Interior. Curzon House. Night.

TYLER (*smiling*). I still think it's a neat idea.

80. Exterior. Frank's car. Night.

FRANK *and* KATHERINE *travelling home.*

KATHERINE. Is he your idea of a scapegoat?

FRANK. I was sure he was doing it for revenge or for his pension to be reinstated or because they probably told him once he'd get a knighthood and he wanted them to keep their promise. But no, I think he's actually realised it's out of control. Not just his team of hi-tech thugs but the whole idea of an England decked out in permanent blue. In a sense you know, he's a English dissenter, a defector even.

81. Interior. Fetter Court. Night.

In the Conference room, VINER, VALENTINE, KATHERINE, FRANK.

VALENTINE. We've done what we knew the country wanted.

82. Exterior. Frank's car. Night.

FRANK *and* KATHERINE *travelling home.*

KATHERINE. Is he?
  There is a pause.
  Frank, it's been wonderful. I think it's time I slept at home again.
FRANK. Yes. I have been worried about your reputation. It's still bugged, I suppose.
KATHERINE. And your home isn't?
FRANK. We don't know, do we?
KATHERINE. Do we have to wait until they spell everything out for us? Do you think the car is bugged?
FRANK. Why?
KATHERINE. I have something to say.
FRANK. What?
KATHERINE. I'm really glad you set up Fetter Court.

83. Interior. Katherine's Flat. Night.

She pushes open the door, she waits, she steps in and puts on the lights. She unplugs all the telephones.

84. Interior. Katherine's flat. Night.

KATHERINE *lays her head to rest on her pillow.*

85. Exterior. English countryside. Dusk.

KATHERINE *is pursued through the farmyard.*

KATHERINE. Run, run.

86. Interior. Katherine's flat. Morning.

She switches on the radio.

RADIO. Though England badly need runs and only the weather can rescue them now.
    KATHERINE *looks at the teeming rain outside her window.*
    And now the news headlines from Clive Russell.
CLIVE RUSSELL. Opposition parties have called for the resignation of the government after last night's announcement from the Attorney-General's office that the charges against MI5 officer David Valentine are to be dropped.

87. Interior. The offices of the National Council for Civil Liberties. Day.

KATHERINE, FRANK, VINER, *sit waiting by a telephone.*

88. Interior. Valentine's flat. Day.

VALENTINE *sits waiting by his telephone.*

89. Interior. Curzon House. Day.

TYLER *watching live TV pictures of* VALENTINE *sitting waiting.*
The telephone rings in VALENTINE'*s room.* VALENTINE *picks it up.*

90. Interior. Valentine's flat. Day.

VALENTINE *listens on the telephone.*

VOICE. I have the Director for you.
    Pause.
DIRECTOR. Well, David?
VALENTINE. It's not enough. I want the Safe Team disbanded.
    There is a pause. The telephone is put down. VALENTINE *replaces the receiver.*

91. Interior. Curzon House. Day.

TYLER *watches* VALENTINE *leave the room and come back quickly with a syringe and a solution in a bottle. He fills the syringe, he looks up at the camera lens, stands on a chair, smiles at* TYLER *and injects cement into the tiny glass fibre optical tube in his wall.*

92. Interior. Fetter Court. Day.

Conference Room.
KATHERINE, FRANK, VINER, VALENTINE *waiting. A knock.* BINGHAM *comes in with* HELEN ROBINSON.

93. Interior. Fetter Court. Day.

Conference Room.
HELEN ROBINSON *brings in* BILL TURNER.

BINGHAM. Bill, Mr Valentine wants to give evidence for the defence in your case. He was once head of the division which took wrongful action against you.
VALENTINE. Mr Turner, I can't undo all the harm that we did you, but I can tell the court how and why you have been the victim of appalling injustice. I hope you'll forgive me.
He offers his hand to be shaken.
BILL *pumps it.*

94. Exterior. Fetter Court. Day.

BINGHAM, ROBINSON, VALENTINE *and* TURNER *emerge into the street.*
TURNER *pumps* VALENTINE's *hand again.*
A cab pulls up, VALENTINE *gets into it, drives off.*

95. Exterior. In a cab travelling through London. Day.

VALENTINE *notices a wrong turning.*
The CABBIE *opens the dividing window.*

CABBIE. The Director wants to see you straight away. The war's over; a lot of us are grateful, David; you've done it.
VALENTINE *smiles.*

96. Exterior. In the cab. Day.

VALENTINE *is relaxing, smoking.*
The CABBIE *locks the windows and doors. A car overtakes with* TYLER *in and escorts them from the front.* VALENTINE *looks behind, another car is escorting them.* VALENTINE *kicks with all his strength with his heels at the windows and doors. The convoy disappears into a subway.*

97. Interior. Turner's dingy bedsit. Day.

BILL TURNER *finishes setting the table for three to take tea. He has*

prepared sandwiches and scones.
A knock at the door. He lets in BINGHAM *and* HELEN ROBINSON.

BILL TURNER. Welcome.
  BINGHAM *looks at the spread.*
  You said you liked cream teas.
BINGHAM. Yes. Bill, the thing is Helen and I have to –
BILL TURNER. Let me just brew the tea. Helen, would you like to
  – ? Can you get your knees in there? James?
  He sits them at the table.

98. Interior. Turner's bedsit. Day.

TURNER, *who sits on the edge of the bed,* BINGHAM *and* HELEN
ROBINSON *taking tea. On the wall above the table are photographs of*
BILL's *former house and his Ex-Volvo.*

BILL TURNER. I built it myself.
BINGHAM. I didn't realise.
BILL TURNER. Yes, not a bad little house. Nothing like yours,
  James.
  BINGHAM *is puzzled.*
  Couldn't resist, I'm afraid. I didn't make a nuisance of myself,
  I just drove past a couple of times. Shall I be mother? (*He
  pours tea.*) Sort of place you secretly dream about really, not
  that I'm complaining. I was happy in my niche, my place on
  the ladder, not as far up as you, but that's how it should be.
  Do you mind if I ask how much is it worth?
BINGHAM. Erm. Well . . . About one point two.
BILL TURNER. Christ! What's the mortgage repayment on that?
BINGHAM. Well: my wife was left it.
BILL TURNER. Ah. Course I had to work for every brick of mine.
BINGHAM. Yes, yes, it's an unfair system.
BILL TURNER (*not liking the idea*). Well presumably your wife's
  father worked for his money.
BINGHAM. No, not really.
BILL TURNER. Well: somebody must have earned it at some point,
  you don't get owt for nowt, as we say.
  BINGHAM *decides not to pursue this.*
  They eat scones.
BINGHAM. The thing is, Bill –
BILL TURNER. The sort of place – you know: you think 'one day'.
  Well. Who knows? I'm only forty-four. I can start again. That's
  the thing about this country. What with you and Helen and
  the Vicar and Mr Valentine all working on my behalf.
BINGHAM. The thing is . . .

BILL TURNER. Bad news?

BINGHAM. David Valentine has disappeared.

BILL TURNER. But he's my witness. I'm relying on him.

BINGHAM. Of course, it doesn't mean we won't win the day. It just means . . . We're back where we were.

BILL TURNER. Oh. Mr Valentine's left me in the lurch sort of thing. Right.

Silence. Tears come down his cheeks as he eats his scone.

99. Exterior. A street. Night.

BILL TURNER *in the back of his van collecting what he needs.*

100. Interior. Dingy bedsit. Night.

BILL TURNER *tapes bare wires to his temples and wrists and plugs the other end into the mains via a timer. He sits in his chair and waits.*

BILL TURNER. Was that fair?

The timeswitch moves on, BILL TURNER *is electrocuted.*

101. Interior. Fetter Court. Morning.

TYLER *and his* FRIENDS *ascending the stairs.*

102. Interior. Fetter Court. Saturday morning.

There's nobody there but BINGHAM, FRANK *and* KATHERINE *sitting by the safe.*

KATHERINE. Accepting the implications of what you know to be true about the secret state means crossing an important but invisible line. Once you cross you're no longer part of the cosy, seamless consensus of sensible political thought. You're in a world where you can't trust the earth under your feet, where it's more important than ever not to lose your grip on reality, but harder than ever to believe what you know to be true.

103. Exterior. English countryside. Dusk.

KATHERINE *is beaten with rubber truncheons.*

104. Interior. Fetter Court. Morning.

TYLER *looks at* KATHERINE *and she at him as his men from the Safe Team cut open the safe, take the documents and go.*

105. Interior. Fetter Court. Morning.

BINGHAM, FRANK *and* KATHERINE *sitting by the safe.*

KATHERINE. Sometimes I feel I'm in a machine. Here's what I
   believe. In England we've forgotten the meaning of liberty,
   and that's why we don't care about justice.

Fade out.